A Handbook of
ANGLO-SAXON FOOD
Processing and Consumption

TO ANT, THOMAS & LIZZIE

For their patience and good company

Abstract

This synthesising study brings together for the first time information from a variety of sources in order to build up a composite picture of food processing and consumption during the Anglo-Saxon period. The period covered is the six centuries from the beginning of the fifth century to c.1100. The area covered is Anglo-Saxon England, with reference to the Celtic west. Occasionally reference is made to continental sites for archaeological evidence to verify points in the literary sources, when, by the accidents of (non) recovery, such evidence is unknown in the archaeological record here.

The primary source material is of two kinds: literary and archaeological. Material in Anglo-Saxon manuscripts in the vernacular has been supplemented on occasion by that in Latin manuscripts. There was no pre-selection of manuscripts, and references to food come from all types of writings: legal, religious, literary and medical. Place-name evidence is also used and reference is made to contemporary illustrations. Archaeological evidence is drawn in the main from the major animal bone assemblages, human skeletal material, and plant remains, as well as artefacts and structures. The problems of interpreting evidence from these sources are considered.

As Anglo-Saxon Food: Processing & Consumption has not been treated as the main subject of any similar multidisciplinary research before, there is no history of research into the subject as such, but it has been necessary to draw on a range of secondary material. This includes classical and later medieval documents. Modern histories of the period and surveys of food in antiquity have been consulted, as have publications on specific foodstuffs, particular areas of processing, and ethnographical works.

This book is published with the
help of a grant from the Isobel
Thornley Bequest Fund of the
University of London to whose
trustees I give thanks.

Ann Hagen

Acknowledgements

First of all I would like to record my thanks to Sir David Wilson who taught me Anglo-Saxon Archaeology, and supervised the earliest stages of this project. A grant from University College London enabled me to visit York, where Peter Addyman was kind enough to conduct me round the excavations. Professor John McNeill Dodgson helped with documentary sources at an initial stage, and it is with great regret that I learned of his death. My late parents, Peggy and Arthur Smallridge, provided support, moral and financial, whereby I could get work under way. Working from home, I relied on the staff of the Information Desk at Bedford Central Library whom I would like to thank for treating my requests as interesting challenges, in particular Robert Napthine, who rarely failed to get his book.

A multidisciplinary work of this kind has to be to some extent a co-operative venture, in that many people have provided me with information. To the specialists listed separately, my colleagues at Clarendon School, and friends who produced books and items of interest, my thanks. I also wish to thank my farming relations in Devon and Bedfordshire, in particular the late Harry Newman and his widow, Iola, who generously lent me books as well as answering agricultural questions, and my brother, David Smallridge, at Chasestead Engineering, Letchworth, where the answer to various questions metallurgical and technical was only a phone-call away.

Debby Banham and Paul Callow helped me more than they know by discussing this thesis with me, and giving me confidence to tackle the task of revision.

I owe an enormous debt of gratitude to Professor James Graham-Campbell at the Institute of Archaeology, London, who has been so generous with his time in supervising my thesis. He has provided me with information, encouragement and made corrections. From him I received counsels of perfection: that the work has shortcomings is due to my own failings.

Pearl and Tony Linsell have made a number of suggestions and improvements at the publication stage, and I am very grateful for their expertise.

Special thanks to Michael Miller at Cambridge.

Ann Hagen
September 1992

Contents

Introduction

The intention of this study is to bring together for the first time information from a number of sources to build up a picture of food processing and consumption from the beginning of the fifth century until c.1100. The area covered is Anglo-Saxon England and the Celtic west of Britain, with occasional reference to continental sites.

Primary material is of two kinds: documentary and archaeological. Material in the vernacular was supplemented from Latin manuscripts. Writings on all kinds of subjects were used, from laws, chronicles and sermons, to poems and medical recipes. Surviving manuscripts have been preserved by chance, so there will always be lacunae in the documentary record. Moreover, this is very heavily weighted towards the end of the Anglo-Saxon period, with few Old English manuscripts surviving from before the tenth century. While place-names are often recorded for the first time after the Conquest, where Old English elements are involved it is reasonable to assume they were in use in the Anglo-Saxon period.[1] Problems of interpretation (for example, where texts are translations of Mediterranean writers, or have a special emphasis) are dealt with in the text.

Archaeological evidence is available for the whole period and is the main source of data for early Anglo-Saxon England, but, as with manuscripts, the recovery of evidence is a matter of chance.

Soils preserve material differentially, and recovery techniques themselves will bias a sample of animal or plant material.[2] Different methods of quantifying the numbers of animals from an animal bone sample produce different results. Problems of interpretation (that the absence of fish bones may indicate not that few fish were eaten, but that many fish were eaten, bones and all, or that animal bones in graves may not represent foodstuffs) are dealt with in the text.[3]

Chemical analysis and electron spin resonance techniques can add to our picture of what the Anglo-Saxons ate and how they cooked it.[4] Human skeletal material provides information about diet not available from other sources. Excavated structures relate to the processing (mills, kitchens) and consumption (halls) of food.

Anglo-Saxon Food: Processing & Consumption has not been treated as the main subject of any similar multidisciplinary study before so there is no history of research to review. However, there is a vast range of secondary material. Treatises by Roman writers such as Varro and Columella may throw light on Anglo-Saxon practice. Medieval and

1

Tudor traditions may reflect Anglo-Saxon conditions, as these are unlikely to have changed rapidly in the interim, since the great improvement in stock was an eighteenth and nineteenth-century phenomenon, and the hybridisation of cereal breeds more recent still. Later medieval works on the Monastic Rule can provide detailed information relevant to the lives of a proportion of the Anglo-Saxon population.

Histories of the Anglo-Saxon period, and surveys of food in antiquity have been used, as have publications on specific foodstuffs and areas of processing, to prevent as far as possible the drawing of any false inferences. Ethnographical parallels have been referred to when this seemed helpful.

The text is divided into two main sections: processing and consumption, which are followed by a review of the main findings and changes over the period. The conclusion ends by looking at Anglo-Saxon attitudes to food and briefly comparing and contrasting Anglo-Saxon and modern English diet and nutrition.

---

[1] Cameron 1985, 96, 183, 204.
[2] O'Connor 1982; Maltby 1979; Grant 1974; Green in Hall & Kenward 1982, 40ff.
[3] Jones, undated paper; Meaney 1981.
[4] Arrhenius 1985, 339; Robins 1988, 49.

Processing

1 Drying, Milling, Bread Making

Drying & Threshing

Drying kilns were used through the Anglo-Saxon period to harden the grain and facilitate threshing.[1] Kilns which could be substantial structures[2] are often clay ovens of elongated form with domed clay roofs, but these have also been interpreted as malting floors.[3] There seems no reason why such kilns should not have had both functions, although, as they were not particularly efficient at drying grain, they may have indirectly speeded up the adoption of naked wheat varieties.

According to *Gerefa*, threshing was a winter occupation, and the Anglo-Saxon calendar illustrates threshing with flails and winnowing for December.[4] The work was done on the *odene* which was thought to be the 'floor of a barn' since it translated Latin *areæ*.[5] But the implication in *Gerefa* is that the two were different: the reeve had to take care of things appropriate to the *scipen oððe to odene* or the effects would be seen *on berne*.[6] Page deals with the problems that the advice 'to build a kiln on the barn floor' (*on odene cylne macian*) would give rise to, and comes to the conclusion that *odene* may represent something more complex than a threshing floor. The suggestion, given by Alfred's version of Augustine's *Soliloquies*, is that it was a place of work, as opposed to a storehouse.[7]

Some structures with opposing doors, as at Chalton, have been interpreted as threshing barns - the draught on a windy day helping with the winnowing.[8] Otherwise a *geflit*, translating the Latin *vannus* (fan), was used. Threshing was probably a humble occupation, which is why it is recorded of St. Eostorwine that 'he threshed corn and winnowed it' (*he corn þærsc and þæt windwode*).[9] Sieving was probably carried out after threshing.[10]

Milling

The process of milling underwent considerable refinement in the Anglo-Saxon period. The simplest method was to pound the grain in a hollow stone with a pestle: 'as a pestle pounds upon barley hulls' (*swylce berenhula punigendum bufan punere*).[11] Saddle querns were also used - the upper stone being rubbed back and forth over the hollow lower stone. Perhaps Alcuin was thinking of a saddle quern when he described teeth as 'the millstones of our food'.[12] Saddle querns and upper rubber stones have been found in several Anglo-Saxon contexts including Southampton.[13] But they were never as popular as the more advanced handmills consisting of two circular stones - the upper moveable with a hole near its circumference for the handle by which it was rotated: 'as one does to the corn - grinds it up - with a pilstaff' (*swa mon corn deð [portige] mid pilstafe).*[14] Such a mill needed less force to operate than a saddle quern. The moveable stone was a 'quern stone' *(cwyrnstan)*: 'the quern stone that turns continually but does not accomplish any journey' (*se cwyrnstan þe tyrnð singallice and nænne færeld ne ðurhtihdð*).[15]

A further development was a mechanically more efficient drive. A long staff replaced the handle of the upper quern stone, with its other end socketed above the stone, perhaps in a hollow in a roof beam. This staff could be turned to whirl the upper stone round. Further improvements included the use of several sockets on the quern in rotation to avoid uneven wear, and even the mounting of a quern on a table, to regulate the fineness of the flour.[16]

Quern stones were made of carefully chosen material. Neidermendig lava seems to have been particularly favoured. Vesicular and hard, it was also light in weight.[17] On the early site of West Stow thirteen Sunken Feature Buildings contained fragments of Neidermendig lava querns.[18] Fragments of rotary querns, often made from Neidermendig/Mayen lavas, have come from most middle and late Saxon sites, including Portchester.[19] Hamwih, Ramsbury,[20] Thetford, Chalton, Canterbury and Ipswich,[21] York from the eighth century on[22] and Cheddar.[23] Native rock traded within the country was also used for querns throughout the period.[24] The late Saxon site of St. Neots produced a number of fragments of Neidermendig lava querns, most from upper stones, and with a diameter of about 18", which seems to have been the standard size.[25] The tenth-century Graveney boat was carrying at least one quern blank of this material and size; it was usual to transport querns as blanks: cutting the central hole weakened the stone.[26]

Grinding corn in a hand mill, even for a small family, might take a considerable time.[27] It seems generally to have been women's work.[28] The laws of Æthelberht of Kent which date from the first decade of the seventh century punish the rape of a king's maiden by a fine of fifty shillings. 'If she be a grinding slave, 25 shillings compensation, the third class, 12 shillings' (*Gif hio grindende þeowa sio, xxv scillinga gebete. Sio þridde xii scillingas*).[29] This suggests that the grinding servants formed an important group and, while they did not have the status of a hand-maiden, they were above the 'third sort'.

Those who did not possess querns or with limited time might have opted for cracked grain. This, after soaking, might be more quickly reduced to fragments of kernel which could be boiled and served up with butter, milk or vegetables, but it seems likely that those who could, would eat at least some of their cereal food in the form of bread.

Oxen were evidently also used to provide the motive power for mills by the end of the period, since a pound was paid by Bury St Edmunds for mill oxen.[30]

The water-mill may have come to England in the seventh century: dendrochronology indicates a late seventh-century date for the mill at Old Windsor.[31] At Tamworth, a mill which may have been part of Offa's palace complex was radiocarbon-dated to the eighth century.[32]

There is some eighth-century charter and place-name evidence for mills, and this becomes plentiful in the ninth century.[33] If the impetus for mill building came from Kent, then the knowledge spread very rapidly north and west to Mercia; an indication perhaps of the value of water mills to those who had large retinues to feed.[34] Tenth-century leases often refer to mills.[35]

By then most large communities had their own mills.[36] The author of *Gerefa* gives instructions that the reeve was to supervise the construction of the mill in association with the fish weir. By Edward the Confessor's reign, mills had become such a hindrance to road and river traffic that he issued a decree limiting the sites at which they could be constructed.[37] A tide mill, either afloat or worked by a reservoir filled at high water, inconvenienced ships 'in the entrance to the port at Dover' (*in introitu portus de Douere*) according to the Domesday Survey.[38] By Domesday some 6,000 water mills were established in England. Often there was more than one mill in a village. Hatfield, Herts., had four by the time of Domesday, but two-thirds of individual manors were without one.[39] Partnerships in mills were frequent.[40] Ordinarily manorial mills were retained exclusively for the use of the lord and yielded no rental. Entries like that for Borhunte, Hants., where there was a mill paying 42 pence 'and another for the hall' (*7 alt. ad aula)* are quite common.[41] There were relatively small numbers of mills in Devon and Cornwall.[42] Some could only be used in winter, and Marcle Hill in Herefordshire rendered only the sustenance of him who kept it, but two in Cambridgeshire, presumably at Grantchester, produced eight pounds in 1066.[43] Seven mills in Battersea that yielded forty-two pounds, nine shillings, and eight pence or corn to that value, must have produced flour for a substantial number of London bakeries.[44]

The place of female slaves was taken by the male miller, such a one as Wine who was bequeathed in Æthelgifu's will of 980-90.[45] The *molendinarius* seems to be a bondsman of the lord's, permanently attached to the estates. By 1086 Bury St Edmunds had '75 p' (*pistores*) which perhaps means millers, but could be translated 'bakers'.[46] Provided that a household had the means to pay for milled flour, and easy access to a mill, women would have been freed from an onerous aspect of food preparation.

The expansion of milling may have been associated with demographic decline - resulting in a shortage of slaves - or an increase in population - more mouths to be fed.[47] Or it might reflect investment to provide income: a church should not be like 'a mill for vile toll' (*an mylne for lyðrum tolle*).[48]

Meal

'Meal' (*meolu/melu*) was the term given to corn, or other material, after grinding. Grube considers that the term was applied to ground grain from which 'siftings/bran' (*sifeda*) had been sieved. He bases this interpretation on a passage from Alfred's translation of Boethius: 'so men sift meal - the meal goes through the holes and the siftings are thrown away' (*swa swa mon meolo seft: ðæt meolo ðurgcrypð ælc ðyrel 7 þa syfeða weorðað asyndred*).[49] However, a reference to *þrittig mittan clænes melowes and sixtig mittan oðres melowes* suggests ground corn in general,[50] and substances other than corn were ground into *meolu*. *Mealan stane* seems to have been an alternative term for *cwern*.[51] Unspecified meal was sometimes mentioned in rents.[52]

Meal could be ground more or less fine, and could be sieved then bolted through various grades of cloth to retain or exclude more or less of the bran, and also spiders and the flour moth.[53] *Leechdoms* refer to 'finely sieved meal' (*getemsud melu*), and Cockayne explains *temse* as a fine hair sieve, a term still in use when he wrote.[54] *Hersyfe* and *tæmesplian* (hair sieves) are referred to in *Gerefa*. Appropriately the *getemsud melu* was to be made into a cake as food for a patient with a delicate stomach. Refined meal - the fine flour - was referred to as *smedma* or *smedema*. One recipe calls for 'fine flour of wheat meal' (*hwætenes meluwes smedman*).[55] *Hlaf smedman* translates 'bread of very fine flour' (*pania smili agineus*), and *smedma* glosses *similia* (the finest wheaten flour). *Pollis* (fine flour) is glossed by *grytt*.[56] Finely divided flour was available in Anglo-Saxon contexts, but it seems probable that only the richer members of society would be able to use it as a matter of course.

Leechdoms are not necessarily representative of substances generally ground into meal, but they are the most prolific source of references. There are ten references to barley meal, plus one to 'fine barley meal' (smæl beren meal); six to wheat, plus one to 'fine wheat meal' (smæl hwætan meolwe), and one to 'fine wheat flour' (hwætenes meluwes smedman); three to rye (as bran, meal, and dust); and one reference each to oat meal and bean meal. All five - barley, wheat, rye, oats and beans - were field crops, and their use for flour is not surprising. 'Worm meal' (wyrm melo) was hopefully purely medicinal, but with the mention of 'acorn flour/powder' (acmeluwes dust) and 'sieved hazel or alder flour' (hæsles oppe alnes asift) we move into the realm of what might have been used to bulk out flour when more desirable materials were in short supply.[57] The very poorest would have ground up more or less anything edible, including 'weed' seeds and bark, and eaten all of the resultant meal.

Ground grain is rarely recoverable from archaeological contexts. Evidence for flour comes from York where quantities of bran were recovered together with parasite ova, indicating that elements of that population probably ate 100% flour: that is, flour from which nothing had been removed by sieving.[58]

Unleavened Bread

By the addition of salt, water and possibly shortening, Anglo-Saxon populations could have made unleavened bread, which may have taken the form of hard, flat cakes, although it could have resembled flat breads - pitta, nan or chapati.[59] Even when yeast is used but the flour is from grain which has started to sprout, then the resulting loaf will be flat and heavy. Unleavened oaten bread hardened on stands in front of the fire may have been made in some areas.[60] The large round was divided into feorth-dæls, or farls.

Baking an unleavened loaf under a pot, rather than on a bakestone or griddle, would draw the dough upwards so that it would rise slightly, resulting in lighter bread.[61] Generally, though, leavened bread is much lighter and easier to digest, particularly when cold, and is likely to have been generally preferred. Moreover, yeast is a good source of B vitamins and lysine, the limiting amino-acid in cereal proteins.[62]

Leavened Bread

Yeast was potentially available to the Anglo-Saxons from three sources. Wild yeasts are present in the air, and a mixture of meal and water left to stand will begin to ferment, and can be used as yeast.[63] Once a household had fermented dough, a lump (sourdough) could be kept from one day's baking and used to ferment a fresh batch of meal some days later.[64]

However, the discovery that fermenting liquor from brewing produced lighter bread had evidently been made on the continent before the beginning of the Anglo-Saxon period.[65] Perhaps *beorma* (yeast), which is etymologically connected with *breowan* (to brew), referred to this kind of liquid yeast source.[66] The Anglo-Saxons may also have used the sediment from bottom-fermenting yeasts - produced by the fermentation at a low temperature of light beers. This is born out by the fact that one Old English term for yeast, *dærst*, is derived from *dros* (dregs).[67] This yeasty sediment was slow-acting, and resulted in heavy, damp, sour bread.[68] Yeast could also have been dried. Coats of well-washed yeast, whisked up in fresh water, used to be spread on a large wooden platter or in a tub. While the yeast was drying, the platter or tub was inverted to protect the yeast from dust, but in such a way as to allow air to circulate. When each coat was dry, another was added until a layer 2-3" thick was achieved. This yeast would keep for several months. Or, as with yeast for brewing, a handful of birch twigs could be dipped in liquid yeast and hung up to dry until the next brewing/baking session when it could be put into wort/water to dissolve off the yeast.[69]

It is possible that *beorma*, *dærst*, and *hæf* (cf. the modern German brewing term *hefe*) derived originally from brewing; *ðæsma*, which is found translating only *fermentum*, originally meant sour dough, and *gist*, the only term not used in religious literature to translate the idea of leavening, was the dried, relatively pure, form. If liquid, it seems unlikely that *gist* could have been stored in a 'chest, box' (*cist*) (*Gerefa*), and it might make sense of the instruction to take new *gist*, i.e. newly dried and not two or three months old, for a brew.[70] The more general term *teage* (container) was used of holding *beorma*, and the term 'barm' was used until recently to indicate a solution of yeast. Although the terms may reflect different origins, they seem to have been more or less interchangeable in Anglo-Saxon times. In one case *gist* translates 'the froth on the ale' (*spuma cerevisiae*).[71] But the common Germanic character of terms for yeast also points to the early production of leavened bread among Germanic peoples, particularly when there were also common terms for unleavened 'low' bread: Old English *þeorfe* and 'raised' bread, Old English *hlaf*.[72]

The procedures of bread making were presumably commonplace; the instructions given for a salve were 'work it as though it were dough' (*gemang þ hit sie swilc swa dah*).[73] The action of yeast must have been very well-known since it is used as the source of a number of metaphors.[74] 'Dough' is the polite answer to Riddle 45 in the Exeter Book.

On contact with water, i.e. when dough is made, wheat gluten forms a tough rubbery material which traps the bubbles of carbon dioxide gas produced by the yeast. After ageing for one or two months, the light yellow colour of freshly milled corn is bleached, and the bonding characters of the gluten proteins are affected so that they form a stronger, more elastic dough.[75] The oils in wheat germ and bran are susceptible to oxidation and develop rancid odours in a matter of weeks, so if flour is to be kept, thus improving its bead-making qualities, then it is better to sieve it until 'white'.[76] Moreover, germ and bran dilute the bread-making qualities of flour, so for superior bread white flour is best.

Barley gluten tends simply to dissolve into a watery suspension.[77] Rye has its own gluten, but this does little to aid the expansion of the dough. There is no appreciable gluten in oatmeal.[78] These factors explain why wheat was sought after for bread making.

Loaves

The common term for bread was *hlaf* (loaf). The word *bread/bræad* (bread) rarely occurs.[79] The dough could be formed into rolls and loaves of various shapes and sizes.[80] The Anglo-Saxons seem to have had two basic sizes of loaf: small and large. For example, Edward the Elder's will (901-8) refers to 'two hundred large and one hundred small loaves' (*tu hund greates hlafes 7 þridde smales*).[81] The Abbotsbury Guild Statutes refer to broad loaves: one is to be provided by every two guild brothers for common almsgiving.[82] Perhaps these were the same as the *greate* loaves. Judging by illustrations, loaves were round,[83] and on the tables of the gentry, as far as can be gauged, were about the size of a present-day medium-sized loaf. The rule of St. Benedict allowed a pound of bread per day, and this would be represented by a present-day medium/large loaf, but may have been allocated as a portion from a 'broad' or 'great' loaf.[84] Large loaves of leavened dough would be difficult to cook properly, other than in an oven, which would suggest the method of baking.

Baking: Hearths & Ovens

In Asser's version of the story of Alfred and the 'cakes', the loaves are burning at the fire; in the Claud MS. the loaves are on a pan with the fire underneath, while Matthew of Westminster's version has the bread under the ashes of the fire to bake.[85] *Axbakenne hlaf* and *heorðbacen hlaf* are two variants in translations of Gregory's Dialogues.[86] One of the *Leechdoms* instructs 'bake him a warm loaf on the hearth' (*bacan him man þanne wearmen hlaf be heorðe*), but another prescribes 'an oven-baked loaf' (*ofen baocan hlaf*).[87] Ovens were enclosed - in their simplest form an inverted pot covered with embers.[88] A clay-lined oven had been built into the chalk rubble walls of a what was evidently a cooking hut on the sixth/seventh-century site at Puddlehill, Beds.[89] In *The Life of Ceolfrith*, written soon after 716, but probably referring to a time before 674, an oven is lit and then cleansed before loaves are placed in it, suggesting a bread oven on conventional lines in which faggots are lit and the ashes raked out before baking.[90] An *ofenraca* is one of the utensils listed in *Gerefa* and while none has been recovered from an Anglo-Saxon context, beech oven rakes were found in eleventh-century levels in Lund.[91] The sides and lower crust of the bread may have been cut off to get rid of ashes: some manuscript illustrations seem to show four slices cut from the sides of loaves.[92]

Bakehouses

Monastic and other large establishments of the middle period had bakehouses.[93] A bakehouse in which a sequence of ovens had been built at North Elmham has been dated prior to 800.[94] At Fladbury, Worcs., a sunken bread oven with similar dimensions to that at North Elmham - about 2 metres across - was found, and associated timbers were radiocarbon-dated to A.D.851 plus or minus 51 years.[95] By the time of the Conquest there were evidently large communal ovens, like that of the Earl at Norwich,[96] and probably commercial bakeries too.[97]

However, in a peasant's household bread would presumably still have been baked at the hearth fire. An eleventh-century scribe glosses *formacula* (a little oven) with *cylen* (kiln/oven) and *heorþ* (hearth), indicating a continuation of the two methods.[98] A griddle, or a small, circular, long-handled pan, such as are found in Scandinavian contexts, may have been used, particularly in areas where oat bread was common.[99]

Bakers

Women were probably responsible for the bread supply of individual households. The term *hlæfdige* (lady) is etymologically derived from **hlaibadigon* (bread kneader).[100] Old English has both masculine and feminine forms for bakers: *bæcere* and *bæcestre*, and the male baker of the *Colloquy* operates in a domestic, or commercial situation, not a monastic one.[101] By the end of the period, the baker was one of the inhabitants of a large estate.[102]

Apart from the monastic and manorial bakers, it seems that there were bakers who were independent tradesmen.[103] By c.1100 Baldwin, the baker of the High Street in Winchester rented a number of properties; and there were at least five other bakers in the town.[104]

Bread

Asked about the importance of his craft, the baker of Ælfric's *Colloquy* says, 'without my skill every table seems empty and without bread all food is turned to loathing, I gladden the heart of men, I strengthen folk, and because of this, the little children will not shun me' (*buton cræfte minon ælc beod æmtig byþ gesewen 7 buton hlafe ælc mete to wlættan byþ gehwyrfed. Ic heortan mannes gestrangie, ic mægen wera 7 furþon litlincgas nellaþ forbigean me*).[105] This suggests that bread was considered an essential part of a meal and was important for young children, particularly perhaps those who were being weaned. The author of *Leechdoms* also considered bread a strengthening food.[106] Each of the craftsmen of the *Colloquy* tends to exaggerate the importance of his own craft, but there is other evidence pointing to bread as the main constituent of a meal.[107] The standard meal was a loaf and something to eat with it. Possibly bread was already being eaten with butter as one of the 'accompaniments': 'Then give barley bread and pure new butter to the invalid to eat' (*þam mannum sceal sellan ægra to suppane, beren bread, clæne niwe buteran*).[108]

Loaves were often mentioned as part of payments in food, either to be made by tenants to the landlord, inheritors to religious foundations, or masters to their servants. In the time of Ine, ten hides were to provide 300 loaves.[109] The numbers of loaves to be paid to religious foundations are particularly high, and perhaps reflect their large establishments. Osuulf's will leaves yearly '120 wheaten loaves and 30 without the bran and 120 well-seasoned loaves for almsgiving' (*cxx hwætenra hlafa 7 xxx clenra, cxx gesuflra hlafa to ælmsmessan*), and these categories recur in other ninth-century wills.[110] Such bequests indicate that the estates were expected to produce a surplus, that they had the facilities for baking large numbers of loaves and that wholemeal flour was more frequently used than 'white', and that 'well-seasoned' loaves were in some way special.

Towards the end of the period, the number of loaves specified tends to increase. For example, Bury St Edmunds was to receive 1000 loaves annually on September 4th, and Leofstan added another 300 to this number, 'and Thurstan relish for 300 loaves' (7 *Ðurstan syflincge to iii hund hlafe*).[111] Again, this suggests bread as the staple and the 'relish' or accompaniment as secondary, if highly desirable. Sometimes, as with a lease of land to Denewulf, bishop of Winchester, the size of the loaves is specified: 'two hundred large loaves and another hundred small loaves' (*tu hund greates hlafes 7 þridde smales*).[112]

It is possible that loaves paid as rent were a special form of bread or rusk that would still be palatable after a number of days in transit.[113] However, the large numbers of bakers recorded for monastic centres may have been fulfilling contracts for food rents, as well as providing bread for pilgrims.

The title 'Lord' is generally thought to have been derived from *hlaford/*hlaidward* (loaf-keeper).[114] This would accord with the fact that the owners of estates owned substantial food resources, and also with the view of the loaf as the staple food. In the early code of Ethelbert (602-3), the first rank subordinate to the *ceorl* was his *hlafæta* (loaf-eater).[115] *The Dialogue of Salomon and Saturnus* states, 'in twelve months you shall give your servants 720 loaves, besides morning and midday food' (*on xii monðum ðu scealt sillan ðinum þeowan man vii hund hlafa and xx hlafa buton morgemetum and nonmetum*).[116]

Wheaten loaves were regarded as superior,[117] white bread being preferred for the Eucharist.[118] Those who chose to eat barley bread did so from ascetic motives.[119] When Bishop Basil offered Julian barley bread such as he ate himself, the emperor was insulted, 'barley is only fit for horses' (*hors mete is bere*), and offered Basil some grass.[120]

On feast days, at least in religious contexts, the ordinary bread was replaced by a finer kind, or by spiced cakes.[121] Feast-day bread may have been made from enriched dough mixtures. *Gesufel* loaves were bequeathed as an offering on Sundays by Ealhburg and Eadwulf (see above), and the Abbotsbury guild loaves were to be *well gesyfled*. *Gesufel* seems to mean 'spiced' or 'flavoured'.[122] Guild loaves were also to be *wel besewen*, which perhaps means 'sprinkled with seeds'.[123] Dill, caraway, poppy, fennel and sweet Cecily seeds could all have been used.

Leechdoms give instructions for making 'a cake' (*anne cicel*) of 'finely sifted flour' (*getemsud melu*) into which cumin and march seed was to be kneaded, so perhaps seeds were incorporated in the dough.[124] Such enriched loaves could have been kneaded with milk instead of water (cf. the *Erce* charm), or cream, and had eggs, butter or other fats incorporated in the dough. They may have been sweetened with honey, or contained fruits, preserved in honey or dried.[125] Local variations of enriched loaves and buns may derive from the special breads of Anglo-Saxon feast days.

The crumpet may also have been available to the Anglo-Saxons. *Crompeht* is used to gloss *folialis*, and Schlutter thought this was a form of thin bread. Grube thought that *folialis=foliatus*, and the *crompeht* was a little flat cake with flowers marked on it, as shown in manuscript illustrations.[126] However, it is more likely that *crompeht* is derived from the Celtic *crempog*, meaning a pancake.[127] A leavened batter will produce a crumpet, in effect a small pancake with holes most of the way down from its top surface cooked in a pan or on a griddle.

[1] Tannahill 1973, 36; Monk 1977, 26, 260, 338.
[2] Owen 1841, 79, 195, 261, 415, 721; Seebohm 1952, 66.
[3] Jones & Dimbleby 1981, 43, 115.
[4] Traill & Mann 1909, 181.
[5] Grube 1934, 145.
[6] Page 1985, 223.
[7] Whitelock 1955, 845; Seebohm 1952, 105.
[8] Monk 1977, 257.
[9] Herzefield 1900, *March 7*.
[10] Monk 1977, 257.
[11] Grube 1934, 146.
[12] Turner 1828, III 439.
[13] Hope-Taylor 1977, 196; Monk 1977, 266.
[14] Grube 1934, 146.
[15] op. cit., 146.
[16] Thomas 1971, 120; Seebohm 1952, 85.
[17] Crossley 1981, 1.
[18] West 1982, 395.
[19] Cunliffe 1976, 227.
[20] Haslam 1980, 6.
[21] Monk 1977, 226; West 1963, 241.
[22] Kemp 1986, 10.
[23] Rahtz 1979, 234.
[24] West 1982, 64; Crossley 1981, 1; Monk 1977, 266; Cunliffe 1976, 227.
[25] Addyman 1973, 89.
[26] Fenwick 1978, 131.
[27] Kuper 1977, 90; Trow Smith 1951, 66.
[28] Kylie 1911, 86.
[29] Attenborough 1922, 5.
[30] Robertson 1939, 255.

[31] Wikander 1986, 6; Rahtz in Crossley 1981, 14; Thomas 1971, 124; Baillie 1981, 61-3; Wilson 1976, 276.

[32] op. cit.

[33] Smith 1964, I, 251; Turner 1828, II 571; Seebohm 1952, 105; Whitelock 1955, 474, 487.

[34] Monk 1977, 269; Hodges 1982, 132.

[35] Robertson 1939, 27, 88; Hart 1975, 83; Whitelock 1955, 533-4, 552.

[36] Grube 1934, 147.

[37] Monk 1977, 269.

[38] Commissioners 1819, 412.

[39] C. A. Wilson 1973, 236.

[40] Bennett & Elton 1899, II 114.

[41] op. cit., 115.

[42] Loyn 1970, 357.

[43] Commissioners 1819, 412; Bennett & Elton 1899, 113.

[44] Loyn 1970, 358.

[45] Whitelock 1968, 6.

[46] Turner 1828, II 369; Bennett & Elton 1899.

[47] Jones and Dimbleby 1981, 115.

[48] Skeat 1881, 253; Robertson 1939, 197, 255.

[49] Grube 1934, 147.

[50] op. cit., 149.

[51] Cockayne 1851, III 215.

[52] Loyn 1970, 304; Whitelock 1968, 8.

[53] Lovell 1988, 1; Holmes 1952, 201; Bosworth & Toller, 1898, I 53.

[54] Cockayne 1851, III 134.

[55] op. cit., II 226.

[56] Grube 1934, 149.

[57] Wilson & Foote 1970, 149; Ashley 1928, 58; Moberg 1973, 45ff.

[58] Hall 1981, 5ff..

[59] Tannur in Fenton & Owen 1931, 179.

[60] O'Danachair in Fenton & Owen 1981, 63-5.

[61] David 1977, 155.

[62] McGee 1986, 290.

[63] David 1977, 89; Renfrew 1985, 40.

[64] McGee 1986, 313; David 1977, 293, 156.

[65] Stewart 1975, 45.

[66] Grube 1934, 152.

[67] op. cit., 152.

[68] David 1977, 98.

[69] op. cit., 95.

[70] Cockayne 1851, II li 1.

[71] op. cit., Herbarium 21, 6.

[72] Grube 1934, 151; Tooke 1798-1815, II 155.

[73] Cockayne 1851, I xlvii 2, II li I.

[74] Swanton 1975, 95.

[75] McGee 1986, 290.

[76] op. cit., 233.

[77] Dr. J. Graham, pers. comm.

[78] David 1977, 67.

[79] Cockayne 1851, II xlix; Robertson 1939, 253.

[80] Wright 1871, 104; Foote & Wilson 1970, 166; Wright 1871, 104.

[81] Grube 1934, 155.

[82] Whitelock 1955, 560.

[83] Temple 1976, figs. 158, 166; Stenton 1957, fig. 49.

[84] Knowles 1940, 462; Ashley 1928, 12.

85 Turner 1828, I 560ff.
86 Grube 1934, 153.
87 Cockayne 1851, III 122, II xxvii.
88 Bosworth & Toller 1898, 729.
89 Matthews 1985, 60, 69.
90 Whitelock 1955, 698.
91 Foote & Wilson 1970, 166.
92 Furnivall 1868, 23.
93 Rahtz 1979, 8.
94 Wade-Martins 1980, 69ff.
95 Monk 1977, 27.
96 Munby 1982, 52d.
97 Smith 1964, II 135.
98 Grube 1934, 153.
99 Foote & Wilson 1970, 166.
100 Grube 1934, 153.
101 Fell 1984, 49.
102 Munby 1982, 52b.
103 Loyn 1970, 324.
104 Barlow et al. 1976, 16, 45, 77, 94, 126, 133, 135-8.
105 Garmonsway 1978, 36-7.
106 Cockayne 1851, II xv 1, xvi 2, xxx, xlix, il.
107 Whitelock 1955, 385, 390, 410, 559, 560, 760; Miller 1890, I, 1 166; Owen 1841, I 69, 395, 677; Miller 1890, I, 2 244.
108 Cockayne 1851, II 220.
109 Whitelock 1955, 371.
110 Grube 1934, 154.
111 Robertson 1929, 13, 193.
112 op. cit., 39.
113 Jaine 1987, 78; Imellos in Fenton & Kisban 1986, 74-5; Weaver in op. cit., 354-5.
114 O.E.D.; Tooke 1805, II 155.
115 Whitelock 1955, 358.
116 Kemble 1848, 192.
117 Owen 1841, 533; Ashley 1928, 129-31; Skeat 1881, St Eugenia 1.404-5.
118 Miller 1898, I, 1 112.
119 Mellows 1980, 37; Swanton 1975, 45.
120 Skeat 1881, St Basilus 1.212.
121 Knowles 1940, 464; Connor 1987, 196.
122 Grube 1934, 156; Knowles 1940, 464.
123 Grube 1934, 156.
124 Cockayne 1851, III 63.
125 Walker & Bennett 1980, 2.
126 Grube 1934, 156.
127 David 1977, 341.

2 Dairying

The Milch Animals

The *Leechdoms* contain ten references to goats' milk, three to cows' milk, two where cows' or goats' milk will do, and two to ewes' milk.[1] The more frequent references to goats' milk may reflect the Mediterranean origin of the text, or the fact that goats' milk is comparatively easy to digest, and good for those who suffer from certain allergies. *Rectitudines Singularum Personarum* refers to the duties of the cowherd, shepherd and goatherd:

'Concerning the cowherd. His right is to receive the milk of an old cow for seven days after she has calved, and the beestings of a young cow for fourteen days...

Concerning the shepherd. The shepherd's entitlement is to have...the milk of his herd for seven days after the equinox and a bowlful of whey or buttermilk all the summer.

Concerning the goatherd. The goatherd is entitled to the milk of his herd after Martinmas, and before that a share of the whey...'

(*Be kuhyrde. Cyhyrde gebyreð, þæt he hæbbe ealdre cu meolc VII niht, syððan heo nige cealfod hæfd, 7 frymetlinge bystinge XIIII niht...*

Be sceaphyrdan. Sceaphyrdes riht is, þæt he hæbbe ...his heorde meolc VII niht æfter emnihtes dæge 7 blede fulle hweges oððe syringe ealne sumor.

Be gathyrde. Gathyrde ge byreð his heorde meolc ofer Martinus mæssedæg, 7 ær þam his dæl hwæges...)[2]

It is clear that the cow, sheep and goat all provided milk, and other dairy products. Archaeological sites provide evidence for the presence of all three animals, and deductions can be made from the age range of the animals concerned. For example, the age range of the goats at Beckery Chapel, Somerset, suggests a dairy function.[3]

Domesday evidence shows that some manors, for example those of the abbot of Bury St Edmunds in East Anglia and some royal manors in Devon, had cattle far in excess of the apparent draught needs. This suggests a cattle husbandry in which milk production was important.[4] This may have reflected a preference in which only those with the necessary resources could indulge, and may have been coupled with another preference - the raising of fat cattle for food.

Households in towns and villages may have kept a cow for milk, the food being hay, or grass gathered from hedgerows.[5] Unimproved breeds, such as the small Kerry cow, comparable to Anglo-Saxon cattle, are able to subsist on very scanty fare and to milk on it.[6]

Their Young

Presumably not all young were reared: if a dairy animal was kept until it was five or six years old only one of its offspring would need to be reared to replace it during this period, so some lactations may have been available just for dairying, provided that, in the case of cattle, the demand for plough oxen had also been met. Calves, lambs and kids would all presumably have been eaten.

Monasteries may have had more cows' milk (and veal) available than lay establishments in that young calves were killed to provide vellum. The three Pandects or Bibles made for Ceolfrith at Monkwearmouth/Jarrow between 680 and 716 needed the skins of some 1,550 calves, though such a large production was the exception, rather than the rule.[7] The extra milk would have played a useful part in a monastic diet.

Dairy Farms

There are records of dairy farms established by mid-Anglo-Saxon times, though these were for milch animals generally, and were not, as today, concerned exclusively with cattle.[8]

Yield

The closest one can come to estimating the yield of Anglo-Saxon milch animals is by extrapolation from present-day breeds. Kerry or Shetland cattle correspond fairly closely and can convert poor-quality fodder into five to seven gallons of milk a day with 4% butterfat up to 3 months after calving.[9]

Evidence for the yield of an early medieval Welsh cow comes from the *Ancient Laws and Institutes of Wales* indicating a minimum of about two gallons a day.[10] A sheep would give about one-tenth of this.[11]

Beestings, the particularly rich colostrum produced by a cow immediately after calving, was sufficiently valued to be the subject of an allocation: the perquisite of the cowherd, according to *Rectitudines Singularum Personarum*.[12]

Problems of Hygiene

The *Leechdoms* include charms (which are not included in the section from 'Apuleius' on which they are based), for milk that has been spoiled,[13] involving plants, often lupins.[14] Plantain, cockle and cress were to be bound together, then laid on the milk pail, which was not to be put down on the ground for a week.[15] It is difficult to know if these herbs would have a disinfectant effect; perhaps allowing the bucket to dry out thoroughly would have been helpful.[16] The incident where St Columba reproves Colomban for not casting out the demon that was lurking in the bottom of the milking pail, by making on it the sign of the cross, is additional indication that the souring of milk was a problem.[17]

A number of outbreaks of disease affecting domestic animals are recorded in the chronicles, and some may have been transmitted to humans, but it is not possible to identify the type of infection with any certainty.[18]

Dairy Workers

On large estates it appears that the men were responsible for milking the animals in their care. The shepherd of the *Colloquy* milked his sheep twice a day and made cheese and butter.[19] According to *Rectitudines Singularum Personarum* the cheese-maker was the only woman specified among the estate workers:

'The cheese maker is entitled to a hundred cheeses, and is to make butter for the lord's table from the whey; and she is to have all the buttermilk except the herdsman's share,

(Cys-wyrhtan gebyreð hundred cyse, and þæt heo of wringhwæge buteran macige to hlafordes beode; and hæbbe hire þe syringe ealle butan þæs hyrdes dæle.)[20]

Usually dairy workers are female.[21] This would seem a reasonable division of labour: the various herdsmen would be too occupied with their animals to spend time making dairy produce. The term *dæge/dey* is cognate with *dige* 'kneader' (cf. *hlafdige* 'loaf-kneader, lady'). The working of butter from cream by hand, of butter to expel brine, the pressing of butter into storage tubs and curds into cheese are forms of kneading.

From the Law code IV Æthelred, which could be as late as the last years of Cnut, and deals with London, comes the information:

'Women who deal in dairy produce - who sell cheese and butter - pay one penny a fortnight before Christmas and another penny a week before Christmas'.

(Smeremangestrae [quae mangonant in caseo et butiro] XIIII diebus ante natale Domini unum den., et septem diebus ante natale Domini unum allium.)[22]

This confirms dairying as women's work, and that dairy products were sold in towns, although, as the reference is to the weeks immediately before Christmas, dairy products may have been a delicacy. Perhaps women also brought dairy products into towns in the summer, when milk would have been more plentiful, but they did not then make the kind of price that attracted tolls.

Fresh Dairy Products

A will leaves 4 pence for milk for the anniversary of a funeral feast.[23] It may have been used for frumenty, syllabubs, sweet curds or junkets, which were associated with festivities, or for making butter or cheese, since the anniversary feast, unlike the funeral feast, could be prepared well in advance.[24] But it may have been to drink with the fish or to cook the fish on the menu. Drinking full-cream milk was a luxury, since there were still drinkable liquids (skimmed milk, buttermilk and whey) after milk had been used to produce the valuable commodities of cream, butter and cheese. References to drinking skimmed milk, buttermilk and whey are much more common than to drinking milk.[25] Ascetics tended to drink milk rather than intoxicating beverages, but even then it might be 'skimmed milk' (*þinre meolc*), or 'milk mixed with water' (*meolc wætre gemenede*) which Cedd took in Lent.[26]

The terminology of other fresh dairy products is problematical. *Flete* derives from *fleotan* (to float), and therefore can refer to cream (cf. modern Danish *fløde*), and, in the plural, to curds or skimmings. A fleeter, in Suffolk dialect, is a skimmer for cream.[27] *Ream* also apparently referred to cream, though perhaps to ripened cream, or cream which had been heated in order to preserve and thicken it.[28] Clotted cream, deriving from the Old English *clut*, may have been made in Anglo-Saxon times.[29]

Obviously milk and fresh milk products had a limited life, turning sour quickly in warm weather. Butter and cheese, however, were forms in which milk products could be preserved for weeks and months, for consumption in the winter when there would be a shortage of fresh milk.

Butter

The Anglo-Saxon invaders were already practised in butter making.[30] In order to make butter, milk is skimmed to collect the cream over two or three days prior to making butter.[31] The cream is then churned until granules of butter form. After the buttermilk has been drained off, the butter granules are given several rinses of water, all cold in summer, but the last warm in winter.[32] Then the butter is worked to expel all the buttermilk which would otherwise quickly turn the butter rancid. Unsalted butter may have been made for immediate use, but most butter was salted, since the salter of the *Colloquy* maintains, 'butter and cheese would be lost to you if I was not there to preserve them' (*butergeweor ælc cysgerunn losaþ eow buton ic hyrde ætwese eow*).[33] The salt would be worked into the butter, and if it was to be stored, it would probably have been pressed down into barrels, with layers of salt, to exclude air pockets.[34] It is possible that butterwort (*pinguicula vulgaris*) was also used to preserve butter.

Around 20 to 30 pints of milk (depending on butterfat content), are needed to make one pound of butter, but skimmed- and butter-milk are also produced, and the rinsings of buttercurd were traditionally used for fattening pigs.[35] However, cheese could be the primary product, and butter made from the whey, which is the situation described in *Rectitudines Singularum Personarum*: the cheese maker is to make butter from the *wringhwæge*. A good deal of cream may be raised from whey by gentle heating, and this form of butter is little inferior to ordinary butter.[36] The practice seems to have been to make the maximum use of a quantity of milk by using it to make butter then cheese, or cheese then butter. The liquid residue in both cases could be used as a drink.

Buttermilk is slightly thickened and soured by the activity of airborne bacteria during churning, and bacterial cultures may have been perpetuated in the wood of the dairy utensils. Since it has only a short life, it was probably consumed on the farms where the butter was made, although some may have found its way into markets near at hand.

The vigorous activity of churning butter is made the subject of Riddle 54 from the Exeter Book. Like Riddle 45, the respectable answer to which is 'dough', the language is packed with sexual innuendo:

> *Hyse se cwom gangan þær he hie wisse*
> *stondan in wincle stop feorran to*
> *hror hægstealdmon hof his agen*
> *hyre stondendre stiþes nathwæt*
> *worhte his willan wagendan buta*
> *þegn unnette wæs þragum nyt*
> *tillic esne teorode hwæþre*
> *æt stunda gehwam strong ær þon[ne] hio*
> *werig þæs weorces hyre weaxan ongon*
> *under gyrdelse þæt oft gode men*
> *ferðþum freogað ond mid feo bicgað.)*[37]

'There came a young man to where he knew her to be, standing in a corner. The lusty bachelor approached her, lifted up his clothes and thrust something stiff under her girdle where she stood, had his way, so both of them were shaking. The thane worked hard; his good servant was sometimes useful, but, though strong, he always became tired and weary of that work before she did. Beneath her girdle there began to grow what good men love in their hearts and buy with money.'

The churn being described here is the knocker churn.[38]

However, *uuellyrgœ* is given as the translation for *smus* (i.e. sinus), 'a vessel in which butter is made' (*uas quo buterum conficitur*). *Uuellyrgœ* is a derivative of *wealwian/wiellan* (roll), and so may refer to a rocker churn.[39]

Cheese making

In cheese making, rennet, a natural curdling agent, and sometimes lactic acid bacteria, which cause fermentation, are added to warm milk. When the milk has coagulated to form a 'junket', this is broken up, and the curds separate from the whey. The finer the curd is cut up, the more liquid drains out, and the harder and drier the final cheese will be. If the curds are heated up to between 70 and 130 degrees Fahrenheit they will become progressively more rubbery, and the resulting cheese will be correspondingly denser, and have better keeping qualities. This is likely to have been done in Anglo-Saxon England.[40]

Some soft cheeses, like Roquefort, are not cooked at all. The whey which is drained off can itself be curdled over heat with acid (vinegar, for example), and made into more cheese.[41] Buttermilk, from which most of the fat has been removed, was also used for cheese. Some cheeses have salt, which will slow down the rate of spoilage, added to the curd before pressing in moulds. Other cheeses are put into a bath of brine for a period after pressing. Salt can be rubbed into the surface of a cheese in order to protect it from spoilage. Cheese which is salted very heavily will not ripen, since all microbacterial activity is brought to a halt.[42]

Anglo-Saxons had rennet available, and lactic acid bacteria were probably present in their wooden utensils.[43] Rennet contains the single enzyme, rennin, of which one part will coagulate five million parts of milk (commercial rennet works only in the ratio of 1:4500).[44] Flowers of the wild thistle, seeds of safflower and 'lady's bedstraw' (*galium verum*) could also have been used to curdle milk for the preparation of cheese.[45] Boiled nettle and the flower of the teasel can also be used, but, unlike rennet, plant proteases digest more casein than they coagulate, and the result is a soft, weak curd.[46] Vinegar can be used to curdle milk for cottage cheese, although milk will separate naturally as it sours, and the curd so formed can be drained and then salted to make cheese.[47] *Leechdoms* state that milk could be 'turned' (*gewyrd*) by heating with hot stones or a hot iron as well as rennet: 'turn the milk with rennet' (*þa meolc geren mid cys[l]ybbe*).[48] The Anglo-Saxons had access to all the curdling agents that have been mentioned. The evidence from one of the *Leechdoms* is that even new cheese had a relatively firm consistency: 'take new cheese and shred it into boiling water...and make as it were small cakes and bind to the eyes' (*nim niwne cysan 7 screda hyne on weallendan wætere...7 maca ealswa litles cicles 7 byd to þan eagan*); this might signify that the cheese was curdled with rennet and the curd heated.[49]

While some cheese was eaten fresh (see below), the addition of salt would seem to have been standard practice. The salter of the *Colloquy* maintained that 'cheese curd' (*cysegerunn*) needed to be preserved with salt.[50] Large dairy farms would have produced more cheese than could have been consumed fresh. The large number of cheeses listed in inventories suggests that they must have been preserved in some way.[51] The Welsh seem to have used the brine bath method for preserving cheese.[52] The cheese was sometimes hung up to keep it out of the way of vermin and domestic animals, but it is possible that it was hung up in order to be smoked, although if it was hung up in the dwelling house it may have been smoked incidentally rather than intentionally.

It is difficult to find any evidence for the size of Anglo-Saxon cheeses. A fragment of a will from Bury St Edmunds leaves 'eight pence for a cheese' (*viii pe. an. cese*) for the first funeral feast, which suggests a large cheese weighing several pounds.[53]

It is not known if there were any Anglo-Saxon blue cheeses. Certainly in France such cheese was a delicacy, and also a rarity, since when Charlemagne encountered it for the first time he had to be instructed not to throw away the *ærugo* (literally 'the rust of copper', i.e. mould), since this was the best part of the cheese.[54] Presumably this was a Roquefort-type cheese, to which the mould *Penicillium Roqueforti* had imparted its special flavour. This is the same mould that flavours Stilton cheese; it may have occurred in some localities where it could have been incorporated into cheese.[55] Dorset Blue is also known as Blue Vinney, *vinney* being a corruption of *vinew/finew*, from the Old English *fynig* (mouldy).[56] It would seem on linguistic grounds to derive from Anglo-Saxon times, although it could be argued that the Anglo-Saxon population would refer to a blue cheese introduced from France at the time of the Conquest as *fynig*. It is a buttermilk cheese, which suggests the Anglo-Saxon dairying economy.

Cheese making was probably practised on a domestic scale by all households which possessed milch animals. Cheese was certainly made on large estates: the reeve was in charge of the cheese vat, and some cheese was made for sale in local markets or abroad.[57] The more prosperous an establishment, the longer its members could wait for cheese to age. Mature cheese was consumed as a novelty by the rich, whereas the poor ate fresh cheese.[58] Perhaps cheese that was to be kept was more time-consuming to make, and expensive, since more salt would be necessary and probably a press of some kind was needed too.

Dairy Products in Food Rents

Butter is not often referred to in Anglo-Saxon food rents, though Ine's Laws call for the provision of an amber of butter from ten hides. Cheeses figure in some of the earliest records of rents. According to Ine's Laws, ten hides were to furnish ten cheeses as well as other food. Forty cheeses were part of an annual food *feorme* retained by Offa from a royal estate at Westbury, Gloucester.[59] Cheeses or weys of cheese are often referred to in rents.[60] Religious communities often received cheeses under the terms of wills.[61] As a protein, cheese was of particular importance to monastic communities.

Dairy Products in Remedies

Milk in *Leechdoms* is sometimes to be taken warm from the cow, ewe or goat, to be drawn at one milking, or to be 'not sour' (*unsure*).[62] The most general use for milk is as a liquid for boiling herbs in, or for making broth.[63] It is sometimes to be boiled, or 'turned' (*gewyrð/geren*) by heating with hot stones or iron, or with rennet.[64] The woman who could not feed her child was to take a mouthful of milk from a cow of one colour.[65]

Ripened or newly-skimmed cream is called for in one recipe; in two others hens' eggs are to be mixed with 'cream' (*fletan*), and three pieces of old lard or butter are to be taken with *fletum*.[66]

'Pure, new butter' (*clæne niwe buteran*) is part of an invalid diet, and the instruction 'drink a bowlful of melted butter' (*drican amylte buteran bollan fulne*) is also given.[67] Butter is recommended too as an antidote to wolf's bane.[68] It is to be added to chicken broth.[69] Very common is the instruction to cook items - usually herbs or vegetables - in butter, sometimes with the addition of honey.[70] One *Leechdom* states that butter is better than milk for boiling herbs in.[71]

'Salt butter' (*sealte buteran*) is also specified.[72] In one *Leechdom* butter is an alternative to oil.[73] *Cu buteran* is specified five times, suggesting perhaps that butter made from sheep's or goats' milk was more likely to be met with, but this may reflect the Mediterranean origin of the text.[74]

Cheese was often to be taken internally. For example, cheese with dry bread was part of an invalid diet for an asthmatic and included in the diet of a 'wit-sick' man.[75] Old cheese taken in goats' milk or sometimes roasted was recommended for dysentery.[76]

Artefacts

A number of factors militate against the survival and/or identification of dairy equipment but butter and cheese churns were identified at Lund.[77]

Conclusion

Cows perhaps became more common as the dairy animal on estates though peasants may have continued to rely on sheep for their own dairy products and in some areas - the marshes of Essex and Kent, for example - dairying continued to be based on sheep.[78]

The impression is that cheese was the most important dairy product; butter was made from the whey, and the buttermilk drunk. Alternatively butter could be made first, and then cheese could be made from the buttermilk, again this would leave whey to be drunk. Consuming dairy products in this way makes an economical use of the resource. There would have been no standardisation and very great regional diversity, particularly where cheeses were concerned.[79]

If the *Leechdoms* reflect general practice, butter was used primarily for cooking vegetables and herbs. Alternatives for this purpose existed - water, milk, oil and lard - and butter may have been something of a luxury. However, butter was to be produced for the lord's table by the cheese maker of *Rectitudines Singularum Personarum*, which may hint at the same use as today, butter for putting on cooked vegetables or as a relish for bread.

---

[1] Cockayne 1851, I ii 5, II xxv, II lxv (2), II xxv; Bonser 1963, 111; Cockayne op. cit., I lxxv.
[2] Leibermann 1898, 450-1.
[3] Rahtz & Hirst 1974, 81 ff.
[4] Trow Smith 1957.
[5] Mitford 1986, 73-4.
[6] Fream 1952, 520.
[7] Dodswell 1982, 94.
[8] Finberg 1972, 105; Loyn 1970, 367; Robertson 1939, 171; Whitelock 1955, 489.
[9] Bowie 1988, 442.
[10] Owen 1841, 271; Herzfeld 1900, *May*.

[11] Seebohm 1952, 126-8.
[12] Leibermann 1898, 450.
[13] Meaney 1981, 56.
[14] Cockayne 1851, I lxvii 1.
[15] op. cit., III liii.
[16] Hartley 1954, 467.
[17] Bonser 1963, 259.
[18] Min. of Ag. 1972, 1,2,6; Burnet & White 1972, 214.
[19] Garmonsway 1978, 22.
[20] Leibermann 1898, 451.
[21] Roberston 1939, 257; Whitelock 1952, 113; Owen 1841, 80.
[22] Robertson 1955, 72.
[23] Robertson 1939, 253.
[24] Kuper 1977, 28, 34; Ayrton 1975, 461, 479.
[25] Turner 1828, III 27.
[26] Miller 1890, I, 2 244; Colgrave 1940, 345.
[27] Evans 1969, 104.
[28] Cockayne 1851, III Gloss.
[29] Hartley 1954, 474.
[30] Brothwell 1969, 51.
[31] Wilkins 1982, 1.
[32] Cockayne 1851, I xliv 2.
[33] Garmonsway 1978, 35-6.
[34] Hartley 1954, 481.
[35] Wilkins 1982, 4.
[36] Seebohm 1952, 107; Trow Smith 1957, 119.
[37] Mackie 1934.
[38] Wright 1871, 105.
[39] Pheifer 1974, 124; Hartley 1954, 479; Cheape in Fenton & Kisban 1986, 118.
[40] Oschinsky 1971, 289.
[41] McGee 1986, 44.
[42] op. cit., 47.
[43] Cockayne 1851, 2 376.
[44] McGee 1986, 37, 44.
[45] op. cit., 37; Harris 1961, 82.
[46] Monk 1977, 124; Lodge & Herrtage 1973, Bk VI stanzas 21ff; McGee 1986, 37, 44; Renfrew 1985, 15.
[47] McGee 1986, 35; Renfrew 1985, 15.
[48] Cockayne 1851, II li 3, II xxv, *Lacnunga* 18.
[49] op. cit., III *Peri Didacheon*, 21.
[50] Garmonsway 1978, 35-6.
[51] Robertson 1939, 197, 249.
[52] Owen 1841, 525.
[53] Robertson 1939, 253; D. G. Wilson 1977, 35; Hartley 1954, 486.
[54] McGee 1986, 37-8.
[55] Hartley 1954, 483-7.
[56] O.E.D. IV, 231, X Part II 216.
[57] Leibermann 1898, 455; Poole 1958, 227, 231; Loyn 1970, 96.
[58] McGee 1986, 38; Skeat 1869, 77; Seebohm 1952, 157.
[59] Loyn 1970, 304.
[60] Whitelock 1955, 489; Robertson 1939, 39, 171, 241 ; Whitelock 1968, 10.
[61] Robertson 1939, 59, 193.
[62] Cockayne 1851, III lxv 2, II ix, xx, I lxvii, II lxv 2.
[63] op. cit., *Peri Didacheon* 37; I ix, II lxv 2.

64 op. cit., II xix, li 3, xxv, *Lacnunga* 17.
65 op. cit., *Lacnunga* 104.
66 op. cit., III x, II li, III xiv 1.
67 op. cit., I i 3, 15, iii 8, viii 2 etc; I xxxi 7, *Lacnunga* XVIIIa, II xxvi, I xl.
68 op. cit., lxxxiv.
69 op. cit., III xliii.
70 op. cit., II li 2,3,4, liii, lvi 1, III xxiii 1, lxv, *Lacnunga* LI, LII, LII, LVI, LX, etc.
71 op. cit., I ii 22.
72 op. cit., II lxv 1.
73 op. cit., *Lacnunga* 3.
74 op. cit., I l 2, II li 4, lxv 2, *Lacnunga* XXXVII, Lac 29.
75 op. cit., III *Peri Didacheon* 52, III xli.
76 op. cit., II lvi 4.
77 Roesdahl 1982, 124; Edlin 1949, 55, 78, 104; Hartley 1954, 481, 486; Liebermann 1898, 455.
78 Seebohm 1952, 157.
79 Furnivall 1868, 85.

3 Butchery

Nature of the Evidence

The bulk of the information comes from animal bone reports, but these do not follow a standard format, nor do they always explore the same questions or give comparable information. The picture then is necessarily a sketchy one.

Place of Slaughter

All skeletal parts of meat animals were found in domestic waste pits in late Anglo-Saxon Exeter,[1] as at Hamwih, Bedford, and other mid/late urban centres.[2] In these cases complete carcasses could have been brought in from the agricultural hinterland, but it seems more likely that slaughter was carried out in the towns. Slaughter on the consumers' premises would have given them the benefit of all the perishable products.

Butchery: the Butcher

Consumers may have slaughtered their own animals, perhaps with the help of kinsmen and friends, or a professional butcher who would have come to their premises. The slaughterman would kill the animal and hang it up, and may have returned to joint and salt the carcass.[3] It would have made sense to pay a skilled butcher: contaminated or damaged meat will deteriorate quickly.[4]

Payments for this service may have been made in kind. Butchers may then have had meat to sell to people who could not afford a whole animal. Rather than depending on a casual supply of meat, butchers may then have bought animals for slaughter if there was a steady demand. In time the households who had had their own beasts slaughtered, might find advantages in buying from a butcher. There are urban sites where the high percentages of waste bones argue for the presence of specialised butcheries. By the end of the tenth century oxen had to be slaughtered in the presence of two witnesses and it might have been easier to arrange for witnesses in a centre of population.[5] The terms 'slaughterer, flayer' (*hyldere*), 'butcher' (*flæsc tawere*), 'meat market' (*flæsc stræt*) and '[retail] butcher' (*flæscmangere*) were in use by end of the period.[6] In the country farmers no doubt continued to slaughter, process and store their own meat.

Evidence for the Sale of Joints

Slaughter was carried on at the late ninth-century Whitehall farm site.[7] There is no evidence that prime - or any - bones had been gnawed or destroyed by dogs, and there is therefore a good case for the dispersal of selected joints: leg and shoulder of mutton, quarters of beef, probably to what was already a substantial market in the city of London.[8] In the case of pigs, the foot bones are in short supply, so trotters may have been disposed of while the main joints of pork were salted.[9] As waste, they could have been fed back to pigs, but they may have been sold as delicacies.

Method of Slaughter

There was a biblical taboo against eating animals that had been strangled, and animals often had their necks severed with an axe.[10] Later, animals were forced to the ground [11]so the sitting cow in the Bayeux Tapestry may represent an animal pulled to its knees prior to slaughter.[12] At Hamwih there was no evidence for pole-axing, so the animals were possibly killed by having their throats cut.[13] One fragment of pig's skull from tenth-century Skeldergate had a round hole 30mm in diameter immediately anterior to the bregma, which may indicate the way it was killed.[14] The pole-axe, with a spike on the back of the blade, was used until very recently in conjunction with a cane, which was inserted through the hole in the skull to destroy the animal's nervous system.[15] At Exeter the fragmentary condition of the skulls of cattle may indicate stunning with a hammer as well as removal of the brain.[16] Presumably cattle were then bled.[17]

Nowadays animals are hung up after slaughter, so that muscles do not set in a contracted position which toughens the meat.[18] There is archaeological evidence that some sheep and cattle were strung up from the middle Saxon period on. Meat is left to age so that the accumulating lactic acid can break down the walls of the cell bodies which store protein-attacking enzymes. These enzymes attack the cell proteins causing them to degenerate into individual amino acids which generally have a strong flavour, and the tissue becomes softer, producing tender meat. This process is best carried out in cool conditions (1-3 degrees Centigrade), and takes from ten days to three weeks for beef, and from one week for lamb.[19] Animals killed in summer would need careful attention or the meat would become high, and this must have given rise to winter as the season for killing. Pork, which goes off more rapidly than other flesh, was traditionally never eaten in summer. A large animal presents the problem of getting the carcass cool quickly from its own body heat. The fact that Anglo-Saxon domestic food animals were smaller than most modern breeds was an advantage when it came to preservation.

Butchery Techniques

There is evidence that the Anglo-Saxons had sharp knives for jointing, and saws may also have been used.[20] The most commonly used instrument for cattle on some sites was a heavy chopper.[21] This technique would be considered heavy-handed in terms of modern butchery practice, where the careful separation of good and poor meat is important, but if the Saxon owner ate all his animal, this was not important.[22]

The Anglo-Saxon period seems to have witnessed a development in the techniques of butchery. On the Flaxengate site, before 900, cattle carcasses were rarely split lengthways to give two sides of beef, but in the tenth-century levels 15-30% of vertebrae had been cloven in the sagittal plane, and this percentage rises to 50% in late eleventh/twelfth-century levels. Sagittally-cloven vertebrae of sheep were also more common after the mid-eleventh century.[23] By the second half of the eleventh century, some cattle vertebrae at Skeldergate were cloven lengthways, indicating some carcasses were butchered as sides by this time.[24] On the eleventh- to thirteenth-century site of St John's, Bedford, cattle and sheep vertebrae were generally split in this plane.[25] At Porchester the vertebrae were not generally found split, and splitting down the dorso-ventral axis was uncommon at Exeter before the post-medieval period.[26] This major development in technique seems to have been introduced first in the east of the country, so perhaps Scandinavian invaders played a part. Traditional methods seem to have continued beyond the area of this influence.

The Bayeux Tapestry shows a carcass from which the lower limbs have been removed, although the head is still on.[27] This may indicate the pig was to be spit-roasted. The picture reinforces the evidence that the hooves and lowest bones of the legs were regarded as waste, not worth transporting.[28]

On both Flaxengate and Bedford sites the evidence of butchery on pig bones was less extensive than on sheep and cattle, indicating that different joints were required.[29] It may be that the pig meat was to be processed differently, probably by salting.

Bones that were split for marrow extraction, but had not been cooked, indicate that some meat was de-boned before cooking.[30] At Exeter knife cuts on the distal epiphysis and lower end of the humerus were the results of cutting meat off the bone, not severance of the limbs, and there were corresponding cuts on the proximal portions of the radius and ulna.[31] Since this is the case, de-boned meat from substantial joints may have been eaten on sites where there is no trace of it in the archaeological record.

Tongue & Brain

There is plentiful archaeological evidence for the extraction of the tongue and brain from all the meat animals throughout the period.[32]

Marrow

A practice for which there is both documentary and archaeological evidence is the removal of bone marrow. 'Gather together all the bones you can, and crush the bones with the back of an axe.' (*Ealle þa ban tosomne ðe man ge gaderian mæge, 7 cnocie man þa ban mid æxse yr.*)[33] The 'marrow' (*mearh*) here was to be used externally in salves and ointments, but there can be little doubt that it was generally used to enrich soups and stews.[34]

At Porchester so few whole bones were found, that the tentative suggestion was made that stews were a popular form of meat consumption.[35] At Yeavering in the early part of the period in a kitchen-like dwelling there was an abnormally high number of bone fragments, never more than two inches across, resulting from the chopping of bones laterally and longitudinally.[36] At tenth-century Skeldergate limb bones were reduced to small pieces, the majority having been chopped through lengthways, either specifically to extract the marrow, or to reduce the size of the pieces of bone for boiling in the stock-pot.[37] Chopping and splitting bones was practised on other sites too, and evidently continued all through the period on sites of different status. The chopping up of bones into small lengths presumably indicates stewing rather than roasting, a cooking method which would release the liquid marrow. The need to make full use of the food resource would have made the effort of chopping up meat and bones worthwhile.

Offal

Offal was probably a low-status food in Anglo-Saxon times.[38] None of the food rents makes specific reference to offal, although that could be because it is more perishable than muscle tissue.

Fats

The various forms of fat: 'grease' (*smeru*), 'bacon fat' (*swices*), 'lard' (*rysele*) and 'suet' (*gelyndo*) are mentioned in *Leechdoms*, often for external use, but sometimes such items as 'half a cup of pure bacon fat melted' (*healfne cuppan clænes gemyltes swices*), or 'suet' (*rysle*) or 'unsalted grease' (*unsylt smeoru*) are to be taken.[39]

Evidence of Site Status

Where there are bones, then they may provide evidence about the status of a site. At one extreme, on the royal site of Yeavering the typical fossil of the early halls is the expensive butcher's joint.[40] In contrast, the heads and feet of older cattle and pigs, and most parts of the low-status sheep seem to 'tell a story of scrupulous making-do' in Viking Age York.[41] However, this interpretation assumes that the inhabitants did not eat boned joints or salt pork, neither of which leaves any trace in the archaeological record.

---

[1] Maltby 1979.
[2] Bourdillon 1980, 185; Grant 1979, 70ff, 141.
[3] Groves in Kuper 1987, 97.
[4] Walker in Fenton & Kisban 1986, 129, 130.
[5] Whitelock 1955, 404.
[6] Bosworth & Toller 1898, I 581, 291, 290, 291; Barlow et al. 1976, 27.
[7] Chaplin 1971, 127.
[8] op. cit., 126, 135-6.
[9] op. cit., 127, 136.
[10] Owen 1841, 71; Turner 1828, III 36.
[11] Walker in Fenton & Kisban 1986, 129.
[12] D. M. Wilson 1985, Pl. 45.
[13] Holdsworth 1980, 9.
[14] O'Connor 1984, 29.
[15] Walker in Fenton and Kisban 1986, 131.
[16] Maltby 1979.
[17] Walker in Fenton & Kisban 1986, 129; McGee 1986, 96.
[18] op. cit., 98.
[19] op. cit.
[20] Holdsworth 1980, 97; Cunliffe 1976, 272.
[21] op. cit., 273; Grant 1979, 59, 103.
[22] Cunliffe 1976, 273.
[23] O'Connor 1982, 16.
[24] O'Connor 1984, 20.
[25] Grant 1979, 106.
[26] Cunliffe 1976, 272; Maltby 1979, 39.
[27] D. M. Wilson 1985, Pl. 38.
[28] Rahtz 1979, 349; Hope-Taylor 1977, 328; Maltby 1979, 39.
[29] Grant 1979, 106.
[30] Holdsworth 1980, 97.
[31] Maltby 1979, 39.
[32] op. cit.; O'Connor 1984, 17; Grant 1979, 106; Hope-Taylor 1977, 328; O'Connor 1982; Holdsworth 1980, 97.
[33] Cockayne 1851, III *Lacnunga* XXXI.
[34] O'Connor 1984, 17; Matlby 1979, 39; Buckland, Holdsworth & Monk 1976, 61ff.; Holdsworth 1980, 97; Cunliffe 1976, 272-3.
[35] op. cit.
[36] Hope Taylor 1977, 105.

37 O'Connor 1984, 17.
38 P. E. Jones 1976, 342; Owen 1841, 25, 71, 667.
39 Cockayne 1851, III *Lacnunga* 116, I Herb. LXXV 5, III *Lacnunga* XXXIX.
40 Hope-Taylor 1977, 327.
41 O'Connor 1984, 26; Whitelock 1955, 222; Maltby 1979, 39.

4 Preservation & Storage

Some foods keep without any processing, and just have to be positioned away from creatures that would eat them. For short-term storage it was enough to hang some items from the wall or rafters.[1] After processing, meats and cheeses could be hung up in the same way for long-term storage.[2] This chapter is divided into three parts: (i) processing; (ii) storage; and (iii) manufacture and supply of salt.

(i) Processing

Drying

Drying - in the sun, in the open air, by a fire, in an oven or kiln - was perhaps the most important method, since it was used for staple foods: cereal crops and beans. *Leechdoms* give instructions on gathering, drying and powdering herbs.[3] It was assumed that if you could not use fresh herbs, then you would have some dried.[4] Mushrooms and other fungi can be dried threaded on a string.[5] Seaweed can be dried, as can peas and beans.[6]

Meat, birds and fish could also be dried.[7] Into recent times in Scotland fish were dried in different ways.[8] There is no reason why Anglo-Saxons should not have experimented and come up with different methods of preserving fish, each imparting its own taste. Less oily fish like flounder and large cod was probably dried, and made a very good reserve food in that it kept indefinitely.[9]

Smoking

Smoke is a complex substance containing alcohols, acids, phenolic compounds and some toxic substances which inhibit bacterial activity and retard fat oxidization, and impart the characteristic flavour of burning wood to the meat, poultry fish and cheese it is used to treat.[10] A combination of salt curing and smoking was often used to minimise fat oxidization.[11] There is some evidence for ceramic fish smokers being used to flavour, rather than cure, the fish.[12]

The wood used for smoking would depend to some extent on the supply available. Traditionally birch wood is used for smoking hams and herrings, oak and beech for kippers, York hams and bacon. Hams are sometimes smoked with juniper wood to impart a gin-like flavour.[13] Dried seaweed was also used to smoke bacon in sea-coast counties. Smoking may also have occurred incidentally as foodstuffs were hung from rafters in smoky rooms.

Pickling

Pickling involves impregnating the foodstuff with acid, either directly with vinegar, though whey and various alcoholic liquids may also have been used, or indirectly by brining, which produces a medium in which acid-producing bacteria grow.[14] Salting was such an important means of preservation in Anglo-Saxon times that it is dealt with separately.

Pickling in honey has a similar effect, since a very sugary solution will also draw water across the cell walls and dehydrate bacteria which might otherwise cause food to decay, and was likely to have been used in Anglo-Saxon times.[15]

Boiling

Fruit will keep much longer when boiled down, so the natural sugars are concentrated.[16] The addition of honey before boiling would enhance this effect. The custom of boiling down rose hips and storing the resulting mush in jars, is continent-wide, suggesting its antiquity; the same method was probably applied to other fruit.[17] Such preserves may have been used as a relish.[18]

Salting

Salt draws water across the cell membranes of some bacteria, dehydrating them when they would otherwise cause decay. Salting also causes the foodstuff to be impregnated with acid.[19]

Salting was essential to food preservation in Anglo-Saxon England. The salter is one of the tradesmen of the *Colloquy*, and ranks in importance with the ploughman, fisherman and smith.[20] When asked 'How does your craft benefit us?' (*Hwæt us fremaþ cræft þin?*), the salter replies,

'My trade greatly benefits you all. None of you would take any pleasure in your meals or food without my hospitable art. How can anyone appreciate very sweet foods to the full without the savour of salt? Who could fill his cellar or storeroom without my skill? Look, you would even lose your butter and cheese, and you can't even enjoy your vegetables without making use of me.'

(*Þearle fremaþ cræft min eow eallum. Nan eower blisse brycð on gererduncge oþþe mete, buton cræft min gistliþe him beo...Hwylc manna þurhwerodum þurhbrycþ mettum buton swæcce sealtes? Hwa gefylþ cleafan his oþþe hedderna buton cræfte minon? Efne, butergeþweor ælc cygerunn losaþ eow buton ic hyrde ætwese eow, þe ne furþon þæt an wyrtum eowrum buton me brucaþ.*)[21]

Leechdoms indicate meat and dairy produce were often salted.[22] As well as preserving fats, fruit and vegetables, salt was important for treating the muscly parts of carcasses.[23]

Bay salt, coarse and heavily polluted with impurities, particularly calcium and magnesium salts, was apparently 'inferior' and did not penetrate meat or fish quickly enough to preserve the flesh.[24] On the other hand it was also said to be 'preferred to finer salts for preserving processes', since fine salt tended to seal the surface tissues, but not to enter further.[25] Traditional recipes reconcile this contraction, since they tend to contain both refined and bay salt.[26] Just how pure Anglo-Saxon would have been is a matter of conjecture, although white, i.e. relatively refined, salt seems to have been preferred.[27] Although it was probably not realised in Anglo-Saxon times that saltpetre (potassium nitrate) was useful in the curing process, nitrites would have built up in the wooden utensils and the salting larders.[28]

Dry salting, or curing, would have been more expensive than brining, as more salt is required, and time and energy would be expended in pounding salt to a powder.[29] With this method it is useful to have pepper to coat the knuckle area of hams, to prevent maggots)[30].

Whatever the method used, bacon was produced in quantity. An inventory of Thorney Abbey listed 43 flitches of bacon and to Peterborough were to go 'a hundred flitches and all the delicacies that go with them' (*hundteongig fliccena 7 eal þa smean ðe þerto gebyriað*).[31] The highest quality bacon comes from lean-fleshed primitive breeds like the Tamworth, which has not been crossed with Chinese pigs.[32]

A traditional curing mixture in Yorkshire and Westmoreland was common salt, bay salt, saltpetre, black pepper and honey. All these ingredients were available to the Anglo-Saxons at least towards the end of the period. The hams were turned and rubbed with the mixture twice a week for a month, then soaked for twenty-four hours and hung up to dry.[33] Even with this cure, York hams were considered inferior to those of Gloucestershire and Buckinghamshire, since pigs in these two counties were fed on beech-mast which gave the hams a special nutty flavour.[34]

If after dry salting the meat was just dried, it was 'green' bacon, but it could then be smoked. Meat pickled in brine could also be smoked subsequently.[35]

A number of animals were probably slaughtered throughout the autumn because they had been fattened up on pasture, or, in the case of pigs, acorns and beech-mast; also flies are absent on cool nights.[36]

Most of the large numbers of fish referred to in food rents must have been preserved, very often by salting.

Other Uses of Salt

Perhaps because of what was seen as its purifying quality, salt was part of a specially consecrated diet for anyone pledged to undergo the ordeal.[37] It was also needed for ecclesiastical ritual, and for the ancient charm addressed to *Erce* for the fertility of land.[38]

Salt was also used much as it is today: as a flavouring with radish, for cooking with beans, with meal and butter to give a savoury pottage, in a marinade for beef, or even for an emetic drink.[39]

Salt intake would need to increase slightly with a predominantly cereal diet, but the Anglo-Saxon population were unlikely to have been short of salt when quantities of salt meat were consumed. The prevalence of salting as a means of preservation perhaps explains the comparatively large drink allowances.

(ii) Storage

Cereals

After harvesting and carting, when they were reasonably dry, sheaves were stacked outside, with heads to the centre of the rick, which was then thatched to keep the rain off, or in granaries (the term *bere ærn* [barn] does not seem to have been used before c.950).[40] Perhaps the owners of large estates had the resources to build barns large enough to accommodate sheaves, and perhaps they needed to do this if they had no one to keep a permanent eye on ricks standing in the open, but a barn came to mean a covered building where a cleaned crop was stored.[41] Peas and beans were also threshed and, presumably, stored in the barn.[42] The official appointed to have charge of the grain was the 'barn-keeper/granger' (*berebrytt*).[43] Those without the resources to build barns, or large supplies of grain or legumes, used pits (not a particularly successful method), or stored the food in their houses.[44]

Like grain, flour and meal had to be kept dry in order to deter insect infestation and the growth of moulds. Flour or meal could be stored in chests or bins, the *cyste* and *mydercan* of *Gerefa*.[45] An ark was generally used for meal, and a bin for flour. It seems likely that the meal ark was a convenient place to store other foods that needed to be kept dry. Moreover, such containers could be padlocked, so that provisions were under lock and key.

Bread could also have been stored in the meal chest, but it was probably not kept for more than a few days, being baked as necessary, although a kind of unleavened bread that would keep for weeks, months, or even years, was traditional in Europe.[46] Such bread may have been baked when there was a surplus of grain, for it was probably a safer way of preserving cereals than leaving them in store in their raw state.

Containers

Storage Jars

'Crock' (*croc*) was probably the Anglo-Saxon term for a storage jar, some of which had a relatively narrow neck and an everted rim, suitable for tying on a cover which may have been greased.[47] Oil or clarified butter may have been used as an airtight seal in the conservation of meat.[48]

Barrels and Boxes

Barrels and tubs were used for the storage of wet and dry goods.[49] Examples of barrels have been found in archaeological contexts, since they were re-used as well linings. It is generally assumed that barrels were used for wine, but the Norman period oval cask found in the bottom of a food storage pit at Pevensey Castle may have been used for pickling.[50] Time-consuming to make, and needing skilled craftsmanship, a new barrel may have been used first for wine, then, if it became tainted, for pickling, before being relegated for use as a well-lining.

The small boxes for which fittings, including locks, were found might have included in their contents particularly valuable spices.[51]

Storage Conditions

Alfred records in his addition to Orosius that Wulfstan told him that 'there is among the Estonians a tribe that can create coldness' (*þær is mid Estum an mægð þæt hi magon cycle gewyrcan*).[52] They used it for preserving dead bodies during a lying-in period, but if 'anyone sets down two vessels full of ale or water, then they cause one or the other to become frozen over, whether it be summer or winter' (*man asette twegen fætels full ealað oðða wæteres, hy gedoð þæt oþer bið oferfroren, sam hit sy sumor sam winter*).[53] This can be effected with saltpetre (potassium nitrate), but is recorded because it was evidently not practised in Anglo-Saxon England. In any case, unheated storerooms were likely to have temperatures not much above freezing for some of the winter months. Stores had probably diminished by the time hot weather came, and restocking of dairy goods and meat would not start until the advent of cooler weather.

Butter needs to be stored somewhere cool, since it will become rancid even when salted.[54] Unsalted cheese would have to be treated as butter, although it would not go rancid as quickly as unsalted butter. In many parts of Britain it was the custom to bury butter in suitable containers, in peat bogs and a similar method may have been adopted for mutton fat in areas of Scandinavian influence.[55] The partial exclusion of air helped keep the fat fresh. Perhaps most households had to make do with cool storerooms. Pots made of porous clay could have been dipped in water which took up heat to evaporate, lowering the temperature of the contents. Salted cheeses could be stored somewhere dry, in the meal chest, for example, or 'hung up'.

Eggs may have been preserved in ash pits, old malt, straw or bran, but results were often less than satisfactory.[56]

Root vegetables could have been stored in cellars or dark storerooms. By spring, when the roots were less palatable, their shoots could be used as early salad.[57]

Storehouses were separate outbuildings, but storerooms could probably be found within large dwellings.[58] The place where salt meat was kept was called, on account of the preponderance of bacon, a 'bacon house' (*spic-hus*).

Cellars

There is archaeological and documentary evidence for cellars, which are ideal for storage, remaining cool in summer and winter.[59] Ad hoc cellars were probably holes in the ground, like the food storage pit from the Norman period at Pevensey Castle.[60]

Responsibility for Domestic Stores

Girdle hangers found in pagan Anglian graves may represent the bunch of keys worn by Roman women as a symbol of their authority and probably indicated the status of their owner.[61] A chatelaine has generally been seen as evidence of matronly authority, and this would seem to be confirmed by Æthelbert's law code: *Gif friwif locbore leswæs hwæt gedeð ... xxx scll. gebete*. This is translated by Fell as, 'If a freewoman in charge of the keys is found cheating...then 30 shillings compensation is to be paid'.[62] This law would seem to parallel the Welsh code where the freewoman had responsibility for her stores.[63] *II Canute* confirms this since it states when legislating about stolen goods:

'But it is her duty to guard the keys of the following - that is her storeroom key and her chest key and her (?)cupboard. If the goods have been put in any of these, she shall be held guilty.' (*Ac ðara cægan heo sceal weardian, þæt is hire heddernes cæge 7 hyre cyste cæge 7 hire tægan; gyf hit under ðyssa ænigum gebroht byð, ðone bið heo scyldig.*)[64]

Pests

Probably both the housemouse and black rat were present in Anglo-Saxon England.[65] Corn had to be kept from these pests which could make inroads on the stores, contaminate the grain they did not eat and transmit pestilence.[66] The reeve was cautioned not to neglect even a 'a mousetrap' (*musfellan*).[67] The remains of cats are found with remarkable frequency on Anglo-Saxon sites, including the earliest, and an accredited mouser was given a value of four pence in the Welsh Laws.[68] Bones of weasels and polecats found on early medieval sites may indicate their importance in the domestic economy, since they were tamed and trained to catch rats and mice.[69]

Flour, cereals and cereal products, cheese and dried fruits can become infested by the flour mite which causes digestive disorders in those who consume infected foodstuffs.[70] Insects can also transmit moulds from one commodity to another as well as disease.[71] Stores would have to be periodically checked, so that if there was infestation of any sort it could be dealt with before it contaminated quantities of food. On a large estate the reeve was responsible for the stores - their security and condition, cautioned to neglect 'neither grain nor sheaf, meat nor fat, cheese nor rennet.' (*ne corn ne sceaf, ne flæsc ne flotsmeru, ne cyse ne cyslyb*)[72] In monasteries this duty rested with the cellarer.[73]

(iii) Salt Production & Supply

Vessels for Salt

A container made of lead and called a *lead* was probably used for salt production and during the salting process as it would not be corroded by the salt.[74] At Bremesgrave, Worcester, which was in the king's demesne, Domesday records six *plumbi* ('leads') for boiling salt, and at Terdeberie were two plumbi.[75] Provided lead was not in direct contact with flames, there was no reason not to use it, as it has a melting point of 327.5 degrees Centigrade. *Gerefa* and inventories list the *lead* with other catering equipment.[76] Archaeological evidence for such containers is likely to be scarce, as lead is a valuable metal, easy to melt down and re-use, but some fairly large lead vessels are known from the later period, like that from Westley Waterless, Cambs.[77]

Salt Production

Salt can be made from the ashes of certain plants, and from seaweed.[78] However, there is no evidence that this method was resorted to in Anglo-Saxon England, perhaps because no district was very far from either the sea, or salt-producing areas. Bede mentioned that England possessed salt pits (*Hit hafað eac þis land sealtseaþas*) which may refer to salt springs and/or pits into which the sea flowed at high tide.[79] Water trapped in the pit evaporated in the sun's heat and the wind to leave a deposit of salt. However, in Domesday salt pans were usually conveyed with 'vessels for the boiling of salt'.[80]

Domesday mentions 285 salt pans in Sussex alone, one hundred at *Rameslie*, a lost place-name, and most other seacoast counties have large numbers.[81] In the main the pans ran from Barnstaple in north Devon, round the south coast, and up round East Anglia. The waters of the Bristol channel may have been too turgid for successful salt extraction, or perhaps the superior salt of Worcestershire with its 50 *salinæ* was near enough at hand. There were also *salinæ* in Cheshire (10), Herefordshire (8), Gloucestershire (7), Shropshire (6), Warwickshire (3) and Oxford (1).[82]

The salt from geological deposits in Worcestershire was being extracted from salt springs at least as early as the late seventh century.[83] Charters of the eighth and ninth centuries include salt pits or salt production plant.[84]

Sometimes the Domesday survey indicates that the salt-works were not objects of great importance: some yield scarcely any revenue. The 285 *salinæ* in Sussex averaged two shillings and five-pence halfpenny, but one salt-works in Devon paid £13.10s.[85] By way of comparison, a salt pan in Droitwich was worth four shillings when a house in Worcester was valued at one; five salt-pans in Halesowen were worth sixty shillings, the mill ten shillings.[86]

At the time of the Domesday survey there seems to have been no standard measure for salt, which is recorded in *ambrae, bulliones, mensurae, mittae, sextaria and summae*.[87] An amber was four bushels, so that we know the production of *v salinae de cx ambris salis* at Wassington in Sussex to have been 11 tons.

Salt Workers

Salt workers seem to have been men working in a small way, renting their own salt pans. It is likely that many were fishermen or closely associated with fishermen.[88] Some may have been full-time salt-boilers, like Picot Sannarius of Winchester.[89] Block salt required considerable effort to reduce to powder, and the individual, Hack-Salt, who is recorded in the Winton Domesday, may have had an occupational name (though equally, this may be a nickname).[90]

Provision of a Salt Supply

Large establishments were anxious to secure the salt supplies necessary for catering on a large scale. The earliest reference to the important Worcestershire salt trade occurs in a charter of King Wulfhere, who reigned from 657-74. He made over 50 *manentes* at Hanbury with all the meadows, woods and brine pits belonging thereto to Abbot Colman.[91] By effecting an exchange of properties, including salt-works, the king and the community at Worcester seem to have finalised the convenient provision of their salt supply in 716/17.[92] There are other eighth-century references to a salt supply, like the exemption from toll of a ship bearing salt in favour of a Kentish nunnery, and in 732 Ethelbert gave land at Sampton, Kent, suitable for the boiling of salt, to Abbot Dunn, plus 120 laden wagons of firewood annually for cooking the salt.[93] It was common to provide 'wood for boiling salt' (*ligna ad coquendum sal*) with grants of salterns.[94]

Similar grants continued to be made in the ninth and tenth centuries, sometimes in connection with weirs, so provision was made for the fish caught there to be preserved.[95] By the end of the period both Glastonbury and Sherborne Abbeys had procured coastal estates in Lyme, whose importance seems to have rested entirely on the salterns.[96]

By the end of the tenth century some ecclesiastical establishments had more than provided for their own needs for salt, and were renting out salt-works as going concerns.[97]

Droitwich, Worcs., the chief salt town of England, was a very specialised community in which, while the majority of the pans belonged to king or earl, many other people had interests.[98] Individuals also negotiated a salt supply. According to the Winton Domesday, Siward the Moneyer owed William of Chesney lodgings, salt and water.[99] Probably most smaller households were dependent on the salt pedlars who transported salt from the salt-pans on the coast, or from the wiches of Cheshire and Worcestershire, by way of the extensive system of salt-ways.[100]

Tolls

A cartload of Cheshire salt drawn by two or more oxen and travelling to another county paid fourpence at the time of Domesday.[101] Salt pedlars from Cheshire were given a preferential rate of one penny per cart.[102] The temptation with tolls based on the pack-load, was to load a horse with as much as it could possibly carry.[103]The rate was twopence for a horse-load or eight men's loads.[104] The fact that salt from Droitwich commanded a higher toll than salt from elsewhere perhaps suggests that it was thought superior. The cost of transport and the taxes probably exceeded the price of the salt itself.

[1] Colgrave 1940, 268-9.
[2] Owen 1841, 753.
[3] Cockayne 1851, I xxii, lxxii, *Lacnunga* XIVa, III xxii 2.
[4] op. cit., *Peri Didacheon*, II xxxix.
[5] Renfrew 1985, 17.
[6] Cockayne 1851, *Lacnunga* 116.
[7] C. A. Wilson 1973, 113; Severin 1978.
[8] McNeill 1963.
[9] Roesdahl 1982, 120; Tannahill 1973, 216; Horander in Fenton & Kisban 1986, 54; Furnivall 1868, 98; Tannahill 1973, 216.
[10] Lauwerier 1986, 210; Cockayne 1851, II xxiv; Ayrton 1975, 11; Moryson 1617, IV 167; Roesdahl 1982, 120.
[11] McGee 1986, 104.
[12] Moorhouse in Aston 1988.
[13] Edlin 1949, 41, 77.
[14] Foote & Wilson 1970, 163; Holmes 1952, 92; Sass 1975, 109, 118-9.
[15] McGee 1986, 370.
[16] op. cit., 171.
[17] Sayce 1946.
[18] Clifton 1983, 19, 32.
[19] McGee 1986, 173.
[20] Garmonsway 1978.
[21] op. cit., 35-6.
[22] Cockayne 1851, II iv, vi, xxxii, *Lacnunga* 39, 112.
[23] Holmes 1952, 92; Sass 1975, 109, 118-9; Kundergraber in Fenton & Owen 1981, 172-3.
[24] Tannahill 1973, 212.
[25] C. A. Wilson 1973, 39.
[26] Hartley 1954, 329ff.
[27] Cockayne 1851, I v, vi, xxxviii 5, II x.
[28] McGee 1986, 509; Hartley 1954, 326.
[29] Horander in Fenton & Kisban 1986, 55.
[30] Kuper 1977, 4.
[31] Robertson 1939, 74-5.
[32] Wiseman 1986, 6, 63, 65.
[33] Ayrton 1975, 79.
[34] op. cit.
[35] op. cit., 78.
[36] Wiseman 1986, 178.
[37] Whitelock 1955, 385.
[38] Cockayne 1851, I 402.

39 op. cit., I xvii 2, xxxi 1, lxxxiii, II vii, I lix.
40 Liebermann 1898, 454; Monk 1977, 278; Owen 1841, 327; Cockayne 1851, III MS. Cott. Vitell. E. xviii. fol. 61; Cunliffe 1976, 126; Bosworth & Toller 1898.
41 Grube 1934, 145.
42 op. cit.
43 Trow Smith 1957, 138.
44 Monk 1977, 341; Hickin 1964, 89; Turner 1828, II 513.
45 Liebermann 1898, 455.
46 Weaver in Fenton & Owen 1981, 355; Moberg 1973, II 38-9.
47 Fenton & Kisban 1986, 114-5; West 1963, 246-72; 1982, 405.
48 McGee 1986, 104; Bonser 1963, 191; Ayrton 1975, 147-9; CA Wilson 1973, 64-5; Kuper 1977, 38, 41.
49 Edlin 1949, 72, 99.
50 Spriggs 1977, 12.
51 Evison 1987, 103; Ottaway 1985, 7-12.
52 Sweet 1954, 22.
53 op. cit.
54 Hartley 1954, 481.
55 Renfrew 1985, 14; Brothwell 1969, 44; Furnivall 1868, 98.
56 Todd 1987, 175.
57 Kundegraber in Fenton & Owen 1981, 173.
58 Colgrave 1940, 346; Olsen & Schmidt 1977, 235; Seebohm 1952, 95.
59 Hodges 1982, 131; Wiseman 1986, 178; Williams 1984, 133; Biddle 1976, 14, 40, 44, 339-40.
60 Spriggs 1977, 12.
61 Meaney 1981, 178-9; Evison 1987, 116-7.
62 Fell 1984, 60-1.
63 Owen 1841, 95, 517.
64 Robertson 1925, 214-5.
65 Prummel 1983, 245; O'Connor 1988, 39.
66 Bonser 1963, 76.
67 Liebermann 1898, 455.
68 Clutton Brock in Wilson 1976, 384; Bell 1977.
69 Seebohm 1952, 133.
70 Hickin 1964, 143.
71 op. cit., 93, 98, 103.
72 Knowles 1940, 462.
73 Liebermann 1898, 453.
74 Loyn 1970, 108.
75 Commissioners 1819, 413-14.
76 Liebermann 1898, 455; Robertson 1939, 75.
77 Wilson 1976, 267; Fox 1948.
78 Kuper 1977, 102; Roesdahl 1982, 120.
79 Miller 1890, I, 1 26.
80 Turner 1828, II 547; C. A. Wilson 1973, 29; Darby 1940, 39.
81 Turner 1828, III 247.
82 op. cit.
83 Finberg 1972, 12, 86.
84 op. cit., 98, 101.
85 Commissioners 1819, 413.
86 op. cit.; Bland, Brown & Tawney 1914.
87 Commissioners 1819, 415.
88 Loyn 1970, 106.
89 Barlow et al. 1976, 85, 115.
90 op. cit., 96.
91 Finberg 1972, 12, 86.

[92] Loyn 1970, 106; Whitelock 1955, 450.
[93] Whitelock 1955, 450-1.
[94] Page 1985, 221.
[95] Robertson 1939, 46.
[96] Keen in Haslam 1984, 229.
[97] Finberg 1972, 110, 126, 133.
[98] Whitelock 1952, 115-6.
[99] Barlow et al. 1976, 106.
[100] Finberg 1972, 73; Hill 1981, map 189; Smith 1964, I 19, 218, 220, 222, III 62.
[101] Langdon 1986, 49.
[102] Whitelock 1952, 116.
[103] Langdon 1986, 49.
[104] Whitelock 1952, 116.

5 Methods of Cooking

Fire

Wood

Securing a Supply

It is sometimes difficult to ascertain for what purpose wood mentioned in grants is intended.[1] 'Wooding' (*uuidigunge*) is the only unambiguous term for fuel.[2]

Cutting and gathering wood is one of the summer tasks listed in *Gerefa*. Wood was taken back to the homestead, sometimes in carts drawn by oxen as illustrated in two early eleventh-century calendars.[3] Splitting the wood was a job for winter,[4] after which it was stacked into a *scidhræc*[5] and kept dry.[6]

A peasant household presumably found its own firewood. *Rectitudines Singularum Personarum* refers to 'the right of cutting wood according to the custom of the estate' (*wuduræden be landside*).[7] A larger household called for more fuel, and the owners of large establishments used their power to ensure that they were supplied with wood. At Hurstbourne Priors, Hampshire, in about 1050, the *ceorlas* had to supply '4 fothers of wood, split and made into a stack in their own time' (*IIII foðera aclofenas gauolwyda to scidhræc on hiora agenre hwile*).[8] Royal charters sometimes granted the right to gather firewood.[9] Tithes and guild dues included firewood.[10]

Different Types Of Wood

Anglo-Saxons who had to make fires for cooking no doubt knew what is now only accessible to most of us in mnemonic poems like 'Logs to Burn'.[11] An analysis of the charcoal in a seventh-century hearth provides evidence of hazel, hawthorn, oak and poplar or willow.[12] Assuming that it is willow rather than poplar charcoal, all the woods are good fuel. Unfortunately there are too many imponderables to make it possible to work out by careful excavation and analysis of hearth material what kind of fire had been made, and therefore what sort of cooking process may have been undertaken.

To spit roast a pig of 120lb dead weight, the ideal fuel is 15 cwt of large oak logs, a foot long and thoroughly seasoned, cloven into halves or thirds and placed on end to form a bed which will burn steadily. On this 15 cwt of ash with a diameter of 4-5" and in foot lengths (cut at least a month previously) is used to provide local areas of fiercer heat in line with the quarters of the animal.

Other Fuel

Glosses give Old English *col* for *carbo* (coal), and *sinder* for *scorium* (cinder, clinker), and since col and sinder are Old English words, this suggests they represent things known to the Anglo-Saxons from an early period.[13] Charcoal may also have been used as a domestic fuel, particularly in braziers. Although reeds and straw produce a hot fire, and were used for baking, they burn very quickly, and processes like roasting would have been difficult.[14] It may be that woodland was decreasing during the Anglo-Saxon period, and that some areas of the Midlands, Yorkshire and the Fens had no woodland at all.[15] If this was the case, then other, less ideal, fuels would have had to have been exploited, with a consequent modification of cooking processes.

It seems that even fires which could call on the best fuel were what we would regard as excessively smoky.[16] Soot (*hrum*) was evidently deposited on utensils in some quantity.[17] Food cooked by direct exposure to the heat of the fire, or in open pans may have had a smoky flavour.

Fire Making

Fire-steels are often found in pagan Anglo-Saxon graves, together with flint or pyrites against which the iron could be struck to obtain a spark.[18] These firesteels very often doubled as pursemounts, the purse almost certainly containing tinder for starting a fire, and sometimes a flint too.[19] They were evidently in use throughout the period, occurring in such late Saxon contexts as the town of Thetford and the palace site at Cheddar.[20] Tinder was often made from touchwood or *punk*, rotten wood decayed by fungal attack, birch bark, dried brushwood, gorse or straw.[21]

'Bellows' (*blestbælg*) were known.[22] Fire tongs are shown also in the Anglo-Saxon calendar, BL Cott. Julius A IV.[23] Pokers and a *fyr-scofl* are recorded.[24] Firecovers were used to keep the fire alive at a time when fires were not particularly easy to light, and to prevent sparks escaping.[25]

Cooking: Direct Application of Heat

Food could be cooked by direct exposure to the fire, or by heating in a utensil placed in, on, above, under or beside the fire. Such fires were often the domestic hearth for warming a room and its occupants, as well as for cooking. The fires may have been lit directly on an unprepared floor or more commonly on a hearth made of clay, tiles and stones.[26] Bede's account, 'A great fire was kindled in the middle of the house'

(*Wæs micel fyr onæled on middum þam huse*) accords with archaeological evidence from West Stow - and elsewhere.[27] Later hearths may have been built against a wall, if this was backed with stone.[28]

There is evidence that hearths were also made in the open.[29] No doubt cooking was carried on outside on suitable days, when the houses could be kept cool and free of smoke.

It is possible that the Anglo-Saxons used chafing dishes and stoves, in effect portable hearths.[30]

Cooking: Indirect Application of Heat

If utensils were available, but were not fire proof, their contents, liquid or semi-liquid, could be heated by 'pot-boilers', stones heated on the hearth and then dropped into the vessels, using tongs or dampened wooden shovels, as was the case at Sutton Courtney.[31] There is evidence that heated stones were used for boiling and roasting material in troughs and hide vessels too.[32] On occasion a heated iron or poker might be used to heat a liquid. Both methods are referred to in *Leechdoms*.[33]

If no utensils were available, then a cooking pit, probably lined with stones, could have been used. Turner deduced that Anglo-Saxons may have cooked their victuals in pits since *seathan* (to seethe, simmer, boil) was derived from *seath* (a pit).[34] An experiment in pot-boiler cookery showed that a ten-pound leg of mutton wrapped in clean straw tied with a twisted straw rope, as indicated in early Irish literature, was cooked after 3 hours 40 minutes uncontaminated by ash or mud.[35]

Ovens

Earth Ovens

Earth ovens used the heat from glowing stones heated on a nearby fire. A pit was dug into the ground, was perhaps lined with stones, and either pre-heated with brushwood, or half-filled with red hot stones on which the meat, packed in clay or leaves, was placed. It was then covered with more stones which, as they cooled, may have been replaced, or they may have been covered with earth or turf to retain the heat. In either case the meat would cook in a time comparable to that taken by a modern oven.[36]

Hot-air Ovens

Ovens in which the contents were cooked in hot air were known to the Anglo-Saxons. The *ofn* which was one of the 'many things a farmstead must have' (*fela ðinga sceal to tune*) was probably of this type.[37] There were three main methods of heating an oven. One, still in use today, is to burn faggots of brushwood in the oven, raking out the ashes before putting in the food to be cooked.[38] Another method was to light a fire beneath, or around or on top of an oven - a small 'oven' could be made by inverting a pot and putting embers around and on it. The third method was to heat the oven by building it into a construction where hot air would be conducted round it in flues. The second and third methods are still in use, as is a combination of them.

According to the literature, ovens could be quite large: big enough for a man,[39] as are some ovens in the archaeological record. At the fifth- to seventh-century site of West Stow half a sunken-floored building was occupied by the remains of a large clay oven, 3'6" along the surviving axis; its floor consisted of a flat plate of clay 2 1/2" thick, incorporating a layer of flints, with walls up to 6" thick.[40] The mid-period site of North Elmham yielded an oven of comparable size. A mid eighth- to mid tenth-century oven at Porchester in building S11, probably a bakehouse serving the hall, had been built largely of re-used Roman tiles and some lumps of limestone set in clay, with walls approximately 15" thick; the floors of the stoking chambers had been worn considerably in use. It had been built over the remains of an earlier oven 3' x 5' in area and 9" deep, the floor of which showed signs of intensive burning.[41]

Ovens were probably a fire risk.[42] It was probably this element, as much as the convenience of having all the baking processes together in a single-purpose building, that caused them to be housed separately.

Use

Perhaps their most important function was to cook bread but they could also have been used for roasting joints, perhaps coated in a flour and water paste which sealed in the juices. After the bread was baked, ovens could have been utilised for a range of dishes that needed long, slow cooking.

Kitchens

Provision of food on a large scale resulted in the use of a detached building as a kitchen, as distinct from a bakehouse.[43] According to Athelstan's Laws, a *ceorl* who had a kitchen could be accounted a thane.[44] From the tenth century the kitchen seems to have been integrated in the manor complex itself.[45]

By the tenth-century monasteries had a *coquina* (kitchen).[46] Everyone had to take their turn 'to work in the kitchen' (*of kycenan to penienne*).[47] At Abingdon Ælfstan prepared food in the kitchen for the builders of the monastery.[48]

In smaller households it is likely that part of the main room was used for cooking.

Cooks

The Old English word *coc* (cook) is a masculine noun and those cooks who are mentioned have male names: 'Ælfsige the cook' (*Ælfsige þene coc*), 'Albold the cook' (*Albold cocus*).[49] The cook of Ælfric's *Colloquy* is also a man and he does not seem to be operating in a monastic context: with his *ge* (you) he seems to be addressing people in general.[50]

A specialist cook is likely to have been male and full-time. Considerable strength was needed to lift large cauldrons and their contents,[51] whilst the quantity of cooking in a large household would have been too great for a part-time worker.[52]

In a peasant household the cooking methods were no doubt adjusted to the amount of time that could be given to this task, which was probably worked in with other jobs. Stews of salt meat and bacon, for example, would have needed little attention, beyond making sure that the fire was kept alight.

The interlocutor in the *Colloquy* suggests most people could cook for themselves: 'we can boil the things that need to be boiled and roast the things that need roasting ourselves' (*we sylfe magon seoþan þa þingc þe to seoþenne synd, 7 brædan þa þingc þe to brædene synd*).[53] Ælfric's cook does not develop the difficulties of his profession, but it is not without significance that one of the dishes he cites - 'rich broth' (*fætt broþ*) may have been a speciality. For providing William I with a dish of farinaceous pottage, his cook, Robert Argyllon, received a carucate of land.[54] *Leechdoms* tell of barley meal or groats 'cooked together as cooks know how' (*togædre gebriwed swa cocas cunnon*) which suggests that some skills were restricted to cooks.[55]

It seems likely that large monastic establishments would have specialist cooks although, according to *The Rule of Chrodegang*, each monk had to take a turn working in the kitchen and to return the *batterie de cuisine* intact and in good condition at the end of his week's work.[56] The *Rule* does however consider the case where 'it is necessary to get in lay cooks' (*neod beo þæt læwede cocas þæder in gan*). They were to leave quickly 'as soon as they had served/done their work' (*swa raðe swa hi geþenod hæbbon*).[57]

As well as specialist cooks in large establishments, the fact that cooks are recorded in Domesday at Bury St Edmunds, may indicate that there were also cooks catering for pilgrims, setting up their cookshops in towns which attracted travellers.[58] In Winchester in 1100 Hugh paid the king four pence for his kitchen, and received from it five shillings, which perhaps suggests a cookshop.[59] As well as Theodoric the king's cook, and Herbert the chamberlain's cook, there were seven others simply described as 'the cook' who rented or owned property in Winchester at this time, as well as a confectioner.[60]

Preparation

Some preparation was doubtless done at table: getting oysters or periwinkles 'out of their shells' (*of scellum*), or peeling apples.[61]

A large variety of leaves was eaten as green salad, but was usually picked over to remove poisonous plants: St Martin 'ate in his food the bitter herb called hellebore' (*on his mete þigde þa ættrian wyrt elleborum hatte*).[62] Most vegetables were probably washed, even when eaten raw.[63]

Some *Leechdoms* call for a 'clean pan, clean container' (*clænne panne, clæne fæt*), but it may have been difficult to clean the various containers used in the preparation of food effectively.[64] This may be why a number of recipes call for new utensils.[65] The success with which metal and soapstone vessels can be cleaned (in comparison with wooden and earthenware containers) added to their value.

After a preliminary scraping and wiping, perhaps with bunches of twigs, leaves or heather, pans could be cleaned with an abrasive sand mixture, or with wood ash.[66] Soap was known at least to later Anglo-Saxons.[67] Presumably the outside of pans was not usually bothered with.[68]

Meat, from large oysters to carcasses, would have needed cutting up with knives or axes.[69] The Anglo-Saxons were able, not only to produce portions manageable enough to be eaten with the fingers, or small enough to be spooned up, but to mince foodstuffs.[70] Minced meat eked out with offal, including such organs as the lights which are not now normally sold for human consumption, cereals, herbs and suet, and sometimes incorporating the blood of a slaughtered - or living - animal, is an ancient dish found in many parts of the British Isles.[71] Mixtures of this type are often put into animal membranes to make sausages or puddings.[72] *Mearh* is used to translate 'a pork sausage' (*lucanica*) in the Epinal and Erfurt glosses.[73] *Mearh-gehæcc, mearh-hæccel* are terms for meat puddings; *haccian* means 'to chop up'.[74] Such puddings or sausages could be made from the meat of virtually any edible animal or bird and could be boiled or grilled: in the latter case no further container was necessary.

For invalids and children who were being weaned, it was necessary to reduce food to a pulp. It could be 'ground in a mortar' (*gegnið on mortere*).[75] Bolting cloths, hair and metal sieves and strainers were known.[76]

Salt meat and fish and dried foods were soaked before cooking.[77]

The principle of marinading was known: beef is marinaded in vinegar and herbs.[78] Vegetables and apples were also marinaded - the latter overnight in wine and honey.[79]

Clay was sometimes used for encasing joints, much as a pastry case would do, and for wrapping seabirds, when the feathers would peel off with the clay.[80]

Other miscellaneous instructions in *Leechdoms* read very like modern recipes. Quantities are not given with the same degree of accuracy, but 'a shilling's weight' (*anes scyllinges gewyht*) or 'a handful' (*hand fulla*) give some idea of quantities.[81] 'Work it into a paste' (*clam of þam ilcan wyrc*), 'sweeten with honey' (*geswet mid hunige*), 'beat two eggs in hot water' (*gehrer twa ægru on hatum wæter*), 'shred up new cheese' (*screda niwne cysan*), 'shred the vegetables' (*gescearfa þas wyrto*), 'bind into mouthfuls with honey' (*mid hunige gewealcen to snædum*) are all perfectly comprehensible.[82] Temperature is indicated: 'on warm embers' (*on wærmum gledum*), 'in front of? a gentle fire' (*æt leohtum fyre*), 'smoke on embers' (*berec on gledum*), 'remove from the heat' (*do of heorðe*).[83] While such instructions sound archaic, because an open fire is generally no longer used for cooking, 'boil strongly until reduced by a third' (*welle swiþe oþ þriddan dæl*), 'until it has the consistency of honey' (*oþ huniges þicnesse*) sound perfectly modern.[84]

Cooking Methods

From a survey of Anglo-Saxon utensils, raw materials and methods of heating, it becomes possible to deduce cooking processes and the kind of meals eaten. However, rather than draw up an exhaustive paradigm of possible combinations and processes, I have drawn only a few inferences directly from the source material.

Cauldrons

Cauldrons are in effect metal cooking pots. They could be larger than their earthenware counterparts and had significance as symbols of the kingly provision of food.[85] The Sutton Hoo ship burial contained three cauldrons. The largest, raised from a single sheet of bronze, but with iron fittings, had a rim diameter of 70 cm, comparable in size to cauldrons from London and Taplow, according also with documentary evidence.[86]

Cauldrons were made of various metals or alloys: 'a copper vessel, or a brass or bronze one' (*cyperen fæt oþþe mæstling oþþe bræsen*), and a 'tin vessel' (*tinum fæte*) is also specified.[87] Cauldrons were also made of iron and although these may not have had the prestige value of bronze, copper or brass items, nutritionally they probably contributed significantly to the diet of their owners by preventing anaemia, since cooking acidic food in iron pots increases the iron content of the food by a factor of thirty to a hundred.[88]

Cauldrons (*hweras*) seem to be the cooking vessel most in evidence in the Anglo-Saxon period, and were associated with mass catering.[89] A late Anglo-Saxon monastic inventory included 'a kettle' (*an cetel*) - a metal container for cooking but differentiated from a 'cauldron' (*hwer*).[90] In one *Leechdom* a *cetele* is the vessel to be used for stewing beet to a pulp.[91] The reeve was to have charge of a range of cooking equipment: 'cauldron, container made of lead, kettle, ladle, pans, crocks, firedogs, dishes, vessels with handles' (*hwer, lead, cytel, hlædel, pannan, crocca, brandiren, dixas, stelmelas*).[92]

Cauldrons had to be suspended over, or supported above, a fire. Pot hangers and suspension chains are recorded in documentary sources and from archaeological evidence.[93] When it was part of the hall furniture, the chain might be very elaborate.[94] A different form of suspension is shown in the Bayeux Tapestry where a pole has been passed through the two rings on either side of the cauldron, and then supported on two forked uprights.[95] The eighth-century Epinal gloss gives 'gridiron/tripod' (*brandrað* for *andeda*), and the slightly later Erfurt gloss gives *brondrað*.[96] 'Trivet' (*trefet*) is recorded in an inventory for Yaxley, and trivets are illustrated supporting round-bottomed cauldrons, although these also have suspension loops.[97] Sometimes feet were an intrinsic part of the vessel.[98]

Cauldrons, used in conjunction with meat forks and ladles, were presumably used for the production of soups and stews for the household.[99] Fires on a hearth suited a hanging cauldron, or a cauldron supported on its own legs or a trivet, which made 'cauldron food' more or less obligatory.[100]

Soapstone Bowls

Soapstone bowls were desirable as being unbreakable on clay floors, easy to clean with good heat distribution and they did not taint the food.

Probably imported from Shetland or Norway they have been found in Anglo-Danish York and elsewhere.[101]

Earthenware Pots

Probably earthenware pots were in general use for cooking throughout the period.[102] Upright pierced lugs on the rims of bowls and horizontal pierced lugs on the shoulders of some of the smaller pots indicate these were for suspension over a fire, and therefore for cooking. Earthenware pots are thought of as being suited to cooking at low temperatures but they were apparently used for boiling too.[103] Good quality pots which were more heat-resistant were imported from widely-spaced centres across northern Belgium and France and Germany into such ports as Hamwih.[104]

Leather Vessels

Leather containers were probably important as cooking vessels.[105] The Anglo-Saxon *sceowyrt* (shoemaker) made *higdifatu* (leather vessels), and it is likely these were used for cooking.[106]

Boiling & Stewing

The Anglo-Saxons seem to have boiled food which we would expect to be roasted, for example, the goose offered by Cuthbert to the visiting brothers.[107] Boiled meat preserves all its juices, making economical and nutritionally effective use of the foodstuff.[108] It has a less luxurious connotation than roast meat which still keeps its special status. Stewing is the ideal way of cooking any part of a carcass that, because of old age, or hard work - in the case of plough oxen - would be very tough if roasted.[109] In tenth-century Skeldergate, the limb bones of cattle were reduced to small pieces, suitable for boiling in the stock-pot.[110]

Boiling, or stewing, that is, cooking with the addition of water, milk, butter or some other liquid, is likely to be the prevailing mode of cooking when salt meat forms a substantial part of the diet, since if cooked in other ways the meat becomes hard. Traditionally, after soaking for 12-48 hours the meat was wrapped in a floured cloth hung from the handle of a cauldron, and dried peas, or - in the case of bacon - beans and/or barley were also cooked in floured bags in the same cauldron.[111] The vegetables, dried or fresh, would absorb the salt. Probably long, slow cooking was the order of the day: 'stew for a very long time over embers' (*seowe swiþe lange ofer gledum*) is the instruction in a *Leechdom*.[112] Salt fish would also be boiled, traditionally in milk or butter.[113] Boiling was evidently such a common way of cooking meat that a *Leechdom* could give the instruction 'boil three times as strongly as water for boiling meat' (*seow swa swyþe þ hit þriwa wylle swa swyðe swa wæter flæsc*) or simply ask for 'fat meat well-boiled' (*fæt flæsc þ beo wel gesoden*).[114]

Not just meat and fish, but a variety of foods were cooked in various liquids.[115] Where no instructions were given as to the liquid, the presumption is that water was used. The instruction for hard boiling eggs, for example, is simply 'take nine eggs and boil them hard' (*genim nigon ægra 7 seoð hig fæste*).[116] Vegetables were probably usually cooked in salted water, since in one case the salt is to be omitted: 'dry beans and boil them without salt' (*drige beana 7 geseow butan sealte*).[117] In one case the instruction was 'boil in milk, butter is better' (*wyl on meolce on buteran is betere*), and in two cases butter was to be used.[118] Honey and butter seem to have been used together in three *Leechdoms*, and honey on its own once.[119] Vegetables were also to be seethed in oil, and seeds in a mixture of oil and ale.[120] 'Many kinds of apples, pears and medlars' (*manigfeald appelcyn peran æpeningas*) were to be stewed in vinegar, wine and water or just wine, on occasion sweetened with honey.[121]

Broth

Broð was the Old English term for broth or soup, which might be enriched with milk or butter.[122] The cook of the *Colloquy* mentions 'fat/rich broth' (*fæt broþ*) as one of the dishes he makes,[123] possibly enriched with bone marrow, as well as dairy products. 'Bean soup' (*beonbroð*) was recommended in *Leechdoms*, as was 'pea soup' (*pysena broþ*).[124] Broths may customarily have included dried pulse,[125] although the recommended *geseaw broðu* were perhaps made from fresh vegetables.[126] Carrot broth and mint broth are also mentioned.[127] *Henne broþe* is referred to, and one recipe for hen and mallow leaf broth confirms the supposition that, like modern soup, Anglo-Saxon broth was a relatively thin liquid).[128] Similarly remedies could be taken 'in hot ale or broth or water' (*on hat ala oððe broð oððe wæter*).[129]

Like stews, broth was a convenient food for mass catering. The *Rule of St Benedict* allowed two dishes of soup every day in monasteries, although peppered broths were classed with dishes of delicacies.[130]

Cereal Pottages

If *broþe* was retained to indicate a thin liquid, the term which supplanted it in the meaning 'pottage', is *briw*. *Briw* originally meant a simple cereal pottage, and even in late Anglo-Saxon times the references of 'make a brewit from rye meal' (*rigenum melwe wyrceað briwas*) and 'new barley meal or groats made into a brewit as cooks know how' (*niwe beren mela oððe grytta togædre gebriweð swa cocas cunnon*) suggest this, even if their preparation seems by this time to have become the province of the professional.[131]

'Groats' (*grytta*) could have been threshed and pounded in a mortar. If the grain had been parched, it needed little further cooking to make it digestible. Unroasted grain soaked in water gelatinises into digestible frumenty.[132] Whole grain preparations are a good source of vitamins A and B, and with milk are a highly nutritious food.[133] Linseed, or other oil-containing seeds, may have been used to enrich cereal-based pottage.[134]

Lacnunga instructs ...'boil [cropleek] in butter, and shred up...add...barley meal and plenty of white salt, boil for a long time and eat hot' (*wyll in buteran þas wyrte 7 scearfa smale ado...beren mela 7 hwites sealtes fela wyl loncge 7 hatne ete*).[135] A similar method is used in other recipes, though with other leaf vegetables and wheat meal.[136] A mixture of 'cream or good skimmings' (*ream oþþe gode flete*) 'good barley meal and white salt' (*god beren mela 7 hwit sealt*) was to be beaten up 'until it is as thick as thin brewit' (*oþ þ hit sie þicce swa þynne briw*) which suggests *briw* was a thick, porridgey mixture.[137]

The serving of cereal or leguminous preparations with meat continues in modern English cooking. Sometimes a direct comparison can be made with an Anglo-Saxon recipe: chicken with a parsley and bread stuffing, for example.[138] Oatmeal (groats) is still used as a thickening agent in stews, as are other flours.

It is possible that such food had a rustic connotation, but while townsfolk may have eaten more cereal as bread, cereals eaten as gruel or porridge probably formed a significant part of the diet in Anglo-Saxon England.[139]

Cereal brewits may also have been fermented.[140] Organic residues from the fermentation process in porridges have been recovered from the Anglo-Saxon period.[141] That such residues have not arisen merely because cereal mixtures were left in pots, is suggested by a traditional Swedish recipe: *blodpalt*, a mixture of salted blood and rye flour fermented for three weeks.[142]

Stews

Stews were the mainstay of the Anglo-Saxon cuisine.[143] In poorer households a stew may have been prepared and reheated with additions over a long period.[144] Such a cooking method would have had much to recommend it to Anglo-Saxons without much in the way of domestic facilities.

Roasting, Grilling & Toasting

These terms are dealt with together, since they cover Old English *gebrædan*: to cook by the direct application of heat from a fire, though an item could also be *gebræde* 'on hot ashes' (*on hatan axan*).[145] Fish could be grilled, so could cheese and apples.[146] Butchery techniques suggest that some cuts of meat may also have been grilled or 'toasted' at a fire. In tenth-century Skeldergate, York, numerous cattle vertebrae were chopped across transversely in a manner consistent with the production of modern fore-rib or T-bone cuts.[147] From the earliest, i.e. ninth-century, levels at Flaxengate, there is archaeological evidence to suggest meat was cooked on the bone and was probably roasted.[148] It has been assumed from the butchery remains at Yeavering that spit-roasted beef was a major item of diet.[149] As well as the cost of the metalwork and a large enough piece of meat for spit roasting, this method is expensive in terms of fuel and time. (A 120lb pig takes about eight hours to cook, it must be turned constantly and the fire also has to be regulated.)

Roasting spits have been found in Viking-age Scandinavia,[150] but the only complete cooking spit known in Britain is from the 'pagan lady' burial at Peel Castle, Isle of Man. It was accompanied by a goose-wing (with feathers) and some seed-bearing plants. Perhaps spit, wing and herbs belong together as a roasting kit, indicative of the prestige of their owner (Graham-Campbell forthcoming). Poultry and other foods are illustrated being delivered to the table on spits in the Bayeux Tapestry.[151] In another scene food on spits is being passed from a stove to what may be a sideboard.[152] A tenth-century manuscript shows three diners, two of whom are being offered food on spits by kneeling attendants. The food here is cylindrical in form, and not immediately recognisable, though it may consist of lengths of sausage, or, more probably, eel.[153]

Griddles/Frying

Food was cooked at or over the fire on a solid support: a griddle or a toasting/baking stone, for example.[154] Griddles/pans occur in the archaeological record in Scandinavia (e.g. Graham-Campbell 1980, no. 48), but were presumably well-known utensils in England since Bede refers to the different cooking methods their use entails in his commentary to the *First Book of Samuel*: 'We are being nourished on food cooked on a griddle when we understand literally, openly and without covering...upon food cooked in the frying pan when, by frequent turning over the superficial meaning and looking at it afresh we comprehend what it contains...' (quoted in Hunter Blair 1970, 300).

In some places in Ireland a shallow pan was used to cook bread.[155] So a frying pan could be used without fat, but a flat griddle could take only a smear of fat to prevent sticking. A frying pan was a necessity if food was to be cooked in any quantity of fat. The Epinal and Erfurt glosses give *bredipannæ* and *breitibannæ* respectively for *sartago* (frying pan).[156] This was presumably the same utensil as the *brade pannan* which was to be 'greased inside with pork fat' (*gesmyre innewearde mid þan rysele*).[157]

Frying pans are found in archaeological contexts from the early ninth century.[158] A much patched iron pan was finally relegated to a rubbish pit in tenth-century York. It has a diameter of 30-35cm and there were clear signs where the handle had been attached. It may have been used for cooking buckwheat cakes.[159] Sheet metal from the iron dish of a smaller pan was also recovered from Anglo-Scandinavian York.[160] A complete iron frying pan of late ninth- early tenth-century date was recovered at Winchester.[161]

Rysele (lard/pork fat/dripping) used for greasing a frying pan, was probably a common medium for frying.[162] Oil and butter were also used.[163]

The term *afigæn/afigan* was used to translate 'fried' (*frixum*) in the Epinal and Erfurt glosses of the late eighth-early ninth centuries.[164] Elsewhere the term for frying seems to have been *gehyrstan*, as in the instruction *gehyrste on hatte pannan*.[165] From written sources it seems that fried dishes often consisted of eggs. *Leechdoms* contain detailed instructions for a sage omelette. 'Take a handful of sage and grind it very small, and twelve peppercorns and grind them up fine; then take eggs and beat them up with the sage and the pepper. Take a clean pan and fry the mixture in oil.' (*Nim salvian ane hand fulle 7 cnuca hy swiþe smale 7 nim twelf piper corn 7 gnind [read grind/gnid] hy smæle 7 nim þanne ægru 7 swing ho togædere mid þam wyrtum 7 mid þan pipor. Nim þanne æne clæne panne 7 hyrste hy mid ele*).[166] Another recipe in *Leechdoms* is also a form of vegetable omelette.[167]

Baking

Abacen is applied to meat as well as bread.[168] Oven-roasted meat may have been encased in a flour-and-water paste before baking so that, technically, it was steam-baked.[169] Baking would also have been the method of cooking complicated composite dishes like 'oyster loaves' (*osterhlafas*), probably made by filling a hollowed out loaf with oysters, suet, minced meat, egg and seasoning.[170]

Anglo-Norman recipes are more complex than those in the French sources and may derive from the Anglo-Saxon cuisine.[171] They include a 'soutil brouet d'Angleterre': chestnuts, hard-boiled egg yolks, and pork liver ground up and made into a paste cooked with spices and saffron. Another unusual combination is cherries, ground chicken and hard-boiled egg yolks.[172] These mixtures were presumably baked.

Desserts

Sweet omelettes containing flowers or fruit were also a possibility, as were egg custard mixtures.[173] Certainly the Anglo-Saxons enjoyed dishes of milk/cream/curds, sometimes with wine, or with the addition of meal.[174] Summer puddings which use bread to contain fruit, often blackberries, raspberries or whortleberries, are also archaic. Cereal-derived flummery produced a slightly acid, solid jelly, and cows' heels and calves' feet may have been used to make jellies.[175]

Sweet dishes - *eft-mettas* (literally 'after-meats', so, desserts) - were regarded as morally dubious.[176] They were seen as a temptation to gluttony, and could result in the stimulation of other appetites. In the Epinal and Erfurt glosses, *sperwyrt* (elecampane) glosses *gallengar*, i.e. galingale, the preserved root of the cypress used in cookery and as a sweetmeat.[177] Elsewhere *sperwyrt* glosses *veneria,* roots used as a confection.[178] Perhaps it was the apparent implications of this semantic association that called down condemnations.

Cakes & Biscuits

Fats and oils were almost certainly used as shortening in biscuits and cakes.[179] The glossing of *crustulla* (a flat cake) by *halstan/heallstan* (hall-stone, possibly hearth- or baking-stone) might suggest a mistranslation.[180] However, *halstan* could have been something like a round of shortbread, and the name a humorous one like 'rock' cakes. The French *gastel*, a type of biscuit or cake recorded in the twelfth century was compared to a flat, round stone.[181] This was made from flour, shortening and honey, and would have been similar to shortbread. The low temperature needed for cooking would have been available in an oven after the bread had been baked, or at the hearth-side. Enriched breads (see Chapter 2) provided another sort of cake.

Other Anglo-Saxon cakes were small: at least *cicel* (cake) is glossed by *pastillus* (a little cake) in one of the later word-lists.[182] *Peri Didacheon* prescribes new cheese pared into boiling water and made into little *cicles* to be bound to the eyes overnight. Here a 'little cake' would only be an inch or so across: perhaps the standard cake size was 2-5" in diameter, our bun or scone size. Grube considers that cake was known to the Germanic peoples long before the Migration period.[183] He thinks that on occasion the term *æppel* (apple) was used to signify a dumpling, as in 'knead it together so that you make it into an apple/a dumpling' (*cnuce tosomne þan gelice þe þu æppel wyrce*).[184] On occasion these may have been sweetened to produce some sort of cake since *hunig æppel* (honey dumpling) glossed Latin *pastellus*.[185] In the post-Conquest period types of cake were made by assembling and binding together ready-cooked ingredients,[186] suggesting the *hunig æppel* of Anglo-Saxon times.

Sauces

A comparison of two later medieval recipes for green sauce, one French, the other English, suggests that the English either had more native herbs or at least appreciated them more.[187] There are several mentions of sorrel in *Leechdoms*, and this was possibly used as a sauce then as it is today.[188]

Some fruit sauces are traditionally served with meat and fish dishes.[189] Fruit sauces are useful in that they 'cut the fat', aiding digestion. Strawberry sauce for boiled meat, recorded in an Anglo-Norman recipe is reputedly subtle and very good.[190]

Vinegar, honey and herbs (cf. modern mint sauce) are mentioned in *Leechdoms* as an appetising sauce, there is no reason to suppose that such sauces were not used as part of the normal diet in Anglo-Saxon times.[191]

'Prepared mustard' (*gerenodne senep*) was apparently used as a flavouring with bread or other food (op. cit.). A mixture is to have 'the form in which mustard is tempered for flavouring' (*þa onlicnesse geworht þe senop bið getemprod to inwisan*), and we learn that this could be spooned up, and so had the pasty consistency that made mustard has today. Cumin is also mentioned as an ingredient in a sauce, and both mustard and cumin were found in the Oseberg ship burial in Norway.[192]

Conclusion

Anglo-Saxon cookery seems to have been based on boiling, a method practised particularly in subsistence economies, where all parts of the animal have to be utilised.[193] The nobility may have been able to indulge a preference which is now widespread for tender joints which do not need stewing. Barley and other cereals, dried beans and legumes were commonly used in stews, brewits and soups.

Some basic procedures were already established in Anglo-Saxon times: clarifying butter, whipping cream, salting vegetables and serving them with butter, or with oil and vinegar, for example, but one important difference is a quantitative one: numerous herbs were used to flavour Anglo-Saxon dishes. That the cuisine used the resources to hand imaginatively, is emphasised by a comparison between Anglo-Norman and early medieval French recipes. The Anglo-Norman recipes make a considerable use of fruit and flowers not found in any French recipes. They are also far more specific and discriminating in the spicing of different dishes.[194] Features of the Anglo-Norman recipes which arguably represent the native English tradition are custard tarts with dried fruit, strawberries, blackberries and pears, hawthorn and rose flowers; white meat stews with elderflowers, mulberries or pears; red meat stews with rose petals, hawthorn blossoms, cherries and strawberries.[195] There seems to have been a predilection for sweet dishes, as a number of the recipes include fruit or honey.[196] There are dessert dishes: hazel nuts used in flour, and flour, milk and elder flowers used to made a pottage, for example.[197]

As well as fruit sauces and seasonings, colourings and garnishes were seen as important as part of the overall visual effect.[198]

This evidence for skilled cookery would seem initially to contradict the *Colloquy*, where the cook is summarily dismissed: 'We don't consider we need him, because we can stew ourselves anything that needs stewing, and roast those things that have to be roasted' (*We ne reccaþ ne he us neodþearf ys, forþan we sylfe magan seowan þa þingc þe to seoþenne synd, 7 brædan þa þingc þe to brædene synd*).[199] The response might be the same today: even if we don't feel we can turn our hand to ploughing or smithing, we feel we can manage to cook for ourselves. However, professional cooks then as now will have produced delicacies - indeed, kings and nobles were certainly able to command a variety of dishes.

---

[1] Robertson 1939, 13; Page 1985, 221.

2 op. cit.
3 Temple 1976, no. 199.
4 Liebermann 1898, 454.
5 Robertson 1939, 241.
6 Bosworth & Toller 1898, 213.
7 Liebermann 1898, 449.
8 Robertson 1939, 241.
9 Whitelock 1955, 484; Finberg 1972, 105.
10 Whitelock 1955, 560; Field 1972, 209.
11 Edlin 1949, 62-3, 156-7, 170.
12 Matthews in Hawkes 1985.
13 Wright 1871, 32.
14 Corran 1975, 37; Mellows 1980, 2.
15 Rackham in Biddick 1984, 75.
16 Owen 1841, 25.
17 Cockayne 1851, I xi 2, lxxii, for example.
18 Meaney 1981, 104; Cunliffe 1976, 195; West 1982, 73; Welch 1983, passim.
19 Brown 1977, 451-77.
20 Rahtz 1979, 267.
21 Edlin 1949, 159: Mellows 1980, 2.
22 Pheifer 1974, 25; Bosworth & Toller 1898, I 82; Riddles 37, 86; Dodwell 1982, 73.
23 Wright 1871, 32.
24 Bosworth & Toller 1898, I 354.
25 Hurst in Cunliffe 1964, 126.
26 West 1982, 37, 38, 41, 62, 71, 141, 194.
27 Miller 1890, I, 1 180-1; West 1982, 37, 38.
28 Owen 1841, 523.
29 Copley 1958, 172-3; Bell 1977, 276-86.
30 Pheifer 1974, 3; Cockayne 1851, III lxii; Wright 1871, 99.
31 Copley 1958, 172-3.
32 Renfrew 1985, 23.
33 Cockayne 1851, II xxv, xxxiii, No. 59.
34 Turner 1828, III 34.
35 C. A. Wilson 1973, 64-5.
36 op. cit., 64-5; Roesdahl 1982, 124.
37 Liebermann 1898, 454.
38 Jaine 1987, 44.
39 Herzfeld 1900, *May 3*; Skeat 1881, *St Sebastian* l.291; Bonser 1963, 248; Cockayne 1851, II li.
40 West 1982, 85.
41 Cunliffe 1976, 30-1, 58.
42 Mellows 1980, 52.
43 Rahtz 1979, 8; Skeat 1881, *St Thomas* 1.97; Hope-Taylor 1977, 63.
44 Turner 1828, III 83.
45 Cunliffe 1976, 126; Davison 1977, 109, 113; Barlow et al. 1976, 293.
46 Symons 1953, xxxi.
47 Napier 1916, 16.
48 Whitelock 1955, 834.
49 Fell 1984, 49; Munby 1982.
50 Garmonsway 1978, 37.
51 Whitelock 1955, 235.
52 Davies 1982, 50; Owen 1841, 47, 49, 355.
53 Garmonsway 1978,37.
54 McKendry 1973, 12.
55 Cockayne 1851, II xxvi.
56 Napier 1916, 16.

57 op.cit., 21.
58 Loyn 1970, 370.
59 Barlow et al. 1976, 98.
60 op. cit., 13, 18, 47, 91.
61 Banham 1991, 36; Cockayne 1851, Vol. 1 358, II i 1, xlix.
62 Skeat 1881, *St. Martin* l.196.
63 Cockayne 1851, I ii 23.
64 Cockayne 1851, *Peri Didachaeon 36.*
65 op. cit., I iii 12, xix, xxi, xliii, xlv 1, xv 5, vi 3, II xli.
66 Edlin 1949, 117.
67 op. cit., 159; Cockayne 1851, I xxxii 2.
68 Herzfeld 1900, *April 3.*
69 Holdsworth 1980, 131; Roesdahl 1982, 125; Hodges 1982, 132; Owen 1851, 581.
70 McGee 1986, 108; Hieatt 1980, 298.
71 Ayrton 1975, 179, 296; C. A. Wilson 1973, 63; Kuper 1977, 51.
72 op. cit., 51, 171; Hartley 1954, 111, 148.
73 Pheifer 1974, 32.
74 Bosworth & Toller 1898, I 674, 497.
75 Cockayne 1851, I iv 2, 1 2, 1 3, vi 5, 1 2.
76 Owen 1841, 723, 725, 95; Cockayne 1851, I i 12, ii 21, xxxi 5, lxiii 1, 3; Bruce-Mitford 1975, 159; Davies 1980, 171-2, 176.
77 Kuper 1977, 19; Herzfeld 1900, *St. Mary of Egypt* l.663.
78 Cockayne 1851, II vii; McGee 1986, 108.
79 Cockayne 1851, III lxvi, II iv.
80 Alcock 1987, 47; C. A. Wilson 1973, 113.
81 Cockayne 1851, *Peri Didacheon* no. 49, I ii 23.
82 op. cit., I i 3, I i 7, I xxxii 2, I iv 3, *Peri Didacheon* 21, III xlviii, II xxxiii.
83 op. cit., I ii 1, 9, I vi 4, iii 12.
84 op. cit., I ii 22.
85 Turner 1828, I 33; Owen 1841, 391.
86 Bruce-Mitford 1983, 488-90; Wright 1871, 38; Skeat 1881, *St George* l.105; *Maccabees* l.117.
87 Cockayne 1851, II Faustina AX fol. 115b; II xxxii, *Lacnunga* 112; Owen 1841, 699.
88 McGee 1986, 623, 548.
89 Wright 1871, 39; Herzfeld 1900, *April 3*; Hodges 1982, 132; Whitelock 1955, 834; Wright 1871, 100; Owen 1841, 77, 437.
90 Robertson 1939, 250.
91 Cockayne 1851, II xxx 2.
92 Liebermann 1898, 455.
93 Hodges 1982, 8; Evison in Haslam 1980, 37.
94 Bruce Mitford 1983, 535-6; Van Es & Verwers 1980, 186; Roesdahl 1982, 122.
95 Wright 1871, 100.
96 Pheifer 1974, 3.
97 Robertson 1939, 75; Wright 1871, 38.
98 Owen 1841, 697; Pheifer 1974, 11.
99 Seebohm 1952, 157; Dunning, Hurst, Myers & Tischler 1959, 56, 59; Pheifer 1974, 3; Wright 1871, 38; Roesdahl 1977, 194; 1982, 125.
100 Gamerith in Fenton & Owen 1981, 92.
101 Roesdahl 1982, 123; MacGregor 1982, 73; Foote & Wilson 1970, 186, 201.
102 West 1982, 11, 404; Cunliffe 1964, 107, 109.
103 Cockayne 1851, *Peri Didacheon* 17; Attenborough 1922, Appendix II.
104 Hurst in Fenwick 1978, 250.
105 Fenton & Kisban 1986, 117; Moryson 1617, IV 199.
106 Garmonsway 1978, 35, 57.
107 Colgrave 1940, 268-9.

[108] Kuper 1977, 225, 6, 8.
[109] Ayrton 1975, 53.
[110] O'Connor 1984, 177.
[111] Ayrton 1975, 50-1.
[112] Cockayne 1851, I lxxxvi.
[113] C. A. Wilson 1973, 40.
[114] Cockayne 1851, *Peri Didacheon* 33, 37.
[115] op. cit., I ii 2, 11, xxxix 3, lix 14, lxxxv, II xix, xxx 2.
[116] op. cit., Vol. 1 380.
[117] op. cit., I xxxi 1.
[118] op. cit., I ii 22, I ii 15, 20.
[119] op. cit., II li 4, III xiii, xiv, *Lacnunga* LIV.
[120] op. cit., II xxv, xxviii, xxviii.
[121] op. cit., II ii 2, II iv, I i 7.
[122] op. cit., *Peri Didacheon* 37; Jackson 1971, 297.
[123] Garmonsway 1978, 37.
[124] Cockayne 1851, II xxiv, xxxix, lvi 4.
[125] op. cit., II xxiii.
[126] op. cit., II xlix.
[127] op. cit., I xviii.
[128] op. cit., II lvi 1, III xliii.
[129] op. cit., Vol. 1, 378.
[130] Turner 1828, III 34.
[131] op. cit., 150-1.
[132] Tannahill 1973, 36-8.
[133] Hartley 1954, 520-1.
[134] Renfrew 1985, 16.
[135] Cockayne 1851, *Lacnunga* LI.
[136] op. cit., LX, III xii.
[137] op. cit., III x, I xxxii 2, xxxviii, *Lacnunga* 116.
[138] op. cit., III xii; Ayrton 1975, 50-1, 299-300.
[139] Seebohm 1952, 157; Bonser 1963, 357.
[140] Vaduva in Fenton & Owen 1981, 338; Gamerith in op. cit., 87ff.
[141] Arrhenius 1984, 343.
[142] op. cit., 344.
[143] Hieatt 1980, 295-6; Holdsworth 1980, 97; Cunliffe 1976, 286.
[144] Moryson 1617, IV 27, 59; Kuper 1977, 224.
[145] Bosworth & Toller 1898, I 375.
[146] Herzfeld 1900, *March 27*; Evans 1969, 45, 66; Cockayne 1851, II lvi 4, I lxi 1; Bonser 1963, 222.
[147] O'Connor 1984, 17.
[148] O'Connor 1982.
[149] Hope-Taylor 1977, 327.
[150] Roesdahl 1977, 190; 1982, 124; Foote and Wilson 1970, 164.
[151] Wilson 1985, pl. 46.
[152] op. cit., pl. 47.
[153] Wright 1871, 35; Banham 1991, 36.
[154] Roesdahl 1977, 194; Bruce-Mitford 1975, 161.
[155] O'Danachair in Owen & Fenton 1981, 63.
[156] Pheifer 1974, 46.
[157] Cockayne 1851, I iv 5.
[158] Evison in Haslam 1980, 37, 39.
[159] Hall 1982, 21; Ottaway 1983, 22.
[160] McGregor 1982, 84.

161 Roesdahl et al. 1987, 169, J12, with illus.
162 Cockayne 1851, *Peri Didacheon* 58.
163 op. cit., II li, li 3, lix 9, xxxviii, *Lacnunga* 3; Holmes 1952, 135.
164 Pheifer 1974, 23.
165 Cockayne 1851, I lxviii.
166 op. cit., *Peri Didacheon* 63.
167 op. cit., 58.
168 Turner 1828, III 34.
169 Weaver in Fenton & Kisban 1986, 44.
170 Cockayne 1851, II xxiii; Ayrton 1975, 245-6.
171 Hieatt 1980, 295-6.
172 op. cit.
173 Ayrton 1975, 418; McGee 1986, 56.
174 Cockayne 1851, III x.
175 Furnivall 1868, 34.
176 Turner 1828, II 36, 102.
177 Pheifer 1974, 134.
178 op. cit., 56.
179 Holmes 1952, 135.
180 Pheifer 1974, 16.
181 Holmes 1952, 91.
182 C. A. Wilson 1973, 250.
183 Grube 1934, 156.
184 Cockayne 1851, I 250.
185 Wright & Wulcker 36, 7, 468,18.
186 Peacocke in Jaine 1986, 58.
187 C. A. Wilson 1973, 40; McGee 1986, 130.
188 Cockayne 1851, I xii, xxxix 3, xli, xlvii 1, II li 3, liii.
189 Ayrton 1975, 182, 206-7, 284.
190 Hieatt 1980, 298.
191 Cockayne 1851, II vi.
192 Foote & Wilson 1970, 163.
193 Kuper 1977, 51.
194 Hieatt 1986, 860.
195 op. cit.; Ayrton 1975, 251.
196 op. cit.
197 Hieatt 1986, 875ff.
198 Hieatt 1980, 296.
199 Garmonsway 1978, 37.

Consumption

6 Meals

Mealtimes

Taking meals at regular times was seen as a good thing in moral terms: 'every mouth needs food; meals shall take place at their proper time' (*muþa gehwylc mete þearf mæl sceolon tidum gongan*).[1] Gluttony consisted of eating before the time of the meal, as well as taking too much.[2] Regular meal-times seem to have been seen as evidence of an ordered, civilised life.

Moreover, in large establishments, serving meals at set hours would have saved time. Punctual meals were particularly important in monasteries where the offices had to be observed.[3]

When meals were taken, or even how many meals a day there were, varied according to the calendar, social class, and personal preference. The novice of the *Colloquy* seems to eat first soon after midday.[4] The novice is being interrogated at this point in his day, so we do not hear the time of any later meals, although this evidence may reflect the fact that children had their main meal at midday. The midday meal is referred to in other monastic contexts.[5]

The *Regularis Concordia* mentions the *prandium ad sextam* at noon, and a *cena* between Vespers and Compline allowed daily from Easter until Whitsun. From Whitsun until September 14 (apart from certain fast days which included Wednesdays and Fridays) and on all Sundays and feasts of twelve lessons there were also two meals a day but the *prandium* was not taken until *none* (3 p.m.).[6] A single meal *ad nonam* between Nones and Vespers was the rule for the winter period from September 14 to Lent; in Lent and on Quarter Tense days the one meal was *ad vesperam* (after Vespers).[7] So it appears there was a main, midday meal, though this might be put back to mid-afternoon, or later, for which the term was *ge-reordung* or *non-mete*.[8]

According to the *Old English Rule of Chrodegang*, if *preostas* ate twice a day then it was at midday and evening, and at Æthelwold's monastery the monks had dinner and supper.[9] There are other references to 'the evening meal' (*æfen-gereord, æfen-gyfl, æfen-mete and æfen-þenung*).[10]

In monasteries a drink was allowed just before *collatio* (the reading at 6 p.m.). By the time of Dunstan, this drink, probably ale, was replaced on certain days by a superior beverage (called the *caritas*), which was accompanied by finer bread and cakes.[11] Frequency of the *caritas* grew to twice a week, and the provision of wine or mead for this was laid as a charge on all the administrative officials.[12]

An earlier meal than dinner or supper is referred to - the *undernswæsendum*. *Undern* was roughly the period of dawn.[13] Aidan was sitting with King Oswald at an *undernswæsendum*.[14] However, this was on Easter Sunday, and 'we eat on Sundays early in the morning and in the evening because Sunday is such a holy day' (*we etað on þam sunnan dagum on undern and on æfen forðan þe se sunnan dæg is swa halig*), so, if there was not to be a midday meal, breakfast may have been eaten instead.[15]

In contrast to the monastic regimen where the main meal was at or around midday, it is possible that in a secular time-table, main meals were at the third hour and again at supper time, to allow a full day's activity between them.

A number of individuals, usually for religious reasons, chose to have only one meal a day. There may have been others whose meals were similarly limited from lack of resources, but we do not hear of them.[16] King Alfred added to his translation of Boethius on the Golden Age, 'They lived naturally and temperately. They always ate but once a day, and that was in the evening'.[17] Everyone was supposed to observe fast days, particularly the period of Lent, and to cut down to one meal a day, but in monasteries dietary observations were strictly observed, so the *Old English Rule of Chrodegang* refers to both eventualities: 'whether the priests eat once a day or twice' (*swa hwæðer preostas ætan on dæg swa æne swa tuwa*).[18]

The ideal meal was the feast, taken in hall, with tables and seating. No doubt most nobles and senior members of their retinues managed to sit at table for their meals, even if the exigencies of campaigning meant this was, on occasion, improvised.[19] Al fresco meals, eaten at a table with servants in attendance, are depicted in manuscripts, but this may reflect Mediterranean artistic influence. Some workers almost certainly ate their meals in the fields.[20]

An anonymous letter to one Brother Edward asks him to try to stop countrywomen at their feasts from eating and drinking in privies.[21] It was the element of gluttony that concerned the writer: eating should be done at table, and perhaps publicly. However, it seems that some saints did not sit at table for meals in order to avoid gluttony.[22]

Diet & Composition of Meals

The composition of meals is hard to assess, though they almost certainly included bread when possible. There was a sound nutritional reason for this. If meat is not accompanied by calorie-rich carbohydrate foods, the protein in the meat will be used as a source of energy and will not be available for other physiological functions.[23]

The baker of the *Colloquy* is pleading a special case, but his reply to the question, 'Can we live without you?' must be close to the truth or it would have been commented on: 'You may for a period of time, not for long, or very well. Indeed without my trade every table would seem empty, and without bread all food turns to loathing. I strengthen the heart of man and am the strength of men. Even the little ones will not despise me.' (*Ge magon þurh sum fæc buton na lancge ne to wel: soplice buton cræfte minon ælc beoð æmtig byþ gesewen, 7 buton hlafe ælc mete to wlættan byþ gehwyrfed. Ic heortan mannes gestrangie ic mægan wera 7 furþon litlincgas nellaþ forbigean me.*)[24]

The legal 'accompaniment' to bread, according to VI Athelstan, might be 'meat or cheese or beans, or what ever one eats with bread according to the season'.[25] Ælfric's *Homily on the Life of St Benedict*, observes of the Italians 'they eat oil...with their food as we do butter', which means that bread was generally eaten with butter.[26] Bread seems to have been eaten with any kind of *smeoru* (literally: smearing), including dripping, new cheese or lard. If there was nothing more substantial, bread might be eaten with a relish of herbs like *gitte* (black cumin), 'the southern wort that is good to eat on bread' (*superne wyrt sio is god on hlafe to þicgenne*).[27]

Even royal meals on feast days included bread.[28] We probably would not know the constituents of two particular meals nor their cost if they had not been itemised for legal purposes in a will, of which only a fragment remains. The first funeral feast was detailed as follows: '7 pence for ale and 2 ores, 1 ore for bread and another ore for a flitch of bacon and for a buck' (*seuen peniges at hale 7 twa ore 7 an ære at bræad 7 hopær hæræ at an flychca 7 at an buch*).[29] At the second funeral feast, when more time could be spent on the preparations, 5 ores were to be provided for malt and fuel and 42 pence for bread, and 17 pence for a pig and 2 ores for a bullock and 1 ore for 3 bucks and 8 pence for a cheese and 3 pence for fish and 4 pence for milk.[30]

At the bottom of the social scale were the destitute. According to Æthelstan's ordinance, one destitute Englishman on each of the royal estates was to receive one amber of meal and a shank of bacon or a wether worth fourpence every month.[31] The meal could have been consumed as bread or pottage. According to *Rectitudines Singularum Personarum*, a male slave was to receive, *inter alia*, about 3 1/2 pounds of corn per day, and a female slave 2 1/2 pounds.[32] This roughly equates to the '4lbs of bread by weight' (*feower punda gewihte hlafes*) provided every day by *The Rule of Chrodegang* for everyone 'from the youngest to the eldest' (*fram þam gingstan oð þone yldstan*).[33]

Bread 'went without saying'. Asked what he eats, the novice replies: 'I still eat flesh-meat because I am still under tutelage...vegetables and eggs, fish and cheese, butter and beans and all things that are not taboo I eat very gratefully.' ('*Gyt flæscmettum ic bruce forðam cild ic eom under gwrda drohniende...wyrta 7 ægra, fisc 7 cyse, buteran 7 beana 7 ealle clæne þingc ic ete mid micelre þancunge.*')[34] The Bury St Edmunds will fragment and the novice's testimony suggest the kind of food that might make up a meal: bread, bacon or pork, beef, cheese, fish, vegetables, eggs, butter, beans and, for special occasions, venison; milk dishes or milk to drink, or ale, or failing that water, with wine for the older, wiser and richer.[35] However, one might be expected, at least under normal circumstances, to limit oneself to one or two dishes.[36]

The monks might not have eaten as well as individuals in a noble household, but probably enjoyed a good diet most of the time. The agricultural labourer of *Rectitudines Singularum Personarum* lacked the variety and choice of the monastic table, but as well as the allowance of meal, the male slave received two sheep carcasses and a good cow, the female one sheep or 3 pence for winter food, one sester of beans for Lenten food and whey in summer or one penny.[37] Both received food at Christmas, Easter, and harvest, and had a strip of land in which to grow vegetables. The swineherd had a pig in sty and the perquisites when he prepared the bacon. The cowherd, shepherd and goatherd all had some milk from their animals, in some cases beestings and whey too. No doubt some bartering went on, so some butter, cheese and other white meats, would be added to the diet.

The Anglo-Saxon peasant's evening meal may very often have taken the form of broth, then chopped meat.[38] Perhaps this was on the lines of the French *pot-au-feu*, which includes a beef marrow bone to provide marrow to spread on the bread served with the broth, and would help to account for the number of split marrow bones found on Anglo-Saxon sites.[39]

About 25kg. of meat per head p.a. may have been consumed, as compared to the present national average of 63.5kg. More than half would have come from beef, pigs provided the second largest amount with sheep providing only a small percentage, although (as has been noted) animal bone evidence takes no account of salt meat. Venison seems to have been a fairly scarce meat. Wild-fowling provided a continuous supply of meat, and, if small in amount, more birds were available in winter when food supplies were short. Fish are often shown whole in illustrations of feasting. Perhaps this is because fish are easily recognisable, as well as because they were a desirable food.[40] Poultry - fowl and goose - was also present on sites throughout the period.

Regional Variations

Inhabitants of coastal districts would probably have included more salt-water fish and shellfish in their diet.[41] Those living near large rivers, or lakes would probably have consumed a fair proportion of fresh-water fish, including eels.

The wetter western and northern counties were more suited to growing oats or barley, and therefore breads and cereal pottages would be likely to include these grains. In the region round Worcester rye was apparently used more than elsewhere. In the eastern counties bread would be more likely to be based on wheat.

Those in western and south-western counties with a climate suited to cattle-raising and dairying based on the cow, may have consumed more beef and dairy products.[42] However, the consumption of beef probably depended more on who you were than where you were.

Seasonal Variations

These were very significant, especially for those with slender resources. A winter diet of bread, salt meat, legumes, with some cheese, was probably short in antiscorbutic foods, but fresh vegetables, particularly early types of cabbage, onions and leeks, but also including 'wild' plants, like Chenopodium, may have been eaten, although these would not necessarily feature in the written record. Lent would have been a time of short commons for some, though vegetables, together with fish, cereals and some fruit and nuts were available. Easter was technically a feast day, and could have been celebrated with fresh meat, probably lamb, eggs, salads of green shoots. The stock pot could be used again for stews of salt meat, lamb and veal. By midsummer some 'grass beef' was ready for eating, and mackerel were plentiful. Dairy products were available, and various white meats were eaten fresh. There may have been a dearth just before harvest. From the summer into autumn various fruits, which may have been eaten with cream, and nuts were available.[43] By

69

Michaelmas fat mutton was available, and at Hallowmas pork, sprats and smelts were in season.

Courses

The *Old English Rule of Chrodegang* refers to courses, so that a meal might have consisted of soft (?new) cheese, then 'delicacies' (i.e. meat puddings/sausages), then fish or vegetables as the *þriddan sande* (lit: third sending), or the order might be meat puddings/sausages, then cheese then vegetables or stewed meat.[44] The Benedictine Rule decreed the *prandium* (lunch) should consist of two cooked dishes and a third of fresh vegetables and fruit.[45] By the end of the period great feasts in rich monasteries might run to a number of courses. Secular meals in important households would seem to have consisted of four to five courses.[46]

Drinks with Meals

The four pence for milk for the second funeral feast detailed in a will fragment from Bury St Edmunds may have been to make white meats, or it may have been to drink, particularly with the fish after which it is mentioned, since the Danish custom was to eat fish with milk.[47] Food allowances never give fish with ale.[48] The monastic diet at Llancarfan included plenty of fish and milk.[49] Otherwise wine (for the senior members of society), ale, mead, cider/fruit wines, or water were drunk.

Conclusion

Monotony may have been a characteristic of the Anglo-Saxon diet. Until recently peasants in central Europe ate the same dishes, basically farinaceous, on five days of each week.[50] Penitents were often given a deliberately monotonous diet, perhaps bread, salt and pease pudding.[51] Hunger would have made repetitious meals more acceptable, and we know that famines did occur.[52]

---

[1] Bloch 1961, 74; Mackie 1934, *Gnomic Verses* 1.124.
[2] Skeat 1881, *Mem. of the Saints* 1.268; *St Mary of Egypt*.
[3] op. cit., *St. Martin* 1.331.
[4] Garmonsway 1978, 44.
[5] Whitelock 1954, 704.
[6] Logeman 1888, Chapter 41; Miller 1890, I, 1 162.
[7] Symons 1953, xxxv.
[8] Wright 1871, 33.
[9] Napier 1916, 14; Turner 1828, III 33.
[10] Wright 1871, 33, 184.
[11] Knowles 1940, 456-7.
[12] op. cit., 430.
[13] Bosworth & Toller 1898, I 424.

14 Miller 1890, I, 1 164.
15 Skeat 1881, *Ash Wednesday* l.3.
16 op. cit., *St Aethelthryth* l.42; Miller 1890, I, 2 244, 318.
17 Turner 1828, II 36.
18 Napier 1916, 14.
19 Wilson 1985, pl. 47.
20 Colgrave 1940, 70.
21 Swanton 1975, 29.
22 op. cit., 57.
23 Harris 1986, 27.
24 Garmonsway 1978, 36-7.
25 Whitelock 1955, 390.
26 Wright 1871, 37.
27 Cockayne 1851, II xxxix.
28 Miller 1890, I, 1 166.
29 Robertson 1939, 252.
30 op. cit.
31 Attenborough 1922, 127.
32 Douglas & Greenaway 1953, 815; Whitelock 1952, 109.
33 Napier 1916, 14.
34 Garmonsway 1978, 46.
35 Robertson 1939, 252; Garmonsway 1978, 46-7; Napier 1926, 14-15.
36 Garmonsway 1978, 46-7.
37 Liebermann 1898, 449-50.
38 Fell 1984, 144.
39 David 1960, 184.
40 Garmonsway 1978, 27.
41 Holdsworth 1980, 131; Bell 1977.
42 Davies 1982, 23.
43 Furnivall 1868, 85.
44 Napier 1916, 14-15.
45 Furnivall 1868, 131, 152ff.
46 Knowles 1940, 463.
47 Groundes Pearce 1971, 12.
48 Ashley 1928, 126-7; Seebohm 1952, 157.
49 Davies 1982, 35.
50 Gamerith in Owen & Fenton 1981, 86.
51 Davies 1982, 35.
52 Napier 1916, 15.

7 Fasting

In Anglo-Saxon society an annual pattern of fasting and feasting was enjoined on the population as a Christian duty; periods of fasting were followed by periods of feasting, and single feast days were preceded by a day of fasting. Fasts were observed by the laity as well as clerics; those exempt were children and the infirm.

The three main forms of fasting were to limit the diet to certain items, to limit the daily amount of food consumed, usually by delaying eating until a certain time, and consuming only one meal a day, but also by limiting the ration of food, and adulterating food with unpalatable additions.

Reasons for Fasting

It has been suggested that there were practical reasons for instituting fasting and that one effect would be the overall saving of food resources, but this can hardly have been a prime concern in a system which also enjoined feasting. However, if food supplies were comparatively short for most of the population at particular times of the year, then there would at least be a psychological benefit if those forced to limit their food intake felt they were gaining merit by so doing. To some extent the pattern of feasts and fasts follows the pattern of the seasons, but a period of fasting is sometimes followed immediately by a period of feasting.

Theoretically at least, fasting freed food for almsgiving, so that food was redistributed to those who needed it most.[1]

In the background was the vision of the ideal world in which man would be freed from the necessity of consuming earthly food. The patristic tradition saw fasting as union with the angels, and that it made the soul clear for the reception of divine truth.[2] Meat eating was seen to reflect Cain's primal crime, and as proof of human weakness and cruelty.[3] To abstain from meat was to go some way to recovering primal innocence. Old Testament models offered pure hearts to God by fasting, and the forty-day fast of Christ in the desert was the model for the forty-day fast of Lent.[4]

Fasting was in some measure reparation for Adam's sin, which was seen as one of 'gluttony' (*oferfylle*), as much as disobedience.[5] It is evident that fasting was a means of purification, and it was so used in various ceremonies (see below).

Apart from these theoretical considerations, it was observed that fasting moderated lust.[6] St Augustine maintained that the body was excited by the full satisfaction of the appetite, but acknowledged the difficulty of keeping the balance between suppression of lust and enfeeblement of the body.[7] Other writers point out the difficulty of carrying out one's duties when following a very ascetic regime.[8] Boniface complained of the perversity of priests who did not eat of the foods which God gave, and others, whose interpretation of the bible was perhaps over-literal, fed on milk and honey, rejecting bread and animal foods.[9]

Fasting was employed to get God on one's side and thereby bring about desired results.[10] The tenth-century *Institutes of Polity* suggest that if misfortune befell the people, then they should consult how amends might be sought from Christ with cleansing fasts and with frequenting churches.[11] There was a belief that choosing a lack would induce God to give plenty.[12]

Periods of Fasting

According to VII Æthelred c.1009, the nation was to fast for three days on bread and herbs and water on the Monday, Tuesday and Wednesday before Michaelmas (and other penitential actions were to be performed). Slaves were to be freed from work during these three days so that they might more willingly observe the fast.[13] This was to 'obtain God's mercy and his compassion that we may through his help withstand our enemies', with the food that would otherwise have been consumed being given to the sick and needy.[14] Saints are recorded as practising or prescribing the three-day fast.[15] The three-day fast perhaps paralleled the three-day feast: both were serious matters. The week-long fast was called for on some occasions.[16] Details of the regular fasts are given in Appendix A, and of fasting practised by individual saints and as penance in Appendix B.

Commuting Fasting

Although fasting could be carried out for the sake of others, fasting as a penance is most often referred to as atonement for one's own sins. Preventing a penitent from feasting cut him off from a normal social life, and reduced his prestige. Donating land, saying psalms, paying for masses to be said, or paying fines were alternatives to fasting. However, it was theologically acceptable to transfer a fast to another individual.[17] This made it possible for a powerful man to avoid fasting for any length of time or making any payment. If fasting was imposed for seven years, he could get twelve men to fast three days on bread, green herbs and water. Then he could get 7 x 120 men to fast for three days, thus making up as many days of penance as there are in seven years.[18]

Conclusion

Fasting and feasting gave an eating rhythm to the week and to the year. However, 'some fasted as though they scorned eating, but on the next day they ate greedily' (*sume fæston eac swa þæt hi forsawon to etanne buton on ðone oðerne dæg and æton þonne grædelice*).[19] Extremes were eschewed: 'eat every day with moderation' (*ælce dæg eton mid gedafenlicnysse*).[20]

One had to be sure of the dates: it was not safe merely to fast, since feast days had to be observed, and 'he who fasts on that day through self-will is to be excommunicated' (*ðe on þam dæge fæsten wile þæt he beo amansumod gif he hi hit for his anwylnysse deð*).[21] It was the mass-priest's duty to tell his communicants the dates of fasts: misinformation was punished by a fine. This is one reason why copies of calendars which gave the dates of fast- and feast-days were in demand.

Like the feast, the fast brought Christians together. To violate the Friday fast was the clearest, most visible way of rejecting the faith.[22] In *Sermo Lupi ad Anglos*, the failure to observe fasts and festivals occurs time and time again and is seen as being in some measure responsible for the state of the country.[23]

Fasting was always supposed to be accompanied by alms-giving: 'then is his fasting pleasing to God' (*þonne bið his fæsten God gecweme*).[24] In theory, those who had food voluntarily forwent some in order that those without food could have something to eat, but it seems unlikely that almsgiving was regularly and generously practised. Altruism was not a prime motive: those who submitted themselves to a rigorous regime of deprivation seem to have been looking ahead to heavenly feasting.[25] For the poor who scarcely had enough to keep themselves alive, visions of the heavenly feast, though infinitely desirable, must have seemed cold comfort.

---

[1] Whitelock 1955, 410.
[2] Bynum 1987, 36.
[3] McGee 1986, 83.
[4] op. cit.; Dembinska in Fenton & Kisban 1986, 153.
[5] Cockayne 1851, III *Lar* l.40, l.74-5; Turner 1828, III 505.
[6] Swanton 1975, 177.
[7] Bynum 1987, 79.
[8] Dembinska in Fenton & Owen 1986, 153; Skeat 1881, *Prayer of Moses* l.104.
[9] Kylie 1911, 116, 122.
[10] Davies 1982, 168.
[11] Bonser 1963, 5.
[12] Bynum 1987, 39.
[13] Whitelock 1955, 409.
[14] op. cit.

[15] Skeat 1881, *St Basilus* l.235; *St Sebastian* l.206.
[16] op. cit., *St Eufrasia* l.211; *St Martin* l.1284; *The Chair of St Peter*, l.262.
[17] Miller 1890, I, 2 233.
[18] Turner 1828, III 86.
[19] Skeat 1881, *Prayer of Moses* l.96.
[20] op. cit.; Napier 1916, 123.
[21] Skeat 1881, *Ash Wednesday* l.4.
[22] Bynum 1987, 41.
[23] Whitelock 1955, 858; Swanton 1975, 120.
[24] Fowler 1972, 13.
[25] Mackie/Gollancz 1972, *The Wonders of Creation* l.95; *The Phoenix, Soul Addressing the Body* l.36.

8 Feasting

Feasts in hall offered a variety of sense impressions - taste, smell, warmth, music and entertainment, the play of light on tableware, colours of hangings, the clothes of the guests. Companionship, a confirmation of one's position in the community, reward, the chance to drink and escape day-to-day concerns were all part and parcel of feasting, and the potent appeal of the feast derives in part from them, as well as the rich and plentiful food.

The Function of Feasting

Although the feast was not primarily a gastronomic event, but a ritual - with religious, aesthetic, legal and societal ramifications - the provision and consumption of food and drink was central. The 'chieftain' provided food and drink that was prestigious in kind and plentiful in quantity. The term *gegadorwiste* meant 'assembly for feasting': *wiste* meant 'plenty' as well as 'feast'.[1] That the image of the king, as a provider of feasts was a particularly important and resonant one, is suggested by the fact that in feeding the five thousand Christ is described in these terms.[2]

The function of royal feasts was to emphasise the ruler's power, and through a lavish display of wealth, attract followers and supporters. Those who partook of the feast were declaring or confirming their obligations to the provider. In return for sustenance, they were pledged to fight to the death for him, sustaining him in his position of power, but also obliging him to continue to provide well for them. Feasting was functional: by keeping his retainers well-fed on a variety of foods, the leader ensured that he had, quite literally, strong supporters. A retainer who ate with the king gained a legal status, but the term *fedesl* used for such an individual occurs elsewhere only in the sense of a fatted animal, and implies special feeding.[3]

A noble king not only provided amply for his retainers, but created a splendid occasion; an image of plenty and assured harmony in a world where shortage, uncertainty and conflict were the experience of many.[4] The feast retained its symbolism as a unifying force, even when the guests were not dependent on the king for sustenance and support.[5]

The lord of the *Rhymed Poem* comments that, when prosperous, 'feasts never failed, guests came and went', and certainly people apart from the king had the resources for a social life that included feasting.[6] The visit of guests was celebrated with a feast, though if the king was the visitor, the royal provisioners would arrive the day before to see everything was ready and suitable.[7] The king could not have his status compromised by attending a feast at which the supplies were insufficiently lavish, or the mead might run out.[8]

Sometimes the guests may have been visiting specifically to consume the food payable as the food rent.[9]

Most people probably only arranged feasts for special occasions, which could be personal, celebrating the arrival of a guest, celebrating or commemorating rites of passage, or seasonal, called forth by the time of year or the date of a religious festival.[10] Victories and coronations were celebrated with feasting.[11]

Funeral feasts and feasts on the anniversaries of deaths are most frequently mentioned. In pagan times the dead person seems to have been propitiated by a grand burial feast.[12] Funeral feasts continued to be held after the introduction of Christianity, and ultimately had to be incorporated into the Christian scheme.[13] Anniversary feasts were often held, particularly in religious establishments.[14]

The Calendar of Feast-days

Gregory realised that pagan religious feasts, being an important part of the life of the people, would be difficult to eradicate.[15] A calendar of feasts commemorating Christian festivals took the place of pagan celebrations.[16] Festivals were holidays and feast days, and while the Church could not enjoin feasting, it could at least state (as above) that there should be no fasting during feast days. The council of all the greater men was summoned to the royal court for all the great festivals, with the Easter feast being the most frequently mentioned.[17] It was the Easter feast which provided the illustration for April in the Anglo-Saxon Calendar.[18]

A well-endowed monastery would have been able to feast on a large number of saints' days, as well as anniversaries of its benefactors' deaths. The arrival of bequests of food was timed to coincide with feasts.[19] *The Rule of Chrodegang* states that those in monasteries would be able on feast days to 'eat twice a day with everyone having plenty to eat' (*eton tuwa on dæg 7 hæbbe ma to eallum þysum fulle þenuncge*).[20]

The seasonal feasts associated with the completion of agricultural tasks and given by the landowner to his workforce were perhaps the only feasts likely to be attended by those of lower classes, including slaves. According to *Rectitudines Singularum Personarum*, 'There are many folk-rights: some are entitled to a winter feast, Easter feast, a feast to celebrate the binding of the sheaves at harvest, a feast at which the drink flows for ploughing, a reward for mowing, food for making ricks, the 'wagon-favour' when loading wood, the 'rick-cup' at corn carting, and many things that I am not able to enumerate'. (*Feola syndon folcgerihtu: on sumre deode gebyreð winterfeorme, Easterfeorm, bendform for ripe, gytfeorm for yrðe, mæðmed, hræcmete, at wudulade wæntreow, at cornlade hreaccopp 7 fela ðinga ðe ic getellan ne mæig.*)[21] The very poorest probably did not participate in feasts directly, though they gathered when and where there was feasting in expectation of left-overs, and they might, on occasion, do much better than that.

Guild Feasts

Feasting together confirmed the unity of those present. Guilds were voluntary associations whose members, usually substantial members of the community, provided mutual support. The benefits were similar to those arising from kinship obligations, and guilds provided a valuable social service in the very late Anglo-Saxon period, in settlements where a substantial part of the population were recent immigrants, without families at hand.[22] Officials of the peace guild in London at the time of Athelstan were to meet once a month and 'feed themselves as they themselves think fitting', an early instance of a civic banquet. The meal was evidently a substantial one since they were to 'distribute all the leavings for God's sake'.[23] The regulations for the guilds at Cambridge, Exeter, and Abbotsbury all refer to feasting.[24] Some of the feasts were fixed for church festivals, others were funeral feasts held at the interment of a member.[25]

Holding a Feast

A feast was arranged and guests *geladod* (invited/bidden/summoned).[26] They dressed in their best clothes 'guests...beautifully dressed' (*giestas...lustum glendon*), according to the *Rhymed Poem* of the Exeter Book, or perhaps their most splendid armour, like the *byrnwiga* of *The Wanderer*.[27] The writer of *The Ruin* saw in hall:

> ....*beorn monig*
> *glædmod and goldbeorht gleoma gefrætwed*
> *wlonc and wingal wighyrstum scan*

(many men, joyful and bright with gold, splendidly adorned, proud and gladdened by wine; their armour shone). According to Cynewulf in his image of the Ascension, the radiant garments of the angels were appropriate to the great feast which was held in heaven to greet Christ's arrival.[28]

Summoning the Guests

Presumably the guests foregathered, and then a horn was blown to summon them to the feast.[29] Such a use of the horn may have been strictly functional, or it may have played some further part in the ceremonial.[30] Hand-washing was the first and necessary part of the ceremonial of feasting.

The Hall

The scene of feasting was the great hall, furnished with trestle tables and benches, and guarded by door-keepers who turned away gate-crashers and prevented anyone from entering while the meal was in progress.[31] The number of compounds using synonyms for hall, e.g. 'hall-cup' (*sele-ful*), 'wine-hall' (*wine-ærne*), 'mead-hall' (*medo-ærne*), 'wine-hall' (*wine-reced*), indicates the importance of the hall for the feasting that took place there.[32] The archaeological record provides much evidence of halls, e.g. one of these at Yeavering was over 80' long and 40' wide and the walls were white-plastered on the inside,[33] whilst at Cheddar there was a hall about 75' long dating from the mid-ninth century.[34]

Other business was also carried on in the hall at mealtimes, so that Harold might receive news of William's landing when he was dining at York, and when Cnut was at table in hall at the end of a feast a crowd of petitioners was occupying his ear, while a bard wanted to sing him a poem he had just composed.[35] In these circumstances it is not surprising that, although communal feasting in hall continued, in the late period we hear that the lady of the household, and sometimes the lord retired to a private room to eat.[36] Some people were no doubt grateful for their entitlement to sleep in the hall after the feast.[37]

Hangings & Table-linen

Hangings, sometimes interwoven with gold, were used to decorate halls from early in the period.[38] Tablecloths were in use, at least on the continent, by the early ninth century.[39] Table napkins (*cneorift* - knee-covering), known of by the eighth century, were certainly in use by the tenth century.[40]

Heating & Lighting

The hall was described as being desirably warm: 'while you sit at the meal with your nobles in the winter and the fire is alight and your hall warmed, while it rains and snows and storms outside' (*swylc swa þu æt swæsendum sitte mid þinum ealdormannum 7 þegnum on wintertid 7 sie*

fire onælad 7 þin heall gewyrmed 7 hit rine 7 sniwe 7 styrme ute).[41]
Some retainers were known as 'hearth-companions' (*heorð-geneatas*), and while this may have been merely a poetic epithet, it may have indicated those whose status entitled them to a seat near the fire, or to sleep in hall. Braziers may have been used in upper rooms; this may possibly have been the case in the first-floor hall at the Cheddar palace site.[42]

The hall was probably lit by lamps and candles, as well as firelight.[43]

Precedence & Seating

A royal feast had some of the elements of a superior dinner party today: fine table-linen, lighted candles, shining tableware. But, aesthetic enjoyment apart, how one fared in hall depended on rank. A visitor to a feast did not necessarily qualify for the rarer dishes unless he was a person of some rank.[44] A thegn was entitled to a seat in the king's hall, but it might be necessary to have had 'high rank' (*heanne had*) before one could say, 'I lacked nothing in hall' (*ne wæs me in healle gad*).[45]

There is evidence that an order of precedence was insisted on in early medieval England as well as Wales.[46] It was possible to buy your way in at a guild feast. If a retainer, as opposed to a guild brother, wanted to sit within the *stig* (possibly a railed-off dais) at a feast of the Cambridge Thegns' Guild, then he could pay a sester of honey to be accorded the privilege.[47]

Hrothgar bids Beowulf, 'sit now to the feast' ('*site nu to symle*'), and we learn that the *medu-benc* is 'decorated with gold' (*gold-geregnað*).[48] Later we are told, 'then the glorious ones sat on the bench, rejoiced in the feast' (*bugon þa to benc blæd-agande/fylle gefægan*).[49] Tenth- and eleventh-century illustrations depicting feasting, show diners sitting on settles or benches which seem to be cushioned.[50] 'Seat coverings' (*setl hrægl*) were bequeathed in wills, so at a feast one might expect to sit on a cushioned or, at least, covered seat.[51] The end of the bench was, for obvious reasons, a desirable position.[52]

Retainers

Guests seem to have been allowed to bring companions to a feast.[53] A guest who arrived with a large retinue assumed his host had considerable resources.[54] If anyone brought a *fotsetla* to a feast of the Cambridge Thegns' Guild, then he was to pay a sester of honey.[55] Whatever sort of retainer the *fotsetla* was (and he could have been a minstrel, since these are recorded as sitting at the feet of their lords, or even a foot-warmer such as the Welsh king had), in the context of a guild feast where the members had to provide the food and drink, he was to be paid for.

Servants

The emphasis on those who 'sat to' the feast was perhaps because sitting down was a privilege in itself, for some of those present at a feast, including the servers, were not entitled to sit, such as the unfortunate apparitor of the Welsh laws, who, though a court official, was not allowed to sit while the king was eating and drinking in hall 'lest the house be burnt while the king is at meat'.[56] At a great feast the servants had to 'scurry to and fro...speed on their tasks'.[57] What they might be doing is illustrated in manuscript illustrations - bringing food on spits from the kitchens and kneeling with it in front of the diners who then helped themselves, serving drink, etc.[58]

Almost all the evidence as to who served food comes from Celtic sources and indicates that men were in charge of the great hall and the serving of food in large establishments.[59] Rank was observed among servants too; high ranking servants served diners of high status. It is possible that men served men with food, women, women.[60]

On occasion it seems to have been the women who served the drink to men at feasts. The *Gnomic Verses* outline the duties of a queen:

> ....*meodorædenne*
> *for gesiðmægan symle æghwær*
> *eodor æþelinga ærest gegretan*
> *forman fulle to frean hond*
> *ricene gereacan ond him ræd witan*

(always everywhere before the band of comrades at the mead-drinking, she shall first of all greet the protector of the nobles, quickly offer the first cup to her lord's hand, and know good counsel).[61] In *Beowulf* it is the queen who offers the cup to Hrothgar and his guest. The wife of a noble who was cured of an illness was then well enough to carry out her duties as hostess and brought the cup to the bishop and the rest of the guests, serving them all until dinner was finished.[62]

In the early period, high born women perhaps poured imported wine through the delicate and expensive sieve spoons which indicated their status and were buried with them.[63] Women's graves also contained bucket pendants, which perhaps symbolised the female role as servers of drink, though buckets were more likely to have been used as intermediate vessels for the serving of mead, *beor* or ale, than wine, which was imported in flasks or casks.[64] Female servants who held the office of 'cup-bearer' (*byrele*) are referred to in the seventh-century laws of Æthelbert, since an *eorl* was entitled to twelve shillings compensation if anyone slept with his cup-bearer; a *ceorl* was entitled to half this amount.[65] What had traditionally been a female role would of course have to be filled by a man in a monastic household.[66] However, it seems that towards the end of the period high-born women were eating with the men at feasts and were not required as servers.

Blessing Food and Breaking Bread

While Hrothgar simply invites Beowulf to sit down and enjoy the feast, after the conversion food was blessed before the eating started.[67] After grace the most important guest seems to have broken the bread or divided the food.[68]

Manners

By the end of the period table-manners were a matter of concern and interest to some.[69] It was not considered polite to gulp down or gobble your food for which the pejorative word *fretan* is used.[70] This word is used to show that it was not the done thing to pick up and eat any morsel of food that had fallen on the floor:

> ðonne snottrum men snæd oddglideð
> ða he be leohte gesihð, lueð æfter,
> gesegnað and gesyfleð and him sylf friteð

(when a chunk of food slips from the hand of one of these clever men, he spots it in the light, bends down to pick it up, blesses it, covers it with seasoning and actually consumes it).[71]

At Coppergate in York the evidence of the faecal layers which contained fruit stones, apple core fragments and fish bones, is that food was bolted, or at least eaten in uninhibited fashion.[72] There is no way of knowing whether hunger was the reason for these foods being bolted, or whether this method of eating was habitual to the inhabitants of Viking York.

The Food

It seems that feast-day food was anticipated with some pleasure, and then enjoyed: Athelstan 'entered joyfully the dinner apartment', and Hrothgar gladly partook of the 'feast and hall-cup' (*symbel* and *sele-ful*).[73] It seems that one might expect better food at a feast - rarer items and choicer cuts - and plenty of it. The better cuts of meat could be roasted, especially as the diners would be on hand to eat the meat as soon as it was done.

Poultry and pork were suitable foods.[74] Beef, particularly from specially fattened bullocks, was feast-day food.[75] The fact that sheep are not mentioned could be an accident of the non-survival of evidence, but is perhaps accounted for by the fact that pigs and cattle will more readily put on weight to give fatty, tender meat.

The game taken by hunting and fowling was considered suitable for feasts since it was expensive to obtain.[76] Fish was also a delicacy, as were broth and cheese.[77]

Bread was the standard constituent of all meals, and specified for funeral feasts, as above; ordinary bread was probably replaced by a finer kind on feast days. A number of festival cakes based on enriched dough mixtures are known from across Europe from Roman times on (Chapter 2).

The most complete picture of food for a feast is that provided by the listing of the major ingredients of the funeral feasts at Bury St Edmunds (see above). The first feast consisted of ale, bread and meat; the second of ale (this time brewed specially for the feast), bread, meat, cheese, fish and milk.[78]

While one might expect Anglo-Saxon feasts to be hearty Homeric affairs, the impression from the documentary evidence is that considerable skill was exercised by cooks to produce delicacies: 'the strange diversity of sumptuous food'.[79] Eating to show social status was a well-developed phenomenon of the medieval period, but was evidently established early in Anglo-Saxon England.

Duration

Day-long feasts were common.[80] It was not generally acceptable to leave before the end of a feast.[81] Some banquets seem to have continued overnight.[82] St Eligius exhorted people - ineffectually as it has turned out - not to make feasts lasting all night nor to indulge in intemperate drinking on the Calends of January.[83] The three-day feast seems to have been the standard for any great celebration.[84]

The Drink

It is clear from the references to feasting that drink was as important as the food. *Ealu* (ale), *beor* (probably fermented fruit-based drinks, including cider), *meodu* (mead) and *win* (wine) are the four drinks frequently mentioned, and all occur in compounds with, for example, *sele/heall* (hall) and *benc* (seat). *Gebeorscipe* was a common term for feasting. The over-riding concern was that there should be plenty of drink.[85]

Drunkenness

The consumption of unlimited quantities of alcohol tended to militate against the preservation of an image of harmony which the feast was calculated to further. Men 'drunken with *beor* renewed old grudges', and in extreme cases the conflict might threaten the king's peace, so this had to be protected by severe penalties.[86] Fines for murder committed at a feast were much higher than if the act was done at an open grave, when feelings might be expected to have been running high.[87]

Gluttony

Although feasting became incorporated into the Christian scheme, the problem was that feasts could and, according to a number of accounts, did lead to the sin of gluttony. Gluttony in respect of Anglo-Saxon feasting was the concern of ecclesiastical writers from the eighth century.[88] When Æthelwold was appointed to Winchester, clerics given over to gluttony and drunkenness attempted to poison him when he introduced a more austere regime.[89] In 1008 Æthelred's law code specifically outlawed over-eating and drinking.[90] The sermon of Wulfstan declares that it was in part gluttony which was causing the destruction of the country.[91] England as a whole had a reputation for heavy eating and drinking all over the continent by the end of the Anglo-Saxon period.[92]

Some people must have had a somewhat ambivalent attitude to feasts: pleasurable as they undoubtedly were, ecclesiastics denounced them as sinful. One way of partially resolving this conflict was to dispose of the left-overs charitably.[93]

Treachery

Eating with someone implied reciprocal social and even legal bonds. Hospitality carried with it a number of obligations - not just the provision of food but the protection of guests. Feasts were used as a cover for premeditated treachery on a number of occasions throughout the period.[94]

Entertainment

Despite the possibility of violence, people went to feasts expecting to enjoy themselves. The sound of people having a good time is mentioned a number of times in the literature; perhaps most dramatically, Grendel is overcome with rage and jealousy when he 'heard the sounds of enjoyment' (*dream gehyrde*) in Heorot.[95] The drink obviously helped people enjoy themselves and everyone might be expected to contribute to the entertainment at a feast. In this connection the story of Caedmon is well known.[96]

Harping must have been a common pastime at feasts since it is used as a metaphor for feasting.[97] The poetic epithet for the harp/lyre was 'the wood of joy' (*gleobeam*), suggesting association with the pleasures of feasting in hall. Such instruments have been found in the archaeological record.[98]

Professional entertainers, jesters, actors and dancers as well as singers and other musicians, were employed as part of their establishment by those who could afford them.[99] Riddles were asked and stories recited. Further details of entertainment at feasts are given in Appendix C.

Nostalgia

Most people saw feasting as an infinitely desirable pastime. Hagiographers even made use of this fact in their writings. St Agatha 'went as cheerfully to the dark dungeon as if she were invited to a pleasant banquet' (*eode þa bliðelice to than blindum cweaterne swylce heo wære geladod to lustfullum beor-scype*), though she was perhaps outdone by some brothers who 'went as gladly to their own deaths as to a banquet' (*swa bliþelice eodon to heora agenum slege swylce to gebeorscipe*).[100] It is the dramatic contrast of the feast in the warm hall where the king sits with his retainers around him and the cold darkness outside that is drawn on for an analogy of human life.[101]

The loss of prosperity evokes nostalgia for feasting. The lord of the *Rhymed Poem* says that, when rich,

> *secgas me segon symbel ne alegon*
> *feorgiefe gefegon*

(men gazed upon me, feasts never failed and they rejoiced in the gift of life).

> *giestas gengdon gerscype mengdon*
> *lisse lengdon lustum glengdon*

(guests came and went, mingled their talk, lingered over delight, adorned themselves richly).[102] The seafarer regrets that he hears now

> *huilpan sweg for hleahtor wera*
> *meaw singende for medodrince*

(the cry of the curlew instead of men's laughter, the scream of the seagull in place of the mead-drinking).[103] The regret for the silent, deserted ruin which was once 'a meadhall full of the sounds of music' (*meadoheall monig mon dreama full*), a place where people had gathered and feasted, where the horn was passed round, is found also in the Celtic literature.[104] The hall was a centre of companionship: the isolated exile has no-one 'who knows my mind in the meadhall' (*þe in meoduhealle min mine wisse*).[105] It is in *The Wanderer* that nostalgia for the joys of feasting finds its most eloquent expression. The lament refers to several essential elements of the noble feast:

> *Woriað þa winsalo waldend licgað...*
> *Hwar cwom symbla gesetu? Hwær sindon seledreamas?*
> *Eala beorht bune! Eala byrnwiga eala þeodnes þrym...*

(The wine-hall crumbles, the walls decay...Where is now the place of feasts? Where are the joys of hall? Alas for the bright cup! Alas for the armed warriors, alas for the might of the nation...)[106]

---

1   Zupita 1959, l.1735-6.
2   Kemble 1848.
3   Whitelock 1955, 357-8.
4   Zupita 1948, l.2431; Huizinga 1977, 24.
5   Whitelock 1955, 258, 280; Turner 1828, III 29, 234.
6   Mackie 1973, *Rhymed Poem*; Miller 1890, I, 1 180-2, I, 2 396-8.
7   Turner 1828, III 29.
8   op. cit.
9   Davies 1982, 165.
10 Bonser 1963, 109.
11 Skeat 1881, *St Eustace* l.387.
12 Meaney and Hawkes 1970, 31-2, 53.
13 Bonser 1963, 135; Whitelock 1955, 557, 707.
14 Kylie 1911, 200; Robertson 1939, 199.
15 Bonser 1963, 123.
16 op. cit., 125; Miller 1890, I, 2 314; Whitelock 1952, 24; Seebohm 1952, 100-11; Skeat 1881, *The Exaltation of the Cross*.
17 Turner 1828, III 210.
18 BL MS., Cott. Tib. B5.
19 Whitelock 1968, 8.
20 Napier 1916, 81.
21 Liebermann 1898, 452-3.
22 Barlow et al. 1976, 335; Turner 1828, III 98; Whitelock 1955, 558.
23 op. cit., 389.
24 op. cit., 557-60.
25 op. cit., 558.
26 Bosworth & Toller 1898, 407.
27 Sweet 1952, l.151.
28 Clemoes & Hughes 1971, 294.
29 Bosworth & Toller 1898, I 431.
30 Wilson 1985, pl. 48; Jones & Jones 1949, 162.
31 Whitelock 1955, 299; Owen 1841, 79; Zupita 1959, l.67 ff.
32 Riddles 55, 56; Whitelock 1955, 559; Barlow et al. 1976, 336, 335; Turner 1828, III 32.
33 Hope-Taylor 1977, 130, 140.
34 Rahtz 1979, 50.
35 Turner 1828, II 344.
36 Owen 1841, 51, 669; Wilson 1985, pl. 3; Turner 1828, III 29.
37 Jackson 1969, 157; Owen 1841, 47.
38 Dodwell 1982, 120-9; Turner 1828, III 50; Whitelock 1968, 12; Fell 1984, 46-7.

39 Hodges 1982, 132; Furnivall 1868, 92-3; Knowles 1940, 452.
40 Wright & Wulcker 1884, I; Wright 1871, 36, 42; Banham 1991, 32.
41 Miller 1890, I, 1 134-6.
42 Rahtz 1979.
43 Jackson 1969, 120, 122; Owen 1841, 669; Roesdahl 1982, 113; Crane 1983, 241.
44 Holmes 1952, 114.
45 Mackie 1973, *Rhymed Poem* l.15.
46 Furnivall 1868, 365, 70-1, 170-1; Owen 1841, 77, 96-8, 363, 641; Garmonsway 1978, 25; Miller 1890, I, 1 196.
47 Whitelock 1955, 558.
48 Zupita 1959, l. 489, 774.
49 op. cit., l.1010.
50 Temple 1976, illus. 158, 197.
51 Turner 1828, III 51; Whitelock 1968, 12.
52 Jackson 1969, 134, 131.
53 Miller 1890, I, 1 162; Owen 1841, 491, 673.
54 Jackson 1971, 30.
55 Whitelock 1955, 558.
56 Owen 1841, 65, 393.
57 Whitelock 1955, 279.
58 Turner 1828, III 36.
59 Jackson 1969, 34; Owen 1841, 355, 643.
60 Whitelock 1955, 706.
61 Mackie 1973, *Gnomic Verses* l.87 ff.
62 Miller 1890, I, 2 396.
63 Meaney 1981, 87-8.
64 op. cit., 247.
65 Attenborough 1922, 6-7.
66 Fell 1984, 50.
67 Miller 1890, I, 1 166; Wilson 1985, pl. 48.
68 Turner 1828, III 420.
69 Holmes 1952, 89; Jackson 1969, 128, 100; Magnusson & Palsson 1960, 117; Garmonsway 1978, 46.
70 Page 1985, 14-15.
71 op. cit.
72 Jones 1987, 29.
73 Turner 1828, III 29; Zupita 1959, l.619.
74 Fell 1984, 144; Davies 1982, 35; Liebermann 1898, 454; Hawkes et al. 1985, 103; Robertson 1939, 199, 252.
75 Davies 1982, 23; Robertson 1939, 252; Whitelock 1968, 10.
76 Robertson 1939, 252.
77 op. cit.; Douglas & Greenaway 1953, 817; Garmonsway 1978, 27; Davies 1982, 35.
78 Robertson 1939, 252.
79 Whitelock 1955, 279, 777; Kylie 1911, 42-3.
80 Zupita 1959, l. 2103ff., 2115ff.; Turner 1828 III, 29, 32; Whitelock 1955, 235; Mellows 1982, 42.
81 Miller 1890, I, 1 162; Whitelock 1955, 234.
82 Turner 1828, II 154.
83 Bonser 1963, 141.
84 op. cit., 140.
85 Turner 1828, III 29; Owen 1841, 63.
86 Gollancz/Mackie 1973, *St Juliana*; Attenborough 1922, 4; Whitelock 1955, 361.
87 Turner 1828, II 507.
88 Kylie 1911, 42-3, 169; Whitelock 1955, 777, 790.

[89] op. cit., 835.

[90] op. cit., 408.

[91] Swanton 1975, 122.

[92] Knowles 1940, 463; Whitelock 1955, 291.

[93] op. cit., 389.

[94] Turner 1828, I 264, 419; Whitelock 1955, 323, 835.

[95] Jackson 1969, 149; Zupita 1959, 1. 88.

[96] Miller 1890, I, 2 343.

[97] Mackie 1973, *Rhymed Poem*, l.25 ff.

[98] Bruce-Mitford 1983, 683, 687-8, 701, 718, 724-5; Evison 1987, 121.

[99] Mackie 1973, *Gnomic Verses* l. 127.

[100] Skeat 1881 *St Agatha* l.97 ff.; *St Cecilia* l.228.

[101] Miller 1890, I,1 134-6.

[102] Gollancz/Mackie 1973, *Rhymed Poem* l.5 ff, l.11 ff.

[103] Gordon 1960, 35.

[104] Gollancz/Mackie 1973, *The Ruin*; Davies 1982, 30; Turner 1828, I 307 *Elegy on Urien of Reged*.

[105] Sweet 1965, 149-151.

[106] op. cit.

9 Special Regimens

This chapter is divided into three sections: special regimens for infants, invalids, and monastics.

(i) Infants

Children were probably breast-fed until they were about two. A woman who could not lactate, and could not employ a wet nurse, would probably lose her child. A Leechdom counsels the woman who cannot feed her child to 'take the milk of a cow of one colour in her hand and then fill her mouth with it and go to running water and spit the milk in and then ladle up with the same hand a mouthful of the water and swallow it' (*nime þonne anes bleos cu meoluc on hyre handæ 7 gesupe þonne mid hyre muþe 7 gange þonne to yrnendum wætere 7 spiwe þær in þa meolc 7 hlade þonne mid þære ylcan hand þæs wæteres muð fulne 7 forswelge*). After that she was to recite some words, but the element of sympathetic magic was no doubt important.[1]

According to Bede, it seems to have been the case that a couple should not resume sexual relations until their child was weaned: 'her man must not go to her bed before the newborn child is weaned from milk' (*to hire gerestscipe þonne hire wer ne sceal gongan, ær þon þæt acennde bearn from meolcum aweneð sy*). However, this tended not to be observed. 'A culpable custom has grown up between the married pair in that the wife neglects to feed her child and gives it to other women to feed.' (*An unriht gewuna wel hwær is arisen betweoh gesinhiwum þæt wiif forhycgað heora bearn fedan þa ðe heo cennað 7 heo oðrum wiifum to fedenne sellað.*)

The late seventh-century Laws of Ine suggest that wet nursing was established. The Laws allow a *gesith*-born man to take with him his reeve, and his smith and his *cildfestre* if he moves elsewhere.[2] *Cildfestre*, translated 'children's nurse' literally means 'child's feeder', and is unlikely to mean simply a nursemaid who would have been easy to replace.

The milk of cattle, goats and sheep, and the whey from cheese making may have been given to babies and young children.[3] The latter is rich in nutrients and easy to digest. Traditionally cows' horns were used as feeding bottles for babies, but there must have been a considerable risk of gastroenteritis as there is no evidence that utensils would have been sterilized, although experience with dairying may have shown the importance of cleanliness. The likelihood would be that a mother breast-fed her baby, supplementing as the child grew older with cereal porridges for which the grain could be finely ground.

Food for Young Children

Babies were probably weaned onto finely ground cereal mixtures. The Welsh Laws provided wheat to be made into pap for a child during the first year of its life, and the 'pan with feet', which was also to be provided, was probably for cooking this gruel.[4] Pap could also be made by soaking bread in milk or water. Probably babies were given bread to suck/chew as soon as they had teeth.[5]

Bread was probably the basic food for children. The baker of the *Colloquy* claims 'I make men strong, and because of this the little ones will not shun me' (*Ic mægen wera 7 furþon litlincgas nellaþ forbigean me*)[6]. Bread was all that the children at the monastery of Abingdon had to eat when Queen Edith came to visit them and decided to make provision for better food.[7] A tradition at St Albans assigned a gift of land in Æthelred's day to the provision of milk and cheese 'for food for the young monks' (*ad alimenta monachorum juniorum*).[8]

Older children, like the novice of the *Colloquy* drank ale or water, not wine because 'wine is not the drink for children or the foolish, but for the older and wiser' (*win nys drenc cilda ne dysgra ac ealdra 7 wisra*).[9]

Relaxation of Dietary Observance

Children were not made to fast. The Penitential of Ecgbert states, for example, 'if he is a grown man, he is to fast one year' (*gyf hit geweaxan man sy fæste 1 gear*). The rigour of the Benedictine Rule was to be relaxed for children and the old on account of their 'feebleness' (*wacmodness*). 'This is to be a kind consideration of them, and permission is to be given them to anticipate the regular hours'.[10] Ingulf says of Editha at the royal court that she used to send him to the larder for refreshment when he was a boy.[11] Lanfranc's *Statutua*, perhaps codifying earlier practice, legislate for a mid-morning breakfast for the children and those monks unable to fast longer, and children could breakfast during the monks' chapter)[12].

The novice of the *Colloquy* says 'I still enjoy meat because I am a child under instruction...vegetables and eggs, fish and cheese, butter and beans and all permitted things I eat with great thankfulness' (*Gyt flæscmettum ic bruce, forðam cild eom under gyrda drohtniende...wyrta 7 æigra, fisc 7 cyse, buteran 7 beana 7 ealle clæne þingc ic ete mid micelre þancunge*). He is not 'such a great glutton that [he] eats all kinds of food at one meal' (*swa micel swelgere þæt...ealle cynn metta on anre gereordinge etan mæge).*[13] It was important that the children were allowed to eat meat, otherwise they could have suffered from zinc deficiency, leading to arrested growth.[14]

Malnourishment

Infanticide was not accounted a crime in the earlier Anglo-Saxon period because it was considered better in times of stress, that a child should die as soon as it was born, rather than that it should linger a short time to die of starvation. By the time of the Pentitential of Theodore infanticide was accounted a serious crime, although more excusable if carried out by an impoverished mother.[15]

Wells suggested that enamel hypoplasia affecting the canines and second molars most often among the Anglo-Saxons indicates that periods of morbidity occurred between the ages of 2 and 4 years, perhaps due to nutritional disturbances associated with weaning.[16] However, Harris's lines in the early Anglo-Saxon communities at Burgh Castle and Caistor, Norfolk, indicate increased frequency around the ages of 4-6 and 8-12.[17] This is probably evidence of the more general 'bread-winner effect'. As in other agricultural communities which depend on the strength of adult males for the heavy agricultural work, children probably ate afterwards with the women.[18] If supplies were scarce, the women and children went short.

(ii) Invalid Diet

A tradition of doctoring, using herbs as the main treatment, was established by the middle of the period, though medical writings date from the late period.[19] The wort drinks so often recommended, are prescriptions rather than food, but so many recipes are given - some hundreds in *Leechdoms* - that they must have been a very common way of treating complaints. They would have been important as a valuable source of vitamins A and C in particular, as well as minerals, apart from containing active principles which may have been effective against the particular complaint for which they were taken. 'Good herb drinks such as doctors make' (*godum wyrtdrencum swa læces wyrcað*) elsewhere called *oxumellis*, contained vinegar and honey, a combination still recommended.[20]

Instructions for invalid or special diets are sometimes given in very general terms: 'eat fresh meat where it is fattest' (*ete fersc flæsc þær þær hit fætost sie*) for example, and there are a number of references to fat meat.[21] 'Light foods' (*leohte mettas*) which included 'juicy broths and fresh peas and beaten eggs and bread broken into hot water and periwinkles removed from their shells with peas' (*geseaw broþu 7 geseawe pysan 7 geslegen ægru 7 bread gebrocen on hat wæter winewinclan adon of scellum mid pysum*) are also called for, and 'delicate food and good drink' (*hnesce mettas 7 godne drincan*).[22]

Sometimes the instructions are specific and worth quoting in full, since they are the nearest we get to Anglo-Saxon recipes, or to an idea of diet: 'he is to eat dry bread and cheese...bake a warm loaf for him' (*sceal he etan drigne hlaf 7 cyse...baca hym man þanne wearmen hlaf*);[23] 'stew chicken in wine and then add walnut oil and drink that' (*cicene mete...seow on wine do þanne ele to þe beo of frencissen hnutu 7 drince þæt*).[24] Beef broth made from beef marinaded in vinegar and oil, cooked with salt, dill and leek was recommended for stomach trouble.[25] So was a diet which included apples, pears and peaches, bread in water, salmon, goose giblets, and pigs' trotters, and another Leechdom recommends the flesh of small birds, stewed and roasted; apples, pears, medlars, and peas cooked in vinegar or sharp wine.[26] Salt meats, hares' and boars' flesh, roots of rue, cresses and easily digested meats were recommended for an invalid with 'a hard swelling of the stomach' (*heardum swile þæs magan*).[27] He was also to be given sweet apples, marinaded in wine, then stewed and sweetened with honey and peppered.[28] An internal stomach injury was treated by giving the patient 'eggs to sup up, barley bread, clean new butter and new barley meal or groats made into a brewit as cooks know how' (*ægru to supanne beren bread clæne niwe buteran 7 niwe beren mela oððe grytta togædre gebriwed swa cocas cunnon*).[29] 'Fresh milk sweetened with honey' (*niwe molcen meoluc mid hunige gesmeþed*), and 'oven baked bread' (*ofen bacen hlaf*) were recommended for other gastric complaints.[30]

Meats 'that make good blood' (*þe god blod wyrceað*) were thought to be 'shellfishes, finned fishes and domestic and wild hens and all the birds that live on the hills, and pigeons, that is, the young chicks of culvers, half-grown pigs' and goats' flesh and the juice of peas with honey somewhat peppered' (*scilfixas finihte 7 ham wilda hænna 7 ealle þa fugelas þe on dunum libbað 7 pipiones þ beoð culfrena briddas 7 healfeald swin 7 gate flæsc 7 pisena seaw mid hunige hwæt hwega gepiperod*).[31] The recommendation of fish was not in the original Greek, and fish remains an 'invalid' food today, as does chicken, recommended elsewhere.[32] The value of eggs, dairy produce and vegetables seems to have been recognised.[33]

'Bullocks' meat, goats' and harts, bucks' and rams' and bulls' and the meat of all old four-footed animals, and birds that have hard flesh -

peacock, swan, and duck' (*hryþeres flæsc gæten 7 hiorota buccena 7 ramma 7 fearra 7 þa þe swiðe ealde beoð on feoporfotum nietenum 7 fuglas þa þe heard flæsc habbað pawa swan æned*) are all recommended in one case.[34]

Avoidance

A pregnant woman was sensibly warned against 'eating salt or sweet things or *beor* or pork or anything fat or drinking to excess' (*sealtes ete oððe swetes oþþe beor drince ne swines flæsc ne naht fætes ne druncen gedrince*).[35]

Instructions about what food is to be avoided is sometimes given in general terms: 'avoid anything sour or salt' (*forga sur 7 sealtes gehwæt*), for example.[36] Food to be avoided by a man with liver disease is given first in general terms: nothing too sharp, bitter or purgative and then in detail: 'all broth must be avoided...eggs are forbidden...crumb of bread can be taken provided it is moistened or sodden...but not to excess. Other moist ?wheaten ?meat-preparations and cookings-up must be forbidden and all moist and greasy things and oyster pies and all sweet things that create wind...no apples or wine' (*ælc broþ is to forganne...ægru sint to forganne...hlafes cruman gif hie beoþ ofþænde oþþe gesodene...ac na to swiþe. oþre wætan mete gearwa 7 cocnunga ealle sint to forbeodanne 7 eal þa wætan þing 7 þa smerewigan 7 osterhlafas 7 eall swete þing þe wyrcað aþundenesse...æppla ne win*).[37]

Other *Leechdoms* warned against vinegar, peas, beans, turnips, apples and nuts because they caused wind.[38] Sometimes 'cold oysters and apples and various vegetables' (*cealde ostran 7 æppla 7 missenlice wyrta þigð*) were to be avoided, elsewhere leek and cabbage are singled out.[39] Cheese, goose, eel, pork, fish and waterfowl could be eaten if salted.[40] Another *Leechdom* forbade 'freshwater fishes and sea fishes that have hard flesh...bullocks' flesh, or pork or mutton...or goat or kid meat' (*fen fixas and sæ fixas þa þe habbað heard flæsc...hriþeres flæsc ne swines ne sceapes...ne gate ne ticcenes*). It also counselled against drinking *þicce win*.[41] Asthma sufferers were given the comprehensive instruction to avoid 'many kinds of meat and drinks and roasted meat and the meat of every kind of animal that chews the cud' (*feala cunna metas 7 drencas 7 wið gebræd flæsc 7 wið ælces orffes flæsc 7 þe cudu ceowe*).[42]

Relaxation from Religious Rule

The Rule of St Benet allowed the flesh of quadrupeds only to the very weak and sick.[43] Æthelwold ate meat for three months when he was ill only at the command of Dunstan, and again during his final illness.[44] The *Rule of Chrodegang* allowed an invalid 'to take food and drink whenever he wants to or is able to, when he cannot observe the proper mealtimes' (*on ælcne sæl æt 7 wæt þicge þonne hine lyste oððe he mæge, þonne he gedafenlicum tidum ne mæg*).[45]

(iii) Monastic

Some Christian hermits, like Old Testament prophets, led a life of austerity in which a restricted, even eccentric, diet played a part.[46] The growth of communal monastic living necessitated meals that were acceptable to a group of individuals. The most famous rule was that instituted by Benedict of Nursia in the sixth century. The standard meal was bread and its accompaniment, as in lay households, and a second dish was offered at mealtimes so that 'he who perchance cannot eat of the one, may make his meal of the other'.[47]

A restricted diet was thought unlikely to inflame the passions, and gluttony and drunkenness would also be avoided.[48] *The Rule of Chrodegang* declared: '...feasts...are to be avoided. But let bread with vegetables and fruit make a pleasant evening meal and if anyone has a fish let it be accounted a great delicacy. He who wishes to reign with Christ, does not care if he consume expensive food and drink which are excreted as dung and urine' (*...gebeorscipas...synt to fleonne...Ac sy eadelic æfenmete, hlaf mid ofæte, 7 amang þam gif ma fisc hæbbe healde þæt for healicne est. Se þe mis Criste wilnað to rixigenne, ne recð he na swiðe hwæþer he of deorwyrðum mettum 7 drincum þæt meox his argancges 7 his micgan gesamnige*).[49] However, there was a problem in balancing food intake so that bodily lusts would be subdued, but the monks would have enough energy to carry out their work. According to *The Rule of St Benet*, 'Everyone hath his proper gift from God, one thus, another thus. For this reason the amount of other people's food cannot be determined without some misgiving'.[50] Fixing reasonable rations was difficult and laxity tended to creep in because no absolute standard could be established.[51]

The capital question concerned the abstinence from flesh meat as Benedict supplied matter for argument. The term 'flesh' was taken not to include fat (*pinguedo*) since an incidental enactment forbids this only during the Advent and Lenten fasts. Because the word 'quadruped' was used, the flesh of birds was considered lawful.[52] The *Regularis Concordia* does not include a chapter expressly devoted to diet, but announces that the Benedictine Rule is to be followed absolutely: that is, the two cooked dishes and one of fruit or vegetables, or, if the field labour was especially severe, other dishes at the abbot's discretion.

A number of religious, or quasi-monastic, communities were established in Anglo-Saxon England as early as the seventh century, among them Canterbury, Ripon, Winchester, Gilling, Whitby and *Icanho*.[53] However, the numbers of men and women living under the monastic rule varied throughout the period, and the dietary regulations were not always observed. At Monkwearmouth and Jarrow, for example, Biscop compiled his guide from the observances of seventeen different monasteries he had visited.[54]

Ascetic individuals, like Cuthbert, and later Æthelwold, who 'thought to subdue himself by abstinence', were revered by their contemporaries.[55] They had their adherents, ready to follow their example, and Æthelwold gave impetus to a movement for monastic reform. However, the respect accorded such individuals on account of their asceticism argues that it was not widespread, even among monastics.

Timetabled Meals

The times of meals, and their number, varied according to the time of year (see Chapter 7), but meals had their place in a regular routine, not to be interrupted by personal circumstances, or the exigencies of work or weather. It is this element of regularity which characterises the monastic regimen. There was a formal, ritual quality to a meal in the refectory.[56] According to *The Rule of Chrodegang*, after washing their hands in silence, a bell would be rung after which the brothers were to kneel and pray, then take their seats one by one. After blessing the food and drink, the prior was the first to eat. The Rule was to be read, and no-one else was to speak.[57] This regimented existence may have been irksome to some of the inmates, but for those who were not guaranteed sufficient food by their personal circumstances, regular meals may have been an attraction.

Food allowed by the Rule

After the *Regularis Concordia*, abstinence from flesh meat was general throughout the monasteries of England until well after the Conquest.[58] Fat, in the form of lard, suet and dripping was eaten, though it was a luxury and therefore to be renounced from Septuagesima till Easter, and in Advent, save on Sundays and feasts.[59] Lent was a time for fourfold abstinence and *pinguedo* (lard) was one of the four items to be abstained from (milk and eggs were two other items specifically mentioned, the fourth was presumably poultry).[60] The flesh of birds and fish could normally be consumed while still keeping to the letter of the law.[61]

The midday meal, the *prandium*, became the chief meal, to consist of two cooked dishes, *twa gesodene sylfian/ twa gesodene sufel*, to be eaten as an accompaniment to bread. These would have been of cereals, beans or other pulse, eggs, cheese and the like. There was to be a third dish of fresh vegetables and fruit if such were available. Bread was the mainstay of the diet with the individual ration set at a pound a day. St Benedict nowhere gave details of the second meal, but it may be supposed that it was a lighter version of the other, since a third of the daily ration of bread was kept back for it.[62]

This information may be amplified by the details given in the plan for the monastery garden of St Gall. Apple, pear, plum, service, medlar, bay, chestnut, fig, quince, peach, hazel, almond, mulberry and walnut trees all featured, and the eighteen great beds of the kitchen garden were to contain onions, leeks, celery, radish, carrots, garlic, shallots, lettuce, parsnip, cabbage, parsley, dill, chervil, marigold, coriander, poppy and corn campion.[63] The vegetables would have made suitable flavourings for cereal or bean dishes or could have been served as an accompaniment to bread.[64]

The Rule of Chrodegang is interesting since it gives a more generous allowance of bread, and mentions 'animal flesh' (*flæsc*) foods:

'give each...four pounds by weight of bread, and...for their midday accompaniment for their bread let each two have a dish of fleshfood and offer other delicacies (e.g. meat puddings and sausages). If there are no delicacies, then let them be given two meat dishes. And for their evening meal let every couple have a meat dish or other delicacies. And at that time they must forego meat, and in Lent, then at midday day every couple shall have sufficient soft cheese and some delicacy, and if fish or vegetables are available, let them have them as a third course. And in the evening, each couple is to have soft cheese and some delicacy, and if the food is plentiful, humbly thank eternal God. When they only have one meal a day, then each couple is to have a delicacy and a serving of soft cheese and vegetable or some kind of stewed meat (?food) as a third course.'

(sylle ma ælcum...feower punda gewihte hlafes; 7...heora middæges sufle, twam 7 twam an[e] flæscsande, 7 syddan oðre smeamettas. Gif man næbbe smeamettas, sylle man twam 7 twam twa flæscsande. 7 [to] heora æfenþenunge sylle man twam 7 twam ane flæscsande oððe oðre smeamettas. On þam tidum þe hi sceolon flæsc forgan, ealswa on

Lengtenne, þonne sylle man to middægþenunge twam 7 twam an tyl cyssticce 7 sumne smeamete; 7 gif man fisc hæbbe oðŏe wyrta, sylle ma him to þriddan sande; 7 on æfen twam 7 twam an cyssticce 7 sume smeamettas; 7 gif it rumre cymŏ, þancion eadmodlice þæs æcum Drihtene. Þonne hi etaŏf to anes mæles on dæg, þonne sylle man twam 7 twam sumne smeamete 7 tyl cyssticce, 7 wyrta oŏðe sumes cynnes gesodenne mete to þriddan sande.)[65]

There are no precise and authentic data for reconstituting the daily monastic meals in the times of Dunstan and Lanfranc.[66] So far as can be ascertained, the arrangements for the common meals remained unchanged between 960-1216, modified only by the addition of more feast days in winter. How far the observance was relaxed in the decades before the Conquest must remain a matter of doubt.[67] When information becomes plentiful, it is clear that, erected upon the basis of an ordinary day's fare of bread, cheese, vegetables, and two or three dishes of cereals, beans or eggs, a considerable fabric of extra dishes had sprung up. The most general form taken by these additions was the pittance, a small dish, usually of eggs or fish, served to each monk or pair of monks. A separate official, the pittancer, had charge of the material for the pittances.[68] At Glastonbury by the end of the period the monks had two pittances on Sundays, Tuesdays, Thursdays and Saturdays, and one on the remaining days of the week. At the same time the Abingdon dietary also allows two pittances on the same four weekdays, and three or four pittances on feast-days, with two dishes of vegetables, one or two of *pulmenta* (cereals/beans) and one *generale* of eggs and fish.[69] In the opening years of Edgar's reign some men had been attracted to Abingdon by its reputation for stricter observance, so other monasteries may have been more lavish in the matter of food, or, perhaps more probably, the laxity had crept in over the ensuing decades.[70]

Wealthy individuals made provision for feasts in particular monasteries on the basis that the monks were to intercede for their souls (see above). Æthelgifu left St Albans '16 measures of malt and 3 of meal and a sester of honey...7 wethers and 6 lambs and a fattened bullock ready for slaughter and 30 cheeses...one *oman* of wine and 20 cheeses and 6 pigs and a bullock...from each estate for the thirtieth day [i.e. after burial - the 'month's mind']' (*xvi mittan mealtes 7 iii melwes 7 an sester huniges...7 viii weþeras 7 vi lomb 7 an slegeryþer 7 xxx cysa...anne oman wines 7 xx cysa 7 vi swin 7 an hryŏer 7 nyme man of æghwilcum tune to þam þryttguþan dæge*).[71]

Laxity & Reforms

There were ideals, but normal practice was not attuned to them. Bede complained to Egbert in 734 that 'certain bishops...are given to laughter, jests, tales, feasting and drunkenness' .[72] He maintained the double abbey at Coldingham was destroyed by fire because of 'gluttony and drunkenness and idle gossip and other unlawful transgressions' (*oferæta 7 druncennesse 7 leasspellunge 7 oðerra unalefedlecra scylda*).[73]

Æthelred instructed in 1008 that clerics, where there was property such that they could have a refectory, were to obey the Rule, but he had to follow this up in 1014 by declaring 'henceforth we desire that abbots and monks live more according to the Rule than they have been accustomed to do until now' (*heonan forð we willað þæt abbodas 7 munecas regollicor libban þonne hi nu ær ðisan on gewunan hæfdon*).[74] The tendency towards laxity was a feature of monastic establishments, although this was checked by a number of individuals throughout the period.[75]

There was an infrastructure of lay servants at monasteries.[76] Cynesige, a monk who was archbishop of York, is recorded as living very temperately when his clerks or household officers were daily feasting in great luxury and splendour.[77] Although there is some confusion over whether those who were feasting were in fact clerics or lay officials, the source indicates the potential for good living in an important ecclesiastical household, even when its head was an ascetic.

Since a monastery contained categories of inmates not bound to observe the Rule, it is not surprising, for instance, that the stores of the monastery of Bury St Edmunds contained flitches of bacon and associated delicacies since the flesh of domestic animals may have been used for guests, servants and the sick, while the lard went to the monks.[78] It is possible to maintain that there is no trustworthy evidence to show meat was ever allowed in the common refectory of a Benedictine monastery between 960 and 1216, even if certain relaxations had begun to come in outside the refectory.[79]

The *Regularis Concordia* stated that all should feed together in the refectory (except in case of illness) and neither prelates not their subordinates should ever presume to be present at worldly feastings, unless perhaps in the case of unexpected hospitality when travelling.[80] However, this dispensation was obviously open to abuse.[81] The difficulty was that high status in lay society was indicated by the consumption of prestige foods in quantity and in the presence of numbers of guests or subordinates.

Monasteries were major landowners, and therefore generally had access to a plentiful food supply. Monks very often came from the ranks of a class used to conspicuous consumption: 'nobly-born men who had been used to eating delicacies' (*æþel-boren weras...þa wæron estlice afedde*).[82] The fact that they subjected themselves to 'the austerity that prevailed in the monastery' (*þære stiðnysse þa þær stod on þam mynstre*) is seen as admirable, and even surprising. In a society where kings, nobles and landowners rewarded their retainers and servants and demonstrated their status by holding feasts, it proved to be difficult to prevent a movement towards feasting in monasteries.

---

[1] Cockayne 1851, *Lacnunga*, 104.
[2] Whitelock 1955, 371.
[3] Bonser 1963, 302; Holmes 1952, 200.
[4] Owen 1841, 51.
[5] Kylie 1911, 95.
[6] Garmonsway 1978, 36-7.
[7] Knowles 1940, 457.
[8] op. cit.
[9] Garmonsway 1978, 47.
[10] Bonser 1963, 91.
[11] Turner 1828, II 354.
[12] Knowles 1940, 45.
[13] Garmonsway 1978, 46.
[14] Morgan 1975, 4.
[15] Bonser 1963, 87.
[16] Wells 1964.
[17] op. cit.
[18] Kuper 1977, 103-4, 107, 164, 175.
[19] Turner 1828, III 4.
[20] Cockayne 1851, II i 1; II xxiii; Hills 1988, 70.
[21] Cockayne 1851, III lxv, lxxii; *Peri Didacheon* 37, 38, II vi, vii.
[22] op. cit., I xlix; *Peri Didacheon* 40, 44.
[23] op. cit., 52.
[24] op. cit., 53.
[25] op. cit., II vii.
[26] op. cit., II i; ii 2.
[27] op. cit., II iv.
[28] op. cit.
[29] op. cit., II xxvi.
[30] op. cit., II xxvii.
[31] op. cit., II xxxvii.
[32] op. cit., II xvi, III lxxii, *Peri Didacheon* 51.
[33] op. cit., II xvi 1, xxv, xxvi, xxvii, li, *Peri Didacheon* 37.
[34] op. cit., II xvi.
[35] op. cit., III xxxvii.
[36] op. cit., I iv 5, 6, xv 2, ii 1, II xliii.
[37] op. cit., II xxiii.
[38] op. cit., II xxiv, xxxix.
[39] op. cit., II xxxvi, I ii 1.
[40] op. cit., II xxii; I xxxvi.
[41] op. cit., II xliii.

42 op. cit., *Peri Didacheon* 52.
43 Logeman 1888, Ch. 39.
44 Symons 1953, xxxv; Knowles 1940, 458.
45 Napier 1916, 47-8.
46 Turner 1828, III 27; Whitelock 1955, 749.
47 Matt & Hilpisch 1961, 114.
48 Garmonsway 1978, 46; Napier 1916, 40.
49 op. cit., 69.
50 Logeman 1888, Chap. 39, 40.
51 Knowles 1940, 150.
52 op. cit., 458.
53 op. cit., Appendix III; Whitelock 1955, 152, 696, 697; Matt & Hilpisch 1961, 149.
54 Knowles 1940, 23.
55 Colgrave 1940, 70; Whitelock 1955, 837.
56 Symons 1953, Sect. 26.
57 Napier 1916, 125-6.
58 Knowles 1940, 460.
59 op. cit.
60 Symons 1953, xxxv.
61 Knowles 1940, 460.
62 op. cit., 462.
63 Stewart 1975, 46.
64 Cockayne 1851, III 408.
65 Napier 1916, 14-15.
66 Knowles 1940, 462.
67 op. cit., 457.
68 op. cit., 464.
69 op. cit., 463.
70 Symons 1953, xix.
71 Whitelock 1968, 11.
72 Whitelock 1955, 737.
73 Miller 1898, I, 2 354.
74 Robertson 1925, 126.
75 Symons 1953, xvi, xxi; Whitelock 1955, 836; Knowles 1940, Appendix III.
76 Symons 1953, Sect. 24, 55, 60.
77 Mellows 1980, 37.
78 Knowles 1940, 460; Robertson 1939, 199.
79 Knowles 1940, 458-63.
80 Symons 1953, xxxi.
81 op. cit.
82 Skeat 1881, *St. Martin* 1.355.

10 Food Shortages & Deficiency Diseases

Hunger

Steorfan did not yet mean 'to starve' but simply to die, though of *hungor/hungre/hungær* was sometimes adjoined, but of the synonyms used for 'to die' only *stearfan/steorfan* and *sweltan* seem to have been commonly employed in the 'of hunger' connection.[1]

Bede mentions hunger and thirst as the first infirmities of nature, following from the sin of the first man.[2] *The Fates of Men* refers to the individual eaten by a wolf, and then states 'another shall be wasted by hunger' (*sumne sceal hungor aliþan*).[3] The eventualities listed by the poem, though perhaps not commonplace, were distinct possibilities. A woman writing to her absent lover feels constrained to point out:

> *Wulf min wulf wena me þine*
> *seoce gedydon þine seldcymas*
> *munende mod nales meteliste*

(Wulf, my Wulf, it was my longing for you, your long absences and my sad heart that have made me sick, not lack of food).[4]

A golden age of plenty was looked back to, but times had changed.[5] Life on earth was 'hard and spent in sweating toil and wearied by hunger' (*geswinc-ful and on swate wunad...and on hungre gewæht*).[6] Some of the writings about hunger are particularly vivid:

> *Þa wæs wop hæfen in wera burgum*
> *hlud heriges cyrm hreopon friccan*
> *mændon meteleaste meðe stodon*
> *hungre gehæfte. Hornsalu wunedon*
> *weste winræced welan ne benohton*
> *beornas to brucanne on þa bitran tid*
> *gesæton searuþancle sundor to rune*
> *ermðu eahtigan.*

('Then was weeping uplifted in the towns of men, the loud outcry of the host, heralds shouted, they moaned the famine, weary they stood, bound by hunger. The spired halls remained, the winehouses empty, wealth needed not men to enjoy in that bitter tide. The wise of thought sat apart in council to investigate on their misery'.)[7]

One way of dealing with misfortune 'through enemy invasions or hunger, through plague or mortality, through crop failure or bad weather' (*þurh here oðþon hunger, þurh stric oððe steorfan, þurh unwæstm oððe unweðer*) according to the tenth-century *Institutes of Polity* was to 'earnestly consult how amends could be sought from

Christ, with pure fasts and with frequenting churches'.[8] Hunger was seen as a punishment for evil living. If monks and their superiors cared for worldly things then God would manifest his disapproval: 'if men cast away the monkly life and hold God's services in contempt what shall we come to but disease and hunger?' (ða þa man towearþ munuc-lif and godes biggengas to bysmore hæfde buton þæt us com to cwealm and hunger).[9]

One specific incidence of famine is recorded by Bede, since for three years before Bishop Wilfred came to Sussex 'there had been no rain and consequently a very severe famine had weakened the people and they died a cruel death. It is said that often forty or fifty people at a time suffering from starvation and in their misery, took each other by the hands, and jumped together from the cliffs, in order to kill themselves by the fall or drown themselves' (þær nænig regn...cwom 7 þonon se grimmesta hungor þæt folc wæs wæcende 7 heo mid arlease cwale fylde wæron. Secgað men þatte oft feowertig monna oðþe fiftig somed, þa ðe mid þy hungre gewæcte wæron, þæt heo earmlice bi honum noman 7 ealle ætgædre of sæsofre ut feollan, 7 woldan heo sylfe oðþe offyllan oðþe adrencan).[10] Wilfred showed the people how to fish, since they knew only how to take eels. What were apparently suicide pacts may have been heathen sacrifices, but the rationale was presumably the same.

Scarcity may also be deduced from the laws relating to stolen food. Thieves were severely punished because 'they have snatched away very often the sustenance of the righteous'. Religious writings too confirm scarcity. Alcuin complains to Æthelred of Northumbria in 793 that 'some are inundated with delicacies and feastings like Dives, clothed in purple, ...and Lazarus dies in hunger at his gate. Where is brotherly love, where the pity which we are admonished to have for the wretched? The satiety of the rich is the hunger of the poor'.[11]

Relief of Hunger

Some charitable individuals of means did make efforts to relieve hunger. A king orders his reeves to supply one poor man on each of his estates with an amber of meal, a flitch of bacon or a wether worth one penny every month.[12] King Alfred left fifty pounds in his will to poor men in need, and another fifty pounds to poor servants of God.[13] Hunger continued a problem in the tenth century, since King Eadred left sixteen hundred pounds in his will to his people that they might be able to buy relief for themselves from famine, and from the heathen army if they had need. Wulfwaru in her will directs her legatees to feed twenty *freolsmen*, presumably freedmen, formerly slaves, on her lands.[14] Another testator left by will that a hundred poor men were to be fed at Ely, annually on St Audrey's day.[15] There was no comprehensive system of organised relief for the hungry, and it is unlikely that relief reached all those who needed it.

Special Circumstances

An individual like Cuthbert, living the life of a recluse and refusing an attendant, was at risk from hunger, if not starvation, if he fell ill. Cuthbert had in fact only consumed half an onion of the five he had with him when he took to his bed.[16] But when the brethren were, after a tempest of five days, able to reach him one of them observed 'I saw by his face that he was greatly wearied by lack of food as well as disease' (*videbam ... in facie eius quia multum inedia sinnul et languore erat defessus*).[17]

Famine Effecting a Change in Economic Circumstances

Theodore's Penitential states 'a father may sell his son aged under seven as a slave if necessity forces him to do so, after that he must have the agreement of the child' (*pater filium suum septem annorum, necessitate compulsus, potestatem habet tradere in servitium; deinde sine voluntate filii licentiam tradendi non habet*).[18] This was not as callous an act as at first appears. Selling oneself into slavery in exchange for food was an established practice throughout the period.[19] Under the terms of her will, written in a hand of the late tenth century, Gætflæd set free 'all the people who sold themselves for food during those evil days' (*ealle ða men ðe heonon heora heafod for hyra mete on ðam yflum dagum*).[20] Slaves who were already part of an estate might be in a reasonably good position in times of dearth. The land would not afford any profit to its owner if it were not worked, and so it was in the landowner's interest to see that workers were fit enough to work.

Monastic

In times of famine gold and silver were stripped from reliquaries, and crucifixes and chalices were melted down - presumably for the poor.[21] St Æthelwold in the tenth century declared that he could not endure the sight of men, created in the image of God, dying of starvation and want, so broke up the church plate to buy food for those in distress.[22] Leofric at St Albans did the same, probably in 1005, adding to the church plate gold and silver vessels from his own table.[23]

Causes of Famine

Weather

After a bad season food might be scarce, but a succession of bad years would bring about serious famine and probably pestilence.[24] Walford made a comprehensive analysis of the causes of famines recorded in the annals and found inclement weather the most serious factor.[25]

Entomological & Zootic Factors

There were occasional plagues of insects - 'locusts' according to the sources, which consumed quantities of the harvest. More important perhaps were the murrains which afflicted cattle and other animals periodically. They may have been influenced by poor pasture and reduced supplies of provender, so that a shortage of animal products might coincide with a reduced crop yield and compound the problem of securing sufficient food.

Human Factors

Walford's 'defective agriculture' may have played a part in food shortages, but the consequences of warfare were a decisive factor.[26] The land itself might be ravaged by troops or agricultural workers might be away campaigning.[27] Transport was certainly not organised on a comprehensive enough basis to make feasible the supply of provisions to an area suffering a shortfall.[28] No doubt landholders with large scattered estates either went to their properties where there was sufficient food or organised supplies to be transported to them.

In some cases there may have been a lack of technological knowledge when it came to exploiting food resources. There is nothing intrinsically unlikely in the fact that the starving inhabitants of Sussex, used to taking eels by spearing them or catching them in weirs of brushwood, did not know how to net fish at sea.

Famine Years

Occurrences of famine were recorded in copies of the Anglo-Saxon Chronicle. These were kept at various religious houses, and local outbreaks may have been recorded in only one copy.[29] The most important, together with comments from the sources, are listed in Appendix D.

Famine Foods

The likelihood is that if supplies were short, important foods like flour would be bulked out with less desirable additions: beans and peas, acorns and ground bark, for example (see Chapter 2). Diseased meat that might normally have been rejected may have been consumed, in some cases infecting the eater. Fruit that was unripe or bad would normally have been rejected, but in times of famine it was probably eaten. Herbs and roots (nettles and wild skirret, for example) would be gathered from the hedgerows to eke out a scanty existence.[30]

In extreme conditions, as were recorded for 695-700, 'men ate each other'.[31] Cannibalism is also recorded in the post-Conquest period. The *Liber Eliensis* records 'consequent famine prevailed with the result that men ate horses, dogs, cats and human flesh' (*fames secuta praevaluit ut homines equinam, caninam, catinam et carnem commederent humanam*).[32] This pattern seems to be generally followed during times of severe famine; taboos play little part when existence is at stake.[33]

Some famine foods, in particular dark green (i.e. high carotene) leaves, including Chenopodium, were nutritionally valuable, high in Iron (4mg per 100gm), Vitamin A (3000IU per 100gm), ascorbic acid (100mg per 100gm), and contained valuable amounts of the B vitamins, thiamine, riboflavin, and nicotinamide. Other leaves with medium or low carotene would also contribute to a healthy intake.[34] Wild rose hips would be a particularly valuable source of ascorbic acid, with an average of 700mg per 100gm.[35] Blood, and human flesh in particular, would have also been valuable nutritionally. However, it seems likely that without the bulk of cereals or dried legumes for bread or stews, the population would gradually have weakened.

Malnutrition

Lack of Vitamin A

The probability is that Anglo-Saxon populations suffered from vitamin A deficiency with consequent skin, eye and urinary tract diseases.[36] The vitamin is present in butter, fish liver, offal and eggs.[37] The vitamin A value of dairy produce and eggs is highest when cows are out at pasture and hens are running loose on grass. Cows fed on dried hay yield milk which becomes progressively poorer in vitamin A. In winter the supply was greatly reduced and consequently reserves in the body would be depleted, so that many may have been in a condition of mild or sub-acute deficiency in the spring.[38] This might explain the high demand for fish experienced by the fisherman of the *Colloquy*, and also the demand for eggs, and fatty foods generally .[39]

Lack of Vitamin C

In the winter and spring a shortage of fresh meat and vegetables may have meant some of the population were in a pre-scorbutic state, suffering from symptoms which included bleeding gums, ulcers and bloody dysentery.[40] A *Leechdom* states: 'there is no time for bloodletting as good as the beginning of Lent when the evil liquid which has been absorbed during the winter has accumulated' (*nis nan blodlæstid swa god swa on foreweardne lencten þonne þa yfelan wæten beoð gegaderode on wintra gedruncene beoð*).[41] This is not an isolated reference: a second Leechdom refers to various complaints, including skin complaints and leprosy, the bacillus of which can feed on human tissue in the absence of vitamin C, and continues 'therefore men should cleanse away the evil humours before the evils come and grow in the winter and run through the limbs' (*Forþon sceal mon ær clænsian þa yflan wætan aweg ær þon þa yfelan cuman 7 geweaxan on wintra 7 þa limo geond yrnen*).[42]

The beet, mallow, Brassica, nettle and elder leaves recommended, contained vitamin C which would remedy the deficiency.[43] It may have been that in the warmer phase towards the end of the Anglo-Saxon period, green plants had a longer growing season than at present, and were readily available in early spring. The numerous green herbs and sometimes bark used in *Leechdoms* may well have been beneficial by reason of their ascorbic properties.[44]

However, the likelihood is that scurvy was prevalent; Bonser considered that during the Danish invasions the populace was always afflicted by a mixture of diarrhoea, dysentery and scurvy.[45] They may also have been affected by relapsing fever which was a famine fever, as is dysentery.[46] In general there is little evidence of scurvy in archaeological material, since it affects soft tissue, rather than bone, but it has been tentatively diagnosed in seven out of 350 Anglo-Saxons from East Anglia, in skeletons at Porchester and a skull from West Stow.[47]

The symptoms of scurvy include anaemia, lassitude, loss of muscle tone and tendency to sudden death on slight exertion. Trouble with sore gums, loosening and loss of teeth was also likely to occur and the Anglo-Saxons had recipes for 'sore of teeth' and 'looseness of teeth', and 'bone-wort' (*banwyrt*) was recommended for 'canker of the teeth from which the teeth fall out'.[48]

Lack of Minerals

Fluorine in the water or from fish would prevent tooth decay. The number of teeth lost *ante mortem* indicates that the teeth of the population at Monkwearmouth were healthier than those of the inhabitants of Jarrow, who would presumably have had a similar diet, but whose water supply would not have contained fluorine.[49] Both groups lost fewer teeth than Anglo-Saxon populations in general, perhaps because of the importance of fish in the monastic diet.[50] It may also have been because the eating habits of monastic groups were more refined, or because they were less likely to use their teeth as tools.

Zinc is particularly necessary for growing children, pregnant and lactating women, and is easily absorbed from animal foodstuffs.[51]

Ignorance was still an element in malnutrition.[52] The bread which young children were given probably did not provide all the nutrients necessary.

Indications of Famine

Evidence of malnutrition came from a number of skeletons from early, mid- and late-period communities in East Anglia of which more than two-thirds were affected in the early and mid periods, about half in the late period.[53]

Fe/male Differences Including Life Expectancy

What evidence we have indicates that girls suffered more than boys from illness, despite their more favourable chromosome pattern, and more from carious teeth; they were probably less valued and had to content themselves with left-overs.[54]

Amenorrhea is one obvious response to malnutrition, and *Leechdoms* dealing with this condition prescribe, among other things, hot herb drinks fairly rich in iron.[55]

On a number of sites the average age of women at death seems to have been several years less than that of the men. That malnutrition was the main cause of earlier deaths is supported by the frequency of enamel hypoplasia and Harris's lines. Women no doubt died from complications of childbirth. At Buckland Anglo-Saxon cemetery most women died in the 20-30 age range, then the 30-45 range, with few surviving to old age.[56] The likelihood is that most of these deaths would not have occurred if the women had been well-nourished from birth: obstetric failures are more likely in malnourished women. The greater increase in male stature over female, from the Roman sample to the sixth-century

Saxon sample found in Hampshire cemeteries indicates that the roles, and importance, of each sex in society varied considerably.[57]

Life expectancy derived from the skeletal series indicates an almost complete absence of elderly people (i.e. over the age of 50 or so). The picture is complicated since there is some evidence that conventional methods for dating skeletal material give the age at death as being younger than was the case.[58] Even so, a larger percentage of Anglo-Saxon adults reached old age than in English parishes in 1800, and the child mortality rate was lower.[59] In fact the Anglo-Saxon statistics for mortality are closer to those of modern Europe, though this may reflect the fact that the Anglo-Saxons were not exposed to as many diseases as later populations so may not simply indicate superior nutrition.

Results of Famine

A longer-lived population indicates higher living standards and a more productive workforce. One serious shortage could start a vicious circle of early death, inability of the community to produce enough food, and further early deaths.[60] The usual reaction to shortage is irritability, complaint and unrest, then lack of initiative, and apathy.[61] So those suffering from a shortage of food would not be in a condition to organise themselves effectively to deal with the situation.

Leechdoms suggest that 'if a woman who is four or five months pregnant often eats nuts or acorns or any fresh fruits then it sometimes happens that her child is stupid because of this' (*gif wif biþ bearn eacen feower monoð oþþe fif 7 heo þonne gelome eteð hnyte oþþe æceran oþþe ænige niwe bleda þonne gelimpeð hit hwilum þurh þ þæt þ cild biþ disig*).[62] It may be that a woman eating nuts, acorns, etc., was scavenging because supplies of the staple foods were not available, and the baby's subsequent defects may have been caused by malnutrition, rather than these particular items.

New-born children may have been killed, since infanticide in times of dearth was not accounted a crime.[63] Those who survived famine during their growing years were likely to be smaller and weaker than those who had not experienced this trauma.[64] However, the stature of Anglo-Saxons was greater than that of either Iron Age or later medieval populations.[65]

The occurrence of famine and pestilence might be stressed as a cause of England's weakness in the time of Æthelred the Unready. The country may have succumbed to Swein and Cnut in part because of the demoralised condition of the people. No outbreaks occurred in the reign of Cnut when the devastation wrought by the Danes ceased with the accession of their own king.[66]

Resistance to disease is lowered by inadequate nutrition and there is a correlation between famines and plagues in Anglo-Saxon times: most pestilences did follow famine.[67] The situation may have been exacerbated by the fact that some people are likely to have moved around in search of food in time of famine.[68] While immune to every common pathogen in their own environment, leaving it to seek food could lead to an outbreak of disease since individuals would then be exposed to different pathogens. Other people might be on the move too, increasing the range of infections.[69]

As well as the plagues which were dramatic in their effects, poor food, combined with poor housing, probably gave rise to chronic 'lowering' diseases, where the sufferer lost strength over a period of months or even years before finally succumbing.

Conclusion

The number of references to hunger in the literature, chronicles and legal documents implies that it was probably a normal experience of life in Anglo-Saxon England, even if it was only the hunger of waiting for mealtimes. In the dialogue of Alcuin and Pepin, the answer to the question, 'What makes bitter things sweet?' is 'hunger'.[70] This probably explains how it was the Anglo-Saxons found palatable food that we would reject today. The higher incidence of caries may indicate not a greater reliance on cereals but the reverse: a dependence on rougher food: siliceous vegetables and stringy meat.[71]

A proportion of the population, in particular women, probably had to make do with a less than adequate diet throughout the period. Some upsets of the metabolism connected with bad diet were probably effectively treated with medicinal herbs.[72]

On a domestic level, the better a woman was as a manager, the more likelihood of her family surviving.[73] Keeping the stores in good condition would be a vital task. The Lenten fast was probably a case of making a virtue of necessity. Easter, when the consumption of eggs and poultry would bring relief, probably brought to an end a season of hunger. Providing the rations laid down in *Rectitudines Singularum Personarum* were met in full and were complemented by vegetables, estate workers may have lived reasonably well most of the time.[74] There is archaeological (as well as documentary) evidence that monastic communities were comparatively well-nourished.[75]

The devastation and disruption caused by Viking raids took its toll on the general health of the people, creating conditions favourable to outbreaks of hunger and pestilence.[76] Bad weather had the same result.[77] Shortages of cereals and hay might mean that their owners could live on the carcasses of their animals for a season, but the following year they would be short of stock.[78] A dearth might take a year or two to make its effects felt, after which it might take several years to re-establish an adequate food supply.

If exacted harshly, the food rents paid by the poor to the rich could lead to very short commons for the poor. Even wealthy men wanted to buy out the right of food farms for considerable sums. Cnut relieves his subjects from what he calls this 'burden'. The powerful were able to strengthen their position during a time of famine by providing food, not as a charitable gift, but as a way of buying slaves.

[1] Bosworth and Toller 1898, I 917; Jember 1975, 21.
[2] Miller 1890, I, 1 78.
[3] Gollancz/Mackie 1972, *The Fates of Men* 1.15.
[4] op. cit., *Wulf and Eadwacer* 1.13.
[5] Skeat 1881, *St Maurice & his Companions* 1.160.
[6] op. cit., *St Cecilia* 1.143.
[7] Kemble 1848, 1.2311.
[8] Bonser 1963, 4-5.
[9] Skeat 1881, *Prayer of Moses* 1.139, 1.152.
[10] Miller 1890, I, 2 302-4.
[11] Whitelock 1955, 77.
[12] Whitelock 1952, 104.
[13] Whitelock 1955, 494.
[14] Kemble 1876, 220.
[15] Whitelock 1952, 104.
[16] Colgrave 1940, 276-7.
[17] op. cit.
[18] Kemble 1876, 199.
[19] Miller 1890, I, 1 54; Walford 1879, 7.
[20] Kemble 1876, 196; Whitelock 1955, 563-4.
[21] Dodwell 1982, 219.
[22] op. cit., 7.
[23] op. cit., 108; Mellows 1980, 70.
[24] Bonser 1963, 86.
[25] Walford 1879, 20ff; Whitelock 1955, 242, 290.
[26] Walford 1879, 108.
[27] Whitelock 1955, 255.
[28] Walford 1879, 107.
[29] Bonser 1963, 14.
[30] Drummond 1958; Fenton & Kisban 1986, 123-4.
[31] Walford 1879, 5.
[32] op. cit., 229.
[33] Victor 1955, 146.
[34] Platt 1968, 14-15.
[35] op. cit., 36.

[36] Bonser 1963, 375, 382, 400.
[37] Platt 1968, 20-1, 24-5.
[38] Drummond and Wilbraham 1958.
[39] Garmonsway 1978, 27.
[40] Holmes 1952, 226.
[41] Cockayne 1851, I lxxii.
[42] op. cit., II xxx; McNeill 1977, 175.
[43] Cockayne 1851, II xxx.
[44] Bonser 1963, 9; Bosworth & Toller 1898, I 344.
[45] Bonser 1963, 86.
[46] McArthur 1949, 169.
[47] Wells 1975, 756; Cunliffe 1976, 240, 255; West 1982, 197.
[48] Bonser 1963, 390.
[49] Wells 1964.
[50] op. cit.
[51] Morgan 1975, 4.
[52] Eydoux 1966, 81.
[53] Wells 1964, 277.
[54] op. cit., fig. 31; Kuper 1977, 107; Harris 1986, 241; Bosworth & Toller 1898, I 348.
[55] Fell 1984, 51.
[56] Evison 1987, 128.
[57] Arnold 1984, 137.
[58] Ascadi & Nemeskeri 1970.
[59] Brothwell in Brothwell & Higgs 1963, 328.
[60] Davies 1982, 42.
[61] Drummond 1958.
[62] Cockayne 1851, III.
[63] Bonser 1963, 87; Whitelock 1955, 754.
[64] Brothwell in Ucko & Dimbleby 1971, 534; Jackson 1969, 117.
[65] Wells in Brothwell & Higgs 1963, 363.
[66] Bonser 1963, 52.
[67] op. cit., 85, 63-4.
[68] Sayce 1946.
[69] Burnet & White 1972, 82, 146, 153.
[70] Turner 1828, III 439.
[71] Brothwell in Ucko & Dimbleby 1971, 537-8.
[72] Sergo in Fenton & Owen 1981, 264-5.
[73] Sayce 1946.
[74] Fenton & Owen 1981, 161.
[75] Wells 1964.
[76] Bonser 1963, 4.
[77] op. cit., 57-8.
[78] Fenton & Owen 1981, 161.

11 Adulteration:
Damage Caused by Dietary Elements

Poisons

Of adulterants poison was perhaps the most dramatic in its effects. It might be taken accidentally: 'at that time Martin ate with his food the poisonous plant called hellebore' (*Martinus on þære tide on his mete þigde þa ættrian wyrt þe elleborum hatte*).[1] As green-leaf salads were served, some knowledge of plants was advisable. If food was short, plants not usually eaten might be tried, which would have increased the likelihood of poisoning. There are also a number of *Leechdoms* in case a man eats or drinks something poisonous. In these cases the poisoning was presumably accidental since there are separate remedies in case you suspect someone may try to poison you, as happened to Æthelwold.[2]

Coccel (cockle) translating 'tares', was presumably corncockle, (*agrostemma githago*). It contains githagenin, which predisposes those who consume it to leprosy, and can be fatal. Corncockle was recognised as a 'baneful weed' of corn at least by the eighth century.[3] Corncockle would need to be rooted up before harvest since the seeds are produced at about the same height and time as ears of corn, and are difficult to separate from cereal grains by sieving as they are not much smaller.[4] As Anglo-Saxon grain size was smaller than that of modern cereal varieties, this difficulty would have been exacerbated. Corncockle seeds turn up in quantity on middle and late urban sites.[5] Perhaps farmers were less concerned with the purity of their corn if they were going to sell it, or the anti-helminthic qualities of corncockle may have been known, and the Anglo-Saxons who consumed it may have been trying to rid themselves of the heavy worm burdens most of them carried (see below).[6] Moreover, the githagenin is probably reduced or destroyed by prolonged heating, so contaminated samples could have been used in stews and porridges.[7]

Ergot (*claviceps purpurea*) was established as a fungus disease of cereals in Europe before the beginning of the Anglo-Saxon period.[8] Ergotism, also known as *ignis sacer*, St Anthony's fire, or erysipelas, was one of the common complaints dealt with in *Leechdoms*, and could produce convulsions, gangrene and abortions in humans and stock.[9] There are several possible instances recorded by chroniclers of the sixth and eighth centuries.[10] Anglo-Saxon populations may have suffered in areas where rye was the main crop: parts of the West Midlands, for example, since ergot is much more common on rye than other cereals.[11]

Ergot flourishes in damp weather which is likely to cause low yields, and so populations may not have been able to afford simply to dispose of contaminated samples. Rye was probably more susceptible to ergot in damper British conditions than on the continent, which may be why wheat became the preferred species.

Moulds which secrete dangerous aflatoxins grow on damp grain, meal and flour.[12] Mouldy samples might not be discarded if food was short.

Parasites

The smoking of cured pork would not have killed trichinae (*Trichuris trichiura*), also known as whipworms, with which it was often infected, because the temperature reached was not high enough.[13] Large numbers of whipworm can lead to moderate to severe diarrhoea.[14] In children the irritation leads to sleeplessness and loss of condition. Whipworm eggs were discovered at West Stow and Anglo-Scandinavian York.[15] Ascarids (*Ascaris lumbricoides*) also known as large roundworms, or maw worms, generally cause little damage to the host, though migrating larva can produce hepatitis and damage the lung tissues, and cause serious trouble if they enter other organs.[16] If these worms are numerous, the symptoms may be severe, simulating those of gastric and duodenal ulcer.[17] A coprolite from Anglo-Scandinavian York was parasitized by a heavy infestation of maw worm and whipworm by today's standards, though it was well within the limits of human tolerance.[18] From the large numbers of parasite ova discovered in York, it seems likely that most people carried worm burdens for most of their lives.[19] It is possible that worm infestation was heavier in urban populations where there was more pressure on space.[20] King Alfred indicates that he also was familiar with internal parasites, since to Boethius he adds, 'the small worms that crawl within and without [man] even sometimes nearly kill him'.[21]

Bacterial Infections

There was, as one might expect, bacterial contamination of dairy products or brewings.[22] Eating food that had 'turned' was recognised as leading to problems.[23] St Gregory told the story of the nun who swallowed a devil through eating a lettuce without making the sign of the cross over it first.[24] Presumably the 'devil' produced unpleasant symptoms, probably the result of eating the unwashed leaves. A general lack of hygiene may have made itself felt in terms of infections.

The common and lesser houseflies are likely to have been significant as carriers of disease. Disease organisms are transferred from faecal matter (which was almost certainly more in evidence in Anglo-Saxon times) to uncovered food.[25] Insects and mice which infested stores could act as vectors of disease [26](see Chapter 4).

Cured pork was a common source of botulism in Europe in later medieval times.[27] There is a strong likelihood that the same situation prevailed in Anglo-Saxon England.

Physical Damage

The teeth of Anglo-Saxons from a number of sites showed marked wear, an indication of a coarse, fibrous diet, probably containing abrasive materials.[28] They suffered from two kinds of tooth decay which arose as a complication of tooth wear, and both gave rise to abscesses.[29] These types of caries differ substantially from caries in modern man and have a different aetiology.[30] In 260 individuals from two cemeteries dating from about 600 and 800, practically all the caries was of the wear-fracture type.[31]

The evidence of arthritis on mandibles also points to a diet which contained tough and chewy materials, perhaps a combination of smoked or salted meat, siliceous vegetable fibres and hard breads or bannocks containing quern dust.[32] Female jaws were more commonly affected which partly reflects the problem the relatively lighter female jaw would have coping with tough food, but may also imply that women took second-best as far as food was concerned.[33]

Cooking & Preserving Methods

There was a high incidence of chronic sinusitis among the Anglo-Saxons.[34] This may reflect the inclement weather, and the winter-long nasal irritation from peat or log fires burning in badly-ventilated rooms.[35] Since cooking was done over such domestic fires, the household cooks, probably women in most cases, may have suffered more from sinusitis and, as a result, from general ill-health.

As well as poisons of vegetable or fungal origin, there is a possibility that Anglo-Saxon populations may have absorbed lead from processing equipment. Salt was evaporated in *leads*, and was probably contaminated with lead in consequence. This contaminated salt might then be used for salting meat in lead containers. Brining creates an acidic medium which can dissolve metal. Lead-lined cider presses and vats may have caused outbreaks of colic and lead poisoning.[36] Brazen cooking equipment may have led to poisoning by copper salts.

Smoke contains a number of carcinogens which are imparted to food preserved by smoking, a traditional method of preservation. The assumption might therefore be that an individual who ate a large amount of smoked food might be at risk from various cancers of the alimentary canal and intestines. On the other hand, if that individual also ate food rich in fibre, any carcinogens would probably not remain in contact with the walls of the digestive tract for long enough to have any serious effect. Since there are so many imponderables, it does not seem to be particularly helpful to deal with the number of scenarios which might conceivably have arisen.

Conclusion

In this area perhaps more than any other, the evidence is incomplete. However, the significant points are that food was contaminated by various substances. In some cases this had a minimal effect on the consumers; in other cases it could have caused ill-health or proved fatal. While ignorance of the effects of, for example, lead poisoning would have been general, possibly most kinds of contamination were less likely in affluent establishments, where sub-standard food samples could be discarded, more tender vegetables and animals were eaten, and where hygiene was practised to some degree.

---

[1] Skeat 1881, *St Martin* 1.196.
[2] Cockayne 1851, II lxv 2, III xliii, I p.84, *Lacnunga* XXVIII, X; Whitelock 1955, 835.
[3] Kylie 1911, 116, 123.
[4] Hall 1981, 5ff.
[5] Monk 1977, 293 ff.
[6] Hall 1981, 5 ff.
[7] op. cit.
[8] Brothwell & Higgs 1963, 178.
[9] Deegan 1986, 20.
[10] Brothwell 1969, 190.
[11] Dickens 1974, 1, 3.
[12] Renfrew 1985, 27; Erlichman 1986, 143.
[13] Kuper 1977, 39.
[14] West 1982, 310.
[15] op. cit.; Jones 1980, 9; Jones in Hall et al. 1983, 228-9.
[16] West 1982, 310; Jones 1980, 11.
[17] op. cit., 11.
[18] Jones in Hall et al. 1983, 228-9.
[19] Jones, undated paper.
[20] West 1982, 309.
[21] Turner 1828, II 34.
[22] Cockayne 1851, I lxvii 1, 2.
[23] op. cit., *Lacnunga* 90.
[24] Bonser 1963, 259.
[25] Hickin 1963, 118.
[26] op. cit., 103; Bonser 1963, 76.
[27] McGee 1986, 512.
[28] Bonser 1963, 338-9, 390; Holdsworth 1980, 79; Wells 1964, 60, 125; Rahtz and Hirst 1974, 85, 87.
[29] Miles 1972, 309.

[30] Miles 1969, 1313.
[31] op. cit., 1314.
[32] Wells 1964, 60; Miles 1969, 1315.
[33] Wells 1964, 60.
[34] op. cit., 81.
[35] op. cit.
[36] Redfern 1987, 16.

Conclusion

The intention of this synthesizing study has been to gather information about the processing and consumption of Anglo-Saxon food from Old English sources, archaeological, place- and field-name evidence, to see what could be established about Anglo-Saxon diet and the ways this might affect the population. It has also been to try to discover what part the consumption of food played in social organisation and to discover changes over the period. From the vast number of references - many more than were expected - it is clear that food production for home consumption was the basis of economic activity throughout the Anglo-Saxon period, and eating together was central to social, and sometimes legal, obligations.

Changes over the Period

As settlement consolidated, the establishment of plough teams brought about an increase in cereal production. As the acreage of cultivated land increased, the habitat of wild animals and birds decreased, and the proportion of wild animals in the diet dropped.[1] Developing preferences were indulged in by those who could afford them, e.g. for lighter wheaten bread, for tender, specially-bred beef, and for certain cuts of meat. In fishing, archaeological evidence suggests the development of the deep-water drift net increased the catch in the ninth and tenth centuries.[2]

The period does not show a consistent increase in the amount of food available for consumption. Malnutrition does not only result in a high death rate, but also in lowered fertility and a low birth-rate as well as a general lowering of resistance to disease. In times of famine, when people left their homes in relatively small communities to look for food, they would have come across pathogens to which they had not developed immunity.

The Role of Women

Eating and drinking seems to have been stereotyped as a male activity, whereas in domestic situations women seem to have prepared and cooked the food, and to have offered drink to guests.[3] There is evidence that women and girls suffered the brunt of shortages, and in this were no different to females in a number of societies.[4] Death in childbirth may have been higher for women who had been undernourished, and there may had been high perinatal and infant mortality rates for babies of such women.

The Importance of Bread

Bread was the staple food without which 'any table seems empty' (*ælc beod æmtig byþ gesewen*), and 'without bread all food is unpalatable' (*buton hlafe ælc mete to wlættan byþ gewyrfeð*).[5] Tastes and textures of the 'accompaniments' usually contrast noticeably with the taste, texture and dryness of bread.[6] These are often oily, have ingredients that are dried, fermented, cured, smoked, salted, or are fresh. Fat and salt (sometimes together as butter) were used to flavour the bread, or the relish might very often be fatty meat, butter, or cheese. The preference for fatty foods can be explained by the fact that the assimilation of fats slows the digestive process, and thus delays the recurrence of hunger.[7] Poorer classes probably had access to bread and some accompaniment, or cereal stews if they were unable to make bread, or vegetable stews with some cereal. The rich were likely to have been the only group with the choice to alter the general pattern of 'bread and its accompaniment', elevating the 'accompaniments' to the most important element of a meal.

Those in positions of power were able to do most to ensure an adequate and varied diet: drawing on food rents from different parts of the country, kings and nobles were not at the mercy of local crop failures. Certain foods, fish and honey, for example are established as luxuries since the king or chief had first claim on them. The diet of the rich was not limited to what could be produced here. Wine, oil, some species of fish and spices were all imported.[8]

Spices would have made dubious meat acceptable, and spices were highly valued in Anglo-Saxon England, but used sparingly. The Anglo-Saxon cuisine seems to have made use of herbs, fruits, and to a lesser extent, flowers as an accompaniment to meat.

Feasting

The ritual of feasting was well established and reflected social status very closely. Only the *hlaford* had access to plentiful food and with this he could repay his retainers. If a *ceorl* had social aspirations he had to own, *inter alia*, a kitchen, and be able to make provision for his own, and others', retinue.

The lord's diet might include beef, mutton, veal, lamb, kid, pork, wild boar, venison, hare, pigeons, fowls, ducks and geese both tame and wild, and other wild birds, fish (freshwater and sea). These foods might be available in fresh and preserved states. Fruit, nuts, honey, dairy products, cereal food, including wheat bread, and eggs were also likely to be available. If he could, the lord would provide such wildfowl as crane and curlew for a feast, since they indicated his ability to pay for and keep expensive hawks, and the presence of venison and wild boar flesh would indicate that his resources enabled him to maintain a pack of hounds. Since the food value of these prestige foods was outweighed by the food resources that went to keeping hawks and hounds, they were symbolic of the conspicuous consumption that would confirm his power. The admission of strangers to royal feasts without question indicates generosity with food was a virtue as well as a measure of status.

Privileged groups maintain high standards of nutrition and the possession of food is a source of power. Access to animal foods bestows health and well-being above and beyond mere survival, as meat is a concentrated source of vitamins and minerals - the only source of B12.[9] A higher percentage by weight of cooked meat, poultry, fish or dairy foods consists of protein than plant foods. This protein is also of a higher quality than any vegetable protein the Anglo-Saxons would have had access to, since the ten essential amino acids occur in ratios which make more of them available for use in the human body.[10] Roast meats were highly desirable in cultural terms as well as nutritionally. 'Good' cuts of meat that can be roasted were top of the food hierarchy.[11]

References to feasting in the literature are so emotionally loaded as to make one realise that such indulgence in food and drink probably took place against a background of deprivation. Feasting was also a way of reinforcing social bonds, particularly the loyalty to the death owed by a retainer to his lord. Virtually every band or village society studied by anthropologists expresses a special esteem for animal flesh by using meat to reinforce the social ties that bind campmates and kinsfolk together.[12] Sharing food is known to reduce individual and intragroup tensions and it was the fellowship experienced during such feasting that would unify retainers into a fighting band if need be.[13]

In a situation where long-term planning was difficult, and storage uncertain, there must have been pressure to celebrate times when food was plentiful, and to indulge the gratification of the moment. Such a feeling would be in conflict with the need to eke food out during the winter months and possibly through the following year if the harvest failed. Feasting for poorer groups was more modest and seems to have been regulated by being connected to the completion of agricultural tasks and holy days. The fact that the church enjoined feasting on occasions made it possible to indulge without guilt, and to endure periods of fasting.

Fasting

Fasting was one way in which God could be propitiated.[14] Fasting was connected explicitly with charity: the food one saved through restricting intake should be given to the destitute. However, for the poor fasting might have been unescapable, even on Sundays: only he who fasted 'through self-will' (for his anwylnysse) was to be excommunicated.[15] It seems likely that the Lenten fast to some extent reflected the non-availability of food, a clear case of making a virtue of necessity. Once again the rich were able to escape the effects of fasting in that they could obtain allowed and acceptable food. Also, if a fast was inflicted as penance, they could pass the fast on to others.

Religious communities found it difficult to make the compromise between allowing food that would provide the necessary calories for labouring work and the necessity of subjugating the body, and particularly sexual appetites, by means of fasting. Adjustments, usually additions, or increased measures, were made to the diet, and this may have reflected the increasing prosperity of religious foundations.[16]

Greater Dietary Range & Flexibility

The greater dietary range and flexibility in Anglo-Saxon times when compared with the situation today is striking, and there were a number of reasons for this. Firstly, perishable products were near at hand for most of the population. Offal was widely eaten and would have included a wider range of items than is now considered acceptable. A similar situation pertained to dairy products, with beestings, whey and buttermilk all being consumed. The availability of all these products was seasonal. With the growth of urban development, some consumers were distanced from the sources of production, and only the less perishable supplies would be brought in from outside towns.[17]

Secondly, there was little standardisation. For example, there would have been a great range of grades of flour, which could contain all the grain, or be sieved and sifted until it was almost white. One cereal was frequently mixed with another, and flour could be more or less contaminated with the dust of querns or millstones, and chemically with the alkaloids of ergot, and the seeds of corncockle or other weed seeds that could not be easily sieved or picked out. Both grain and flour could have been contaminated during storage by rodents or insects. Baking was attended by some risks, and some batches of bread would fail to rise.

Processing was necessary to preserve surpluses. Milk, from sheep as well as cows, was converted into butter and cheese, both of which will keep longer than milk. While the poor probably ate green cheese, the rich could afford to wait and enjoy matured cheese, even blue cheese. Preservation of meat and fish was also necessary, and salting, smoking and wind-drying were effective methods, but different local circumstances and varying conditions from year to year would have resulted in different flavours. Food was not uniformly fresh or well-preserved, and there is evidence that it was eaten in what would now be an unacceptably 'high' state.

Thirdly, a much wider range of plants, birds and animals was eaten than now. This was in part because they were at hand, whereas now some of the animals and birds are extinct in this country, and may have been getting scarcer and therefore have become prestige items for feasts during the Anglo-Saxon period. A number of plants which we think of as inedible are not only eatable, but rich in vitamins and minerals.[18] However, one item of diet - horse - had to be relinquished during the period because of religious pressure.

Seasonal variation would have been apparent, particularly in relation to plants, which would not have been available during the winter, apart from one or two exceptions like cole-wort and leeks. The tender shoots of spring would give way to the much more siliceous, and in the case of bracken, poisonous, mature leaves. A summer diet: bread, milk, curds, butter, vegetables, for example, might give way to a winter diet of bread, butter, cheese, salt meat, dried peas and beans.[19] If fish was part of the diet, then the varieties available changed with the seasons. Wildfowl were more likely to be trapped in winter.

Regional variation was probably an important factor. Nearness to the sea would mean fresh fish and shellfish could be added to the diet. Closeness to a river could mean the addition of fish, fresh-water mussels and eels. Dairying based on cattle became established in the south-west.

Natural circumstances imposed variation on meals, but so did the church. It decreed periods and days of fasting and feasting which were closely regulated and therefore probably observed by most people. Feast-day and fast-day meals were different in kind as well as quantity.

Finally, necessity resulted in people eating what was not normally considered food. Cereal flour was bulked out with ground peas, beans or acorns. Grass and the bark of trees may in fact have had some nutritive value, but these foods were not resorted to if there were more palatable alternatives available.

Nutrition

It is difficult to arrive at any definite conclusions as to how nutritious was the Anglo-Saxon diet. Certainly crops were organically grown, and free from pesticide residues. It was thought that the protein content of wheat may have been higher than in modern varieties, but in fact this would have depended on the ground being sufficiently manured, since this is the factor which largely determines protein content.[20] What we know of the composition of meals: meat with vegetables or cereal products, suggests the Anglo-Saxons were aware empirically that such combinations were more satisfying without realising the scientific explanation - that these made available a greater proportion of the protein in the foods. The preference for white, leavened bread also made nutritional sense in that the effect of phytic acid, present in the outer layer of the grain, which prevented the absorption of essential minerals (iron, zinc and calcium) was lessened.[21] Certainly wheat bread was preferred, since it will rise more than other breads, and in consequence, be lighter.

Fermented drinks were especially valuable. Yeast cells synthesize proteins and vitamins as they grow, and make a fruit juice or cereal mash much more nutritious. Today yeast cells tend to be skimmed or filtered out, but these beverages when consumed 'whole' or 'live' are a valuable part of the diet.[22] Liquid intake was probably higher, because of the consumption of items preserved by salting.

Relatively small amounts of milk, butter or cheese (3-4 oz. daily) will supply the recommended daily allowance of calcium, which is also present in significant qualities in oysters and some greens.[23]

A lack of fresh vegetables may have meant that some of the population were in a pre-ascorbic condition by the spring of some years; others may actually have suffered from scurvy. Lack of vitamin C may also have disposed individuals specifically to leprosy. Because of a general lack of hygiene, it seems likely that many people ingested the ova of parasitic worms, which made their own demands on the food consumed by their host. Teeth seem to have been at risk from stone dust in flour, tougher meat and vegetables as well as less inhibited table manners.

In bad years a lack of adequate food caused a number of deaths, but it seems likely that a proportion of the population was perpetually undernourished and therefore able to work at less than optimum efficiency, as well as being more susceptible to disease. In some monasteries, *The Rule of Chrodegang* seems to imply, food might be short, and rations vary according to the harvest. Probably those well-endowed monasteries, where hygiene was better, would offer the members of their communities a healthier than average life.

Table-Manners

It is apparent that the knife was used almost exclusively at table, and that eating from communal plates and using a communal wine jug was standard practice.[24] It seems to have been considered politic to bless food, by making the sign of the cross over it, in the Christian era. Grace was said before meals in monasteries and visiting ecclesiastics to a secular meal seem to have said grace and blessed the food.

Comparisons & Contrasts

There are some elements of Anglo-Saxon food and drink that are familiar to us: meat and two vegetables, meat with fruit sauces, green salads with onions, garlic, oil, vinegar and salt dressing. Candle-lit dinners, with imported glassware, wines, exotic foods, fine table-linen and silver tableware are still occasions for impressing guests. Feasts were occasions for escaping the concerns of everyday life.

> ....lyt him gepenceð
> sepe him wines glæd wilna bruceð
> siteð him symbelgal sip ne bemurneð
> hu him æfter pisse worulde weordan mote

(he little thinks, gladdened with wine, enjoying pleasures, flushed at the feast, what must become of him after this life).[25]

There were those who mourned the passing of feasts, and good fellowship in the meadhall, but there were those for whom heaven would be the only 'dwelling place of plenty'.[26] Anglo-Saxons were only too aware on a personal level of the importance of food as 'a primary and recurrent want', recognising more acutely than their descendants that 'our transitory life is sustained by food' (ure hwilendlice lif bip mid mettum gefercod).[27]

---

[1] Holdsworth 1980, 99.
[2] Hodges 1982, 143.
[3] Bynum 1987, 190-1; Laurence 1986, 22.
[4] Cole-Hamilton & Lang 1986, 2, 65.
[5] Garmonsway 1978, 36.
[6] Mintz 1985, 11.
[7] McGee 1986, 530.
[8] Hodges 1982, 54.
[9] Harris 1986, 22, 35.
[10] op. cit., 31-3.
[11] Laurance 1986, 22.

[12] Harris 1986, 27.
[13] Marshall 1961, 236.
[14] Bynum 1987, 34-5; Whitelock 1955, 858.
[15] Skeat 1881, *Ash Wednesday* 1.4.
[16] Dembinska & van Winter in Fenton & Kisban 1986, 152ff., 612-3.
[17] Hodges 1986, 152.
[18] Harris 1961, passim; Ayrton 1975, 304; Monk 1977, 124, 131.
[19] Fenton & Owen 1981, 161.
[20] Ucko & Dimbleby 1971, 80; Dr J. Graham, pers. comm.
[21] McGee 1986, 284; Weicholt 1987, 53-7.
[22] McGee 1986, 437.
[23] op. cit., 546.
[24] Freeman 1970, 192.
[25] Mackie 1934, *The Day of Judgement*.
[26] Jackson 1971, 251.
[27] Richards 1932, 1; Bosworth & Toller 1898, I 391.

APPENDICES

Appendix A: Fasting

The Regular Fasts

Some fasts were only day-long. The important weekday fast was on Fridays, though Saturday was also a day of fasting in anticipation of the following feast day. Some monastic institutions also observed a fast on Wednesdays. The ancient church followed the Jewish custom of fasting on two days a week, but instead of Monday and Thursday, altered the fast days to Wednesday and Friday.[1] Bede tells us that Aidan and his community observed both these days: 'it became their habit through the year, except for the fifty days after Easter, to fast till the ninth hour on the fourth and sixth days of the week' (*þæt hi him to gewunan genamen þæt heo þurh eall ger buton fifig neahta ofer Eastron þæt heo þy feorðan wicdæge 7 þy syxtan feaston to nones*).[2] Possibly Cuthbert observed the Wednesday fast too, but in the sense that he did not eat until the ninth hour, since he did not abstain from flesh on Fridays.[3] There was much variation in the matter of abstinence, especially among the laity in the early medieval church.[4] The eves of feast days were observed with a fast. The periods of fasting were Lent, September and Advent. The eves of feast days are specifically mentioned in Ethelred's Code of 1008, which states that all festivals of St Mary are to be diligently observed, first with a fast and afterwards with a festival, and the same for festivals of every apostle, except there should be no fast for the festival of SS Philip and James because of the Easter festival.[5] The *Regularis Concordia* of a few decades earlier had specifically stated that the fast should not be observed on the Vigil of the Epiphany, so perhaps by imposing a fast then too, the law code was simplifying matters by removing exceptions.[6] Ethelred's Code went on to say that there should be a fast every Friday, except when it was a feast day.[7] The Lent and Ember day fasts were specifically mentioned in the *Be fæstene* (Concerning Fasting), section of the later Code of Canute: 'That one must observe fasts, whether it be the Ember Day fasts, or the Lenten fast, or if it be any other fast, with all conscientiousness' (*Þæt man ælc beboden fæsten healde, sy hit ymbrenfæsten, sy hit lenctenfæsten, sy elles oðer fæsten, mid ealre geornfulnysse*).[8] The Council of Placentia in 1095 confirmed the Ember day fasts as the Wednesday, Friday and Saturday following the first Sunday in Lent, Whitsun, 14th September and 13th December.

Periods of Fasting

A fast lasting a few days before Easter was practised in the second century, emerging in the fourth century as a fast of 36 days. This was expanded to 40 days in the seventh century in the west.[9] According to the *Old English Martyrology*, Pope Telesphorus was the first to decree 'that one fast for seven weeks before Easter in Rome' (*þæt man fæste on rome syfon wucan ær eastran*).[10] It was not until nearly fifty years after the arrival of Augustine's mission that a Kentish king ordered the final suppression of paganism, and 'that the forty-day fast be held before Easter on pain of punishment' (*þæt feowertiglice fasten healden beon ær Eastrum bi witerædenne*).[11]

It seems that violating the Lenten fast might invite more than legal punishment, and the following cautionary tale was recorded for the beginning of Lent. 'In that same week some buffoon came to the bishop's household and went to the kitchen while the bishop was saying mass and began to eat. He fell down backwards in a faint at the moment when he took his first mouthful, and vomited blood and his life was preserved only with difficulty.' (*On þære ylcan wucan com sum trud to þæs bisceopes hirede se ne gymðe nanes lenctenes fæstenes ac eode him to kicenan pa hwile ðe se bisceop mæssode and began to etenne. he feoll þa æt dærne forman snæde under-becc geswogen and spaw blod ac him gebyrede swa ðeah þæt feorh.*)[12]

The fact that a *presbyter et Scottus* had eaten meat in Lent caused Charlemagne enough concern for him to mention it in a letter to Offa. Charlemagne sent him to be judged by the bishop, as he could not remain at his post because of the infamy of the sin, and the fact that others might be induced to violate the sacred fast.[13]

On the other hand 'Many deeds foolishly injure mankind...like those do who foolishly fast beyond their strength in Catholic Lent as we ourselves see until they become ill.' (*Fela dyslice dæda deriað mancynne...swa swa men doð þe dyslice fæstað ofer heora mihte on gemænelicum lenctene swa swa we sylfe gesawon oð þæt hi seoce wurdon.*) Ælfric went on to explain that England was on the outer edge of the world and therefore not as strong as lands in the middle and there men might fast more easily. Moreover 'men now are not as strong as they were in the beginning' (*ne nu nis man cynn swa mihtig swa men wæron æt fruman*).[14]

The later medieval period records a period of fasting called the 'Lent of Pentecost' which ended on SS Peter and Paul's Day, June 29, but this is not often referred to in the Anglo-Saxon sources.[15] One occasion where it does occur, is when Ecgbehrt says that he will keep to a very strict diet 'the forty days after Pentecost' (*for þæt feowertig daga æfter Pentecosten*).[16] The other sustained fast period in Anglo-Saxon England was the forty-day Advent fast, beginning on November 14, which developed originally as an expression of penance at the year's end, but then became seen as the forerunner of the Christmas feast.[17]

Although there were three forty-day fast periods, most references are made to the Lent fast. Bede gives an account of how Bishop John used to retreat to an oratory and church for the Lenten fast, with a few companions whom he asked to find 'a poor and needy man suffering from great infirmity and poverty, so they might have him with them at that time, and give him alms. For it was his custom always to do this' (*sumne earmne ðearfan, se ðe wære micel untrumnisse 7 woedelnisse hefigað, ðæt hie meahton in ðæm dagum mid him habban 7 mid him ælmesse doan. Forðon his gewuna wæs, ðæt he symle swæ dyde*).[18]

However, while Bishop Eadberht also took himself off, this time to an island, for the Lent fast, he did the same for the forty days before Christmas, so he could live in great abstinence, fervent prayers and outpourings of tears.[19]

Instructions as to the observation of a fast are given with reference to the Lenten fast, which may indicate its importance, although, as the first feast of the year, it would be logical to give regulations about fasting at that point. The Old English version of the *Rule of Chrodegang* gives the following details: 'We beg that on the forty days before Easter our community conduct itself with all soberness of mind and body and eats only one meal and takes drink with the abstinence that God decrees, and each day except Sunday from the beginning of Lent until Easter eats after evensong in the refectory and everyone is to keep to the food that the bishop and the prior has appointed and not to eat elsewhere, either in the town, or in the minster or in any place, nor even in their own house during these forty days, except out of necessity, in that they do not have enough time to get back for the brothers' meal.' (*We beodað þæt on þam feowertigum dagum ær Eastron mid alre syfernysse modes 7 lichaman ure preosthyredas hi sylfe gehealdon 7 an metes þigene 7 drinces habbon swa micle forhæfednysse swa him þonne God geunne 7 ælce dæg butan sunnandæge fram Lenctenes aginne oð Eastron æfter æfensange etan on beoderne 7 fram þam metton dricum hi forhæbbon hi [þe] se bisceop 7 se ealdor þonne gesetton 7 elles nahwer ne an þære ceastre ne an þam mynstrum ne on nanum stowum, ne furðon on heora agenum husum þissum feowertigum dagum ne gereordigen hi, butan*

hwa for hwiclere nytwyrdnysse swa feor beo þæt he þam gefenlicum
tidum to broðra gereorde cuman ne mage.)[20]

It is clear that laymen were to observe fast days, but it is also evident
that lay fasting, fasting practised by monastics, and the virtuoso
performances - admired if not emulated - of saints were different in
degree, and so I propose to deal with these three types of fasting
separately.

Fasting for Laymen

Evidence for fasting is almost entirely documentary, though there is a
possibility that stones sometimes found in the boxes which were
excavated from tenth-century Fyrkat, and normally belonged to women,
were sucking stones to relieve hunger or thirst, and they may have been
used during fasts.[21]

The attitude laymen took towards fasting varied considerably. Alfred
added to his translation of Boethius on the Golden Age, 'They lived
naturally and temperately. They always ate but once a day and that was
in the evening'.[22] In this he seems to have been more abstemious than
the clerics with whom Cuthbert was dining one Christmas. Exhorted by
Cuthbert to 'earnestly engage in prayers and vigils' they understandably
replied, 'You give us good, yea excellent, instruction, but nevertheless,
because the days of fastings, prayers and vigils abound, today let us
rejoice in the Lord'.[23]

The fast-day food of the poor may not have been very different from
their normal diet. In the fifteenth century in the west, the poor on fast
days ate mainly vegetable foods, since fish was more expensive and
even a comparative rarity.[24] This is likely to have been the case in
Anglo-Saxon England. The nobility and rich religious establishments
took pains to secure a supply of fish, fish featured at feasts, and were in
short supply (see previous chapter). Some dried cod or salted herring
may have been available; these were eaten by the poor with linseed or
rape oil in later medieval Europe as fast-day food.[25]

Originally a religious requirement, fasting became a legal one.
According to the *Laws of Wihtred*, 'If a man gives meat to his household
during a fast, he shall redeem free and slave by payment of his
healsfang' (*Gif mon his heowum in fæsten flæsc gefe, frigne ge þeowne
halsfange alyse*). 'If a slave eat of his own accord, he shall pay six
shillings or be lashed.' (*Gif þeow ete his sylfes ræde, vi scll oþþe his
hyd.*)[26] Later Laws repeat and amplify the legal requirement for fasting.
It was obviously important that people should be told when the fasts
were, and apparently this was the duty of the parish priest. The

legislation enacted by Alfred and Guthrum states 'If a mass-priest misinforms the people about feasts and fasts, he shall pay thirty shillings in an English district, three-and-a-half marks in a Danish one.' (*Gif mæssepreost miswyssige æt freolse oððe æt fæstene, gylde xxx scill. mid Englum 7 mid Denum þreo healfmarc.*)[27] It continued: 'If a freeman break an official fast, he is to pay compensation. If a slave does this, he is to suffer a beating, or pay a fine in lieu.' (*Gif frigman rihtfasten abrece gylde wite oððe lahslite. Gif it þeowman gedo, ðolie his hyde oððe hydgylde.*)[28] The same situation is recorded in Canute's Laws, in that if a free man were to break a legally ordained fast, he was to pay a fine. Fasting is here further defined in that it was wrong to eat during a time of fast before the mealtime, and worse still to defile oneself with fleshmeat. If a slave was to do this, he was to suffer a flogging, or redeem himself from one, in proportion to the wrong-doing.[29] Canute's proclamation of 1020 repeated that 'all men, poor and prosperous...should observe strictly the legal fasts and conscientiously celebrate saints' days, as the mass-priests tell us' (*ealle men, earme 7 eadige...ælc beboden fæsten geornlice healdan 7 þa halgan georne weordian þe us mæssepreostas beodan sceolan*).[30] This again confirms the responsibility of the masspriests. The purpose of right observance was so that all 'may attain to the joy of the heavenly kingdom' (*to heofena rices myrðe becuman*).[31] About the same time the Laws of the Northumbrian priests also specified a fine for anyone violating a festival or a legal fast, fixing the amount at 12 ores.[32] King Edgar's Code at Andover (959-63) had repeated that ordained fasts were to be observed with all diligence, and added that the fast every Friday was also to be observed, unless it was a festival.[33] Evidently the importance of observing fasts was felt from the mid-seventh century on, since most law codes referred to it. Fasting as an institution presumably met with resistance from some individuals, since penalties for breaking fasts had to be imposed.

Fasting by Monastics

Whereas laymen were to observe only the legal feasts and were otherwise free to eat what and when they wanted, monastics generally were restricted as to diet, as to mealtimes and quantity. Moreover, their regime on fast days was probably more austere than that of laymen. According to the *Rule of Chrodegang* there was some restriction on diet for almost all the year. 'From Easter to Pentecost the brothers eat twice a day and can eat flesh with permission except for Wednesday and Friday. From Pentecost till the birthday of John the Baptist they also eat twice a

day but forgo flesh. From John the Baptist's birthday until the anniversary of St Martin's death, they also eat twice a day and forgo flesh on Wednesdays and Fridays. Then from Martinmas to midwinter, they forgo all flesh and fast till nones and on all of those days they eat in the refectory, and during that period they forgo flesh on Wednesday and Friday. If one of those days is a festival it lessens the fast, and if the prior gives permission they may eat flesh for the sake of their health.'
(*Fram Eastron of Pentecosten tuwa on dæg etan preostas 7 etan flæsc be leafe, butan þa dædbetendan buton Wodnesdæg, 7 Frigedæge. Fram Pentecosten oð Sancte Iohannes gebyrdtide þæs fulwihteres, ealswa eton tuwa on dæg 7 forgan flæsc. Fram Sancte [Iohannes] gebyrdtide of Sancte Martinus forsiðe ealswa eton tuwa on dæg 7 Wodnesdæge 7 Frigedæg forgan flæsc. Þonne fram Sancte Martinus mæssan oð midne winter forgan ealle flæsc 7 fæstone to nones 7 ælce þara dage eton on beoderne 7 on þone timan Wodensdæge 7 Frigedæge forgan flæsc. Gif þonne þam dagum hwilc freolsdæg gescyt, gif se ealdor lifð hi moton flæsc etan for untrumnysse.*)[34]

However, a Vegan diet was not encouraged, perhaps because it weakened members of the community who would not then be able to do their share of the work. This effect was recognised as early as the fourth century on the continent, and caused concern, since it ultimately diminished the amount of food available to the whole community.[35] 'Indeed abstinence in these days consists in giving up almost all delicacies and in living soberly and ascetically. He who is genuinely able to abstain from eggs and cheese and butter and fish and wine is of great strength/virtue. He who cannot really abstain from them because of weakness or any other reason may eat them; provided he solemnly fasts until evening before a feast and doesn't get drunk on wine they may be consumed to preserve his body. He who abstains from cheese and milk and butter and eggs when he is not fasting is very wrong and completely mistaken. Truly wine and every intoxicating drink and gluttony is forbidden, but not milk and eggs. Certainly the apostle did not say "Don't eat milk and eggs"; what he said was, "Don't get drunk on wine, gluttony lies there".' (*Forhæfdnes soðlice on þysum dagum sceal beon forneah ealra esta 7 syferlice and clænice to lybanne. Se ðe soðlice fram ægrum 7 cyse 7 buttan 7 fixum 7 wine forhabban mæg he is mycles mægenes. Se ðe witodlice fram þæm for untrumnesse oððe ahwylcum weorce forhabban ne mæg, he bruce, for an þ he þæt fæsten of æfen symbellice breme, 7 win næs to drucenesse, ac he gereorde his lichaman nyme. Ðæt hwa fram cyse 7 meoluc 7 buteran 7 ægrum forhæbbe 7 ne fæste is gewolenlicost 7 fram eallum gesceade ascyreð. soþlice wines 7 ælces wætan druncennes 7 galne synt forbodene, næs meoluc 7 ægru. Ne cwæð witodlice se apostol, 'Nellen ge þicgan meoluc 7 ægru,' ac he cwæð, 'Nellen ge beon gynddrencede of wine, on þam is galnes'.*)[36]

The very austere regimes of the east where dry eating and raw eating were practised seem to have been admired. At the monastery where Zozimus went to live the brothers kept themselves alive 'on bread and water' (*mid hlafe and mid wætere*) to demonstrate their devotion.[37] But there was the realisation, voiced by Ælfric, that such a diet was not sufficient for monastics in the colder climate of England. Towards the end of the period the larger abbeys secured supplies of eels for Lent. They were Lenten food at Abingdon, and the abbot and brethren of Ramsey, who probably had a plentiful supply of eels for themselves, were to give 4000 in Lent to Peterborough.[38]

Monastics who ate outside the cloister were presumably able to avoid some of the restrictions imposed on those who ate in the refectory, which is why monks were expected to make the effort to eat together in the refectory during fasts, unless it was too far for them to get back to. Bishops presumably could have eaten out on a number of occasions: when a gesith invited Bishop John to a meal 'the bishop refused, saying his minster was near, and he ought to go there' (*widsoc se biscop 7 cwæth þær his mynster neah wære þæt he scold þyder faran*). However, he did ultimately accept the invitation when the gesith promised to fast and give alms to the poor.[39] A section in the report of the Legates to Pope Hadrian prohibits ecclesiastics taking food in secret.[40] This was presumably to limit the abuse whereby an individual might appear to be observing food restrictions, but was in fact consuming extra rations. On the other hand, an individual could not elect to fast without the permission of the abbot.[41] In both cases the food resources of the monastery were affected, either directly, as in the first case, or indirectly, if the faster could not maintain his contribution to production.

Monastic meals in mid-fifth-century Gaul consisted of two cooked dishes, one a vegetable/cereal soup, the other a puree of pulses with oil, flour or cheese, and a third dish of raw vegetables with salt, oil and vinegar. Bread was also available, but was probably hard dried rusk, which had to be softened in liquid before it could be eaten. Meat was generally prohibited but some wine was permitted.[42] The strict fasting diet consisted of restricting intake to one meal of this sort per day taken in the evening, or to bread and water only. Those who could not comply with this regime were allowed to divide their meal into two, one part to be eaten not before three in the afternoon, and the other in the evening. In the mid-sixth century Benedict laid down the 190-200 fast days in the year. Periods of strict fasting included the forty days of Lent, from Whit Sunday till the autumn equinox, and thirty days before Christmas. There were additionally the two or three fast days each week (Wednesdays, Fridays and in some communities, Mondays) and the eves of twenty-five holidays particular to the monastery, when abstinence from fats, eggs, cheese and fish was called for. When two meals a day were still taken quantitative restrictions were achieved by serving the normal single ration in one bowl which was then shared by two monks.[43] This was probably close to the fasting regime for early Anglo-Saxon monasteries. According to the later *Regularis Concordia*, the Lenten abstinence from milk and eggs was to be observed from Quinquagesima, and on the Ember Days.[44] However, it proved necessary to increase the amounts of food available under the strict fasting diet, since it did not allow for the fulfilment of duties.[45] Fish were originally classed as 'delicacies' (*deliciae*), to be eaten only with the abbot's permission on holidays. Later in the period after monasteries had acquired grants of land and rights to the fish in lakes, rivers and ponds fish became a fasting dish.[46] The growing wealth of monasteries in England and on the continent led to some degree of laxity. The regime laid down by Benedict of Nursia was reformed by Benedict of Aniane, although this rule in turn was relaxed, since Cluny was founded in the tenth century to revive the strictness of the original Benedictine rule.[47] In England too, reforming ecclesiastics like Æthelwold worked to bring back a more rigorous regime.

The *Regularis Concordia*, produced in the reign of Edgar, confirmed that flesh was prohibited, but the evidence of the novice of Ælfric's *Colloquy* 'I still eat meat because I am a novice' (*Gyt flæscmettum ic bruce, forðam cild ic eom under gyrda drohniende*), indicates that the importance of an unrestricted diet for growing children was recognised.[48] According to *The Rule of Chrodegang*, 'no food or drink is to be taken before or after mealtimes, except by the sick and children if permission has been previously given by the prior' (*ær tide oððe æfter tide naht metes oððe drinces hi na underfo ut asyndrodum untrumum 7 cildrum þæra wacmodes fram þam ealdre is toforan sceigende*).[49]

---

[1] Colgrave 1940, 344.
[2] Miller 1890, I, 1 162.

[3] Colgrave 1940, 344.
[4] op. cit.
[5] Whitelock 1955, 407.
[6] Cockayne 1851, III.
[7] Whitelock 1955, 407.
[8] Robertson 1925, 65, 166.
[9] Bynum 1987, 37.
[10] Herzfeld 1900, *Jan. 2.*
[11] Miller 1890, I, 1 172.
[12] Skeat 1881, *Ash Wednesday* ll.59.
[13] Turner 1828, I 416.
[14] Skeat 1881, *Prayer of Moses* ll.91, 106.
[15] Bynum 1987, 37.
[16] Miller 1890, I, 2 242-4.
[17] Bynum 1987, 37.
[18] Miller 1890, I, 2 388.
[19] op. cit., I, 2 376-7.
[20] Napier 1916, 42-3.
[21] Roesdahl 1977, 194.
[22] Turner 1828, II 36.
[23] Colgrave 1940, 247.
[24] Kisban in Fenton & Kisban 1986, 3.
[25] Dembinska in Fenton & Owen 1981, 162.
[26] Attenborough 1922.
[27] op. cit., 102-4.
[28] op. cit.
[29] Whitelock 1955, 425-6.
[30] Attenborough 1925, 144.
[31] op. cit.
[32] Whitelock 1955, 438.
[33] op. cit., 396.
[34] Napier 1916, 43-4.
[35] Dembinska in Fenton & Kisban 1986, 153.
[36] Napier 1916, 114-115.
[37] Skeat 1881, *St Mary of Egypt* l.93.
[38] Cockayne 1851, III; Harmer 1952, 265.
[39] Miller 1890 I, 2 394.
[40] Whitelock 1955, 771.
[41] Dembinska in Fenton & Kisban 1986, 154.
[42] op. cit., 153.
[43] op. cit., 154.
[44] Cockayne 1851, III.
[45] Dembinska in Fenton & Kisban 1986, 157.
[46] op. cit., 155.
[47] op. cit., 163.
[48] Garmonsway 1978, 46.
[49] Napier 1916, 123.

Appendix B

Part I: Fasting by Saints

Saints, and others not officially canonised, either observed fasts more strictly than was ordained, or followed a regime of deprivation, the rationale being that increasing austerities increased merit. No doubt fasting was also used as a demonstration of moral superiority, and to try to influence opinion.

The fact that the early saints of the Christian church tended to fast strictly must have influenced their later followers. For example, Mary of Egypt 'lived on vegetables' (*be þam wyrtum leofode*), and on one occasion was satisfied with a pinch of dried peas.[1] Bread and water was a standard diet.[2] St Eufrasia occupied herself in fasting and vigils day and night and 'was very thin on account of her strict and austere life' (*wæs swiðe geþynnod for þære micclan and stiðan drohtnung*).[3] Some individuals emulated these practices with similar results: a twelfth-century hermit who ate nothing but roots became so thin from fasting that he could hardly stand.[4]

On occasion the fasts might not be voluntary, as when St Ananias was imprisoned for twelve days without food by Diocletian, or when St Thomas told Migdonia to fast earnestly for seven days.[5] Or they might be incidental: Enbolus was so desirous of Basil's doctrine 'that he had no wish for any food... for three days... he took no heed of any meals' (*þæt he hlyste nanes metes...ðry dagas...ætes ne gymdon*).[6] But fasting seems to have been an attribute of saintliness, and not the prerogative of one or two individuals.[7]

During the Lenten fast Ecgberht 'only ate once a day, and then only had a small loaf and some thin milk' (*æne siða in dæge gereorde 7 elles ne þeah nemne medmicel hlafes mid þinre meolc*), while Bishop Cedd ate only half a loaf and a hen's egg and milk in the evening.[8]

Cuthbert, who from other evidence was a man of considerable bodily strength and stamina, found it difficult in his early years to fast for long periods, lest he should become unfitted for the labour required of him.[9] He did not abstain from flesh on Fridays, but always fasted until nones.[10]

Once he had settled at Crowland, Guthlac 'tasted nothing except barley bread and water and when the sun was set, then he ate the food on which he lived' (*nahwiht ne onbyrigde buton berenne hlaf and wæter; ond þonne sunne wæs on setle, þonne þigede he þa andlyfene þe he bigleofode*).[11] He rejected the suggestion of two devils that he should fast for seven days 'instead he took a moderate meal, that is the barley loaf, and ate it and preserved his life' (*ac feng to medmycclan bigleofan, þæt wæs to þam berenan hlafe, and þone þigede and his lif bileofode*).[12] A passage in the Exeter Book tells us that 'Guthlac loved fasting and was refreshed by that noble meal', i.e. the Eucharist (*Gudlac fæsten lufiað ead-mod þy æplan gyfle*) and certainly he did not begrudge the visiting brethren their *beor*, since he found amusing the incident where they buried the container so they could recover it after visiting him.[13] The fiends by whom he was persecuted had warned him that 'hunger and thirst will be hard foes' (*beoð hungor and þurst heard gewinnan*), but he said that God sent by the hand of men his necessities each day.[14] Presumably procuring the blessing of so holy a man by taking him what was a relatively cheap food, was motive enough to ensure that individuals took him enough to eat.

Neither Aidan nor Guthlac generally accepted invitations to eat out, though Aidan did on occasion eat with the king, and Guthlac dined with the bishop who ordained him 'though it was not his habit to do so' (*þeah hit his life ungeþeawe wære*).[15]

According to Bede, Aidan influenced all monastics of his time in the matter of fasting. 'By the example of this holy man at that time, all religious people, whether men or women, were so confirmed, that it became their habit throughout the year, except during the fifty days after Easter, to fast up to the ninth hour on the fourth and sixth days of the week'. (*Mid þyses halgan mannes bysenum wæron getrymeðe on þa tid gehwilce æfeste ge wæpnedmen ge wimmen, þæt hi tim to gewuman genaman, þæt heo eall ger buton fiftig neahta ofer Eastron, þæt heo þy feorðan wicdæge 7 þy syxtan feaston to nones.*)[16]

Bede cites a number of saintly individuals who fasted strictly, like Cenred who 'in prayers and fasting and alms-giving lived until his last day' (*on gebedum 7 on fæstenum 7 on ælmesdæum awundade oð ðone ytmestan dæg*).[17] Dryhthelm, having seen a vision of heaven, purgatory and hell, was so shocked, that he embarked on a regime which 'by daily fasts' (*dæghæmlice fæsteno*) left him 'exhausted and subdued' (*swæncte 7 temede*).[18]

Columba once fasted on a diet of nettle soup because a poverty-stricken old lady living nearby was reduced to this extremity. However, his cook added milk to the broth, and when Columba was complimented on how well he was looking, the deception was discovered. Far from being annoyed with the cook, he blessed him.[19]

Monastic situations were generally perceived as too lax by saintly individuals. In the mid-fifth century, Sampson, dissatisfied with the life he had tried at three monasteries for this reason, withdrew to an isolated community, and then used to retreat to a cave for seven-day fasts, when the brethren provided him with food (though of course no meat or alcoholic drink).[20] This withdrawal from even a strict monastic regime was paralleled by Cuthbert's retreats to Farne, after he was made bishop of Lindisfarne.[21] Occasionally an abbot like Æthelwold succeeded in imposing a more austere regime against considerable opposition. Æthelwold only ate the flesh of animals and birds once for three months when forced by infirmity, and this, moreover, at the command of Archbishop Dunstan, and again during the sickness from which he died.[22]

Anglo-Saxon women are also recorded as practising lives of austerity. Leoba, Boniface's chief woman helper in his mission, ate and drank very sparingly, though she practised the greatest kindness to others. The little cup from which she used to drink was called 'the little one of the loved one'. In her case fasting was accompanied by hospitality: she would produce a feast while fasting herself.[23] After Ætheldrida had received the veil, 'seldom, except at greater festivals and seasons or in case of greater need, would she touch food more than once a day' (*seldon, buton maran symbelnysse 7 tidum oðþe maran nydþearfe, ma þonne æne siðe on dæge þæt heo wolde mete þycgan*).[24] Eadgyth, the sister of Athelstan, remained strong to the end of her life, at Polesworth, in fasts and vigils.[25] Perhaps the lives of those important by virtue of their family connections are more likely to have been recorded, but we do hear occasionally of other individuals, like a certain widow called Oswyn, who lived near the burial place of St Edmund in prayers and 'fasting for many years afterwards' (*fæstendum manega gear syððan*).[26]

Part II: Fasting as Penance

The view that fasting was an efficacious penance presumably received a boost from the account of purgatory given by a Northumbrian, who returned from the dead to say that souls could be aided by - inter alia - the fasting of other men so that they could be rescued before Domesday.[27] After the death of a much-hated prioress at Wimborne, the younger nuns danced on her grave, and the consequent subsidence was seen as evidence of the dead woman's sinfulness. In order to obtain absolution for her, the mother of the community enjoined a three days' fast for her soul, together with psalm singing and prayers. The depression in the grave duly filled with soil, indicating the success of their penance.[28]

However, fasting is mostly mentioned as penance to be carried out by an individual to atone for his own misdeeds. Fasting was given as penance for such crimes as administering a love potion, passing a child through a hole in the earth for the sake of its health (40 days' bread and water), fasting in honour of the moon on health grounds (1 year's bread and water).[29] These were presumably more likely to be lay misdemeanours, but the lazy monks of Winchester who refused to get up and sing the Te Deum every time St Swithin effected a cure, were threatened by the bishop that they 'should heavily atone for it with seven days' fasting' (*sceolde hit mid fæstene seofon niht on an swarlice gebetan*).[30] According to Wulfstan's *Canons of Edgar*, 'The regulation says if any man in orders goes hunting then if he is a cleric he must abstain from fleshmeat for one year, a deacon for two years, a masspriest three, and a bishop seven.' (*Se canon segð gyf hwylc gehadod man on huntaþ fare, gyf it bid clerec forga xii monað flæsc, diacon twa gear, mæssepreost þreo, bisceop vii.*)[31]

As in Wales, penance might involve a limited diet for days or years.[32] Monastic penances ranged from missing one meal to foregoing flesh and alcohol and most fats for several years.[33] Welsh sources give in detail the fasting diet for the monastic priest or deacon found guilty of a sexual offence: bread without limitation and a titbit fattened slightly with butter on Sunday; on the other days a ration of dry bread and a dish enriched with a little fat, garden vegetables, a few eggs, a British cheese, a Roman half-pint of milk in consideration of the body in this age, also a Roman pint of whey or buttermilk for his thirst , and some water if he is a worker.[34] According to the Old English *Rule of Chrodegang*, no-one was to sleep in the interval between *utsange* and *dægeredsange* (a period of time in which a man may say forty or fifty psalms), but 'if he does, then he must abstain from that day's drink' (*gif hwa elles do, sy he ascreð fram þæs dæges drince*).[35] Or for various 'small offences' (*litlum gultum*) 'he must abstain from meals...and eat his food after the brothers' meal, so that...if they eat at midday he must eat at 3pm , and if they eat at 3pm he must wait until the evening' (*ascyreð fram gereorde...7 ete ana his mete æfter broðra gereorde, swilce...gif broðra etam to middæges ete he to nones, gif broðra to nones, he to æfenes*).[36]

'Adamnan only took meat and meals on Sundays and the fifth day of the week...the other days he fasted' (*Adamnan næfre mete onfeng ne swæsendo þeah, buton Drihtenlecan dæg 7 þy fiftan wiicdæge...oðrum dagum he swa fæstende awunade*).[37] This austere existence was imposed on him by a priest who said that a week of fasting was excessive and 'two or three days' fasting is enough to observe' (*twydæglic fæsten oðþe þreodæglic fæsten is genoh to healdenne*), and that he would shortly return and tell Adamnan how long his penance should continue. However, he suddenly returned to Ireland, and as the penance was not rescinded, Adamnan continued with the regime, first 'on account of divine terror' (*for intingan þæd godes eges*) and then on account of the eternal reward.[38]

An example of penitential fasting is recorded from 735 when a lady of noble family in Oxford is recorded as mortifying herself by lying on the ground and subsisting on broth made of the poorest herbs and a small quantity of barley bread.[39]

According to Edgar's Laws, part of the penance of a rich man was that he should fast on bread, green herbs and water, and that he should eat no flesh nor drink anything intoxicating.[40]

Special penitential bread was sometimes eaten. In monastic institutions it was made from the lower grades of the unsifted flour of rye, barley, oats and pulses, or a mixture of these flours.[41] Individuals like Gwynllyw and his wife ate barley bread with added ashes.[42] The Cistercian Rule established in the eleventh century envisaged bread made of bran with some bitter herbs added.[43]

Those who chose to fast were probably always outnumbered by those who preferred not to. Even though ascetics were held in very high regard, they were no doubt seen as different by most people who were not prepared to emulate them, even though fasting was a route to eternal feasting. Fast day dishes could be elaborate delicacies, so that even if a noble was observing the fast legalistically, and limiting himself to fish, he might be able to enjoy a luxury meal. This problem was commented on by - inter alia - St Thomas Aquinas. Moreover with a certain amount of sophistry one could have reclassified the tail of the beaver, frogs, puffins and barnacle geese as fish, and unborn or newly born mammals as 'not meat' as had happened by the fifteenth century.[44] There is no evidence for these evasions in Anglo-Saxon England, but we do not have a menu for a 'fish feast' like that held for the Archbishop of Canterbury in 1504-5) where these items are listed.

Bishop Theodred imposed a penance on himself (for having thieves at St Edmund's shrine hung there and then) and then called on the people 'that they fast completely with him for three days' (*þæt hi him mid fæstan fullice þry dagas*).[45] Alcuin thought that a fast should be declared because Æthelheard had fled his post as Archbishop of

Canterbury in 797. The whole people were to join in this, and in addition, prayers were to be said, masses celebrated and alms given.[46]

Fasting as Part of Particular Rituals

Fasting was used to sanctify places and occasions. Cedd fasted to purify the site for his church, and various ceremonies were consecrated by fasting. As Lent was a sanctified period, the fine for breaking and entering according to Alfred's Laws, was to be doubled if these offences were committed 'during the Lenten fast' (*in lencten fæsten*).[47] In a sense, feast days were sanctified by the fast on the preceding day(s). The *Canons of Edgar* stated that 'we instruct that any man who has eaten, unless because of illness, may not take communion' (*we lærað þæt ænig unfæstende man husles ne abirige buton hit for oferseocness sy*).[48] Individuals were expected to refrain from eating and drinking in church, but 'Now men nevertheless will foolishly weaken very often and recklessly drink within God's house...he who wants to drink and make a foolish noise let him drink at home, not in the Lord's house.' (*Nu doð men swa þeah dyslice foroft þæt hi willað wacian and wodlice drincan binnan Godes huse...and se de wile drincan and dwæslice hlydan drinc him at ham na on drihtnes hus.*)[49]

The protagonist of the ordeal was expected to prepare for the ceremony with three days' fasting. 'If anyone is committed to go to the ordeal, he shall come three days before to the mass priest who is to consecrate it, and live off bread and water and salt and herbs until he has to go to it.' (*Gif hwa ordales weddige, ðonne cume he þrim nihtum ær to þam mæssepreost þe hit halgian scyle, ond fede hine sylfne mid hlafe 7 mid wætre 7 sealte 7 wyrtum, ær he togan scyle.*)[50] According to another account, an equal number from each party were allowed to enter the church as witnesses, 'all having fasted' (*beon ealle fæstende*).[51]

There are several instances in *Leechdoms* where the patient is to fast before taking a cure.[52] This may have been to make the remedy more effective - taking the medicine before meals, but equally it may have been to purify the patient and consecrate the treatment. Proverbs declared quite sensibly that 'If you want to be healthy, drink in moderation; all surfeit and all idleness nourishes sickness'.[53] Fasting was supposed to dry up bodily humours, and put demons to flight, so that it was seen as medicine for the body and the soul.[54] Gluttony was the first of the eight sins that troubled man, because it brought about sickness and caused early death through immoderate drinking.[55] One of the chief virtues on the other hand, is 'Temperance, which is moderation in English, that is that a man be moderate and does not eat or drink too much, nor eat before mealtimes...but a wise man shall observe his mealtimes...then may he overcome such as gluttony.' (*Temperantia þæt is gemetegung on englisc þæt is þæt man beo gemetegod and to mycel ne ðicge on æte and on wæte ne ær timan ne gereordige...ac se gesceadwisa man sceal cepan his mæles...þonne mæg he oferswiðan swa þa gyfernysse.*)[56]

[1] Skeat 1881, *St Mary of Egypt* 1.569.
[2] Herzfeld 1900, *July 9, January 17, July 7, June 2.*
[3] Skeat 1881, *St Eufrasia* 1.173, 236.
[4] Holmes 1952, 125.
[5] Herzfeld 1900, Jan. 19; Skeat 1881 *St Thomas* 1.296-7.
[6] Skeat 1881 *St Basilus* 1.43-4.
[7] op. cit., l. 478.
[8] Miller 1890, I, 2 244, 232.
[9] Bonser 1963, 113.
[10] Colgrave 1940, 344.
[11] Goodwin 1848, 27.
[12] op. cit., 35.
[13] Mackie/Gollancz 1972, *Guthlac*; Swanton 1975, 54.
[14] Mackie/Gollancz 1972, *Guthlac*
[15] Miller 1890 I, 1 162; Goodwin 1848, 27.
[16] Miller 1890 I, 1 162.
[17] op. cit., I, 2 448.
[18] op. cit., 436.
[19] Jackson 1971, 279.
[20] Davies 1982, 152.
[21] Miller 1890, I, 2 360.
[22] Whitelock 1955, 837.
[23] op. cit., 722.
[24] Miller 1890, I, 2 318.
[25] Whitelock 1955, 257.
[26] Skeat 1881, *St Edmund* 1.191.
[27] Miller 1890, I, 2 432.
[28] Whitelock 1955, 720-1.
[29] Bonser 1963, 149, 240, 249.
[30] Skeat 1881, *St Swithun* 1.261.
[31] Fowler 1972, 15.
[32] Davies 1982, 192.
[33] op. cit.
[34] op. cit., 151.
[35] Napier 1916, 24.
[36] op. cit., 35.
[37] Miller 1890, I, 2 352.
[38] op. cit.
[39] Turner 1828, III 27.
[40] op. cit., 30.
[41] Dembinska in Fenton & Kisban 1986, 154.
[42] Davies 1982, 192.
[43] op. cit.
[44] Furnivall 1868, 37; Tannahill 1973, 112.
[45] Skeat 1881, *St Edmund* 1.229.
[46] Whitelock 1955, 789.

[47] Attenborough 1922, 82.
[48] Fowler 1972, 8.
[49] Skeat 1881, *Prayer of Moses* l.72.
[50] Attenborough 1922, 138.
[51] op. cit., 172.
[52] Cockayne 1851, II vi, xxv, xxxii, etc.
[53] Swanton 1975, 177.
[54] Bynum 1987, 41.
[55] Skeat 1881, *Memorial of the Saints* l.267.
[56] op. cit., l. 314.

Appendix C

Entertainment at Feasts

Minstrels

It seems that the professional minstrel or the amateur singer ideally accompanied himself on a harp or lyre. According to the professional scop Widsith,

> *þonne wit scilling sciran reorde*
> *for uncrum sigedryhtne song ahofan*
> *hlude bi hearpan hleopor swinsade*
> *þonne monige men modum wlonce*
> *wordum sprecan þa þe wel cuþan*
> *þæt hi næfre song sellan ne hyrdon*

(when Shilling and I, with clear voice raised the song before our victorious lord - loud to the harp our speech made music - then many men bold of heart who well knew, declared in words that they had never heard a better song).[1] Listening to the feast in Heorot, Grendel distinguishes

> *Hludne in healle ... hearpan sweg*
> *swutol sang scopes*

(loud in the hall ... the sound of the harp and the sweet song of the minstrel).[2] The phrase to learn or say *by rote* apparently comes from the practice of reciting to harp accompaniment, since one of the types of harp was called a *rota*.[3]

The harp of a chief was a valuable instrument, probably decorated with gilt mounts, like the lyre found at Sutton Hoo.[4] This instrument had been kept in a beaver-skin bag, which was probably valuable in itself, since the Welsh Laws give the value of a beaver skin at 120 pence, that of a stag, fox or wolf as eight pence.[5] At the Welsh court the harp of the chief of song (provided for him by the king) and the harp of the king were both worth 120 pence according to the Welsh Laws, while the harp of the *gwrda* was worth 60 pence.[6] A harp was one of the three pledges that never lapsed, and the fee for tuning the keys was 24 pence, so that it was a prestige object.[7] It seems to have been in the keeping of the chief of the household at the Welsh court - at least, he was to place the harp in the hands of the bard on the three principal festivals, and was entitled to a song from the bard whenever he wanted one.[8] (However, if the queen wanted a song, then the bard had to sing it in a low voice, so that the hall should not be disturbed by him.)[9]

The form of harps is indicated in the manuscript illustrations. There seem to have been a large harp of seven or twelve strings which was held on the knee and the *rota*, a zither-like harp of five strings.[10] The two sorts are shown in a manuscript of between 1030-1050.[11] One has a narrow trapezium shape, while the other is rectangular. One illustration from the mid-eighth century shows King David playing the lyre,[12] and harps are also shown in later manuscripts, like one dating between 1030-50.[13] There is considerable archaeological evidence for harps/lyres. As well as the example from Sutton Hoo, there was also a lyre in the burial of Tæppa, a chieftain or minor king buried at Taplow.[14] This confirms the documentary evidence that harping was a fashionable accomplishment. Dunstan, for example, was accustomed to play his *cythera* 'which we in the native language call "harp"' to entertain a noblewoman and her ladies.[15] Only the bone yoke facings from an instrument survive in a mid-fifth century immigrant's grave at Abingdon.[16] The remains of a lyre, consisting of two metal plates, plain and undecorated, in a poorly furnished burial at Burgh Apton, and remains at other sites, Morning Thorpe, and Buckland, Dover, may indicate the grave of a professional scop.[17]

According to the Welsh Laws, the professional bard was entitled to protection in his 'circuit of minstrelsy'; bardism and the science of a harpist, together with metallurgy, were the three domestic skills with special rights.[18] The chief harper seems to have trained minstrels who then set out on their own account as professionals.[19] According to *The Fates of Men*

> Sum sceal mid hearpan æt his hlafordes
> fotum sittan feoh þicgan
> ond a snellice snere wræstan
> lætan scralletan sceacol se þe hleapeð
> nægl neomegende biþ him neod micel

(one shall sit at his lord's feet with his harp, receive wealth, and ever pluck the strings rapidly, let the leaping plectrum, the ringing nail shrill loudly, great is his eagerness).[20] This suggests a permanent post with a lord, and Deor was the minstrel of the Heodnings for many years, until he was replaced by Heorrenda, 'a man skilled in song' (*leodcraftig monn*).[21] However, the minstrel Widsith had been to very many courts:

> ....folgaðe wide
> forþon ic mæg singan ond secgan spell
> mænan fore mengo in meoduhealle
> hu me cynegode cystum dohten...

(I served far and wide so I can sing, tell my story, declare before the company in the banqueting hall how men of high rank were noble, generous to me).[22] He sang the praises of Queen Ealhhild 'throughout many lands' (*geond londa fela*),[23] and concludes:

> *Swa scripende gesceapum hweorfað*
> *gleomen gumena geonde grunda fela*
> *þærfe secgað þoncword sprecað*
> *simle suð oþþe norð sumne gemetað*
> *gydda gleawnbe geofum unheawne*
> *se þe fore duguðe wile dom aræran*
> *eorlscipe æfnan oþþæt eal scæceð*
> *leohte ond lif somod lof se gewyrceð*
> *hafað under heofonum heahfæstne dom.*

(Roving thus as is their destiny, the minstrels of men wander over many lands. They tell their need, they speak words of thanks. North or south, they always find someone skilled in lays who wishes to exalt his fame among his retinue and do heroic deeds until all passes away, light and life together. He gains praise and enduring glory under the heavens.)[24] This passage establishes the fact of the wandering minstrel, readily admitted to the feasts of the great, as were also Alfred, Athelstan, and Olaf, who were able to trade on this, and disguising themselves as minstrels, were received into enemy camps where they managed to do some useful spying.[25] The old poem about Athelstan's coronation feast quoted by William of Malmesbury suggests with its juxtaposition of 'stomachs are filled with delicacies, minds with song' that the music accompanied the meal.[26] The story of Olaf confirms that the singing went on during the meal, and once the nobles had eaten enough, the conversation turned to war, and he was ordered out.[27] It also confirms the connection between feasting, and adding to the prestige of the ruler, since the minstrel was paid in many cases to sing his employer's praises: 'one makes the harp resound, another contends with praises'.[28] There is also a link between the feasting, the minstrel and the pagan concept that a man's immortality would rest in the commemoration of his deeds after his death.

Widsith received a jewelled bracelet from Gudhere of the Burgundians, as a reward for his song.[29]

This was a suitably noble reward, within the heroic tradition. A ninth-century Irish poem complains of a boorish patron that he does not give horses for songs of praise 'but what is natural to him - a cow', but we also hear of a chief praised because he did not leave his court deliberately on the calends of January, and so was a profit to the ministrels of Britain, since the New Year's feast was when gifts were traditionally given to minstrels, among others.[30] So while employing a minstrel was prestigious, a suitable return had to be made for their services. The names of famous minstrels were recorded, like that of Gorthyn who provided song at a New Year's feast.[31] Grants of land are recorded to minstrels: 'to Æthelwearde, my faithful minstrel' (*meo fideli ministro Æthelwearde*), or 'to Ealdbert, my minstrel' (*Ealdberhto ministro meo*).[32] William the Conqueror gave his minstrel 3 vills and 5 carucates of land in Gloucestershire.[33] More immediately, the minstrel seems to have been given a horn of liquor as soon as he finished his song.[34]

The council of Clovesho in 747 decreed that monasteries must not be *ludicrarum artium receptacula*, and these arts are defined as those of versifiers, harpers, minstrels or buffoons. The canon law forbade the clergy from having anything to do with mimes, jesters or play actors. The word 'minstrel' applied to all these variety performers associated with bawdy songs and comic acts, as well as to the respectable gleemen who recited epics.[35]

However, it was not so easy to eradicate minstrelsy from the religious life. Wulfstan's *Canons of Edgar* were still trying to prevent priests from being an *ealu-scop* (ale-minstrel) or acting the *gliwige* (gleeman).[36] *Gliwig-manna* (gleeman) glossed *ganeones*, a term which covered vagabonds, ribalds and jokers.[37] *The Laws of the Northumbrian Priests* in c.1020 repeated that if a priest practised drunkenness or became a gleeman or ale-minstrel he was to compensate for it.[38]

Musicians

While the minstrel had his harp, the Welsh Laws refer to two other Chiefs of Song to be provided with appropriate instruments by the king. These were a *crawd* and pipe.[39] A riddle in the Exeter book, describes a bagpipe which:

> *siteð æt symble sæles bideþ*
> *hwonne ær heo cræft hyre cyþan mote*
> *werum on wonge ne heo þær wiht þicgeð*
> *þæs þe him æt blisse beornas habbað...*
> *hwæþre hyre is on fote fæger hleopor*
> *wynlicu wodgiefu*

(sits at the feast and awaits the time when it may first make known its art to men on earth. It receives nothing there of what men have for their enjoyment yet it has in its foot beautiful music, a gift of pleasant sound.)[40] Manuscript illustrations show other instruments.

It is possible that, while the minstrel sung to his harp during the meal, after the eating louder instruments were played, since the horn, trumpet, drums and the flutes, which could be played two at a time, were hardly likely to have been used as continuo.[41] A short trumpet, curved horn and organs are also shown in illustrations, and Bede mentions a drum and cymbals.[42] A violin-like instrument with four strings played with a bow is also shown.[43] The other instrument illustrated is a bell.[44] *Clochetes*, a series of small bells strung on a rod and played with a hammer from a sitting position were known from twelfth-century France.[45] The musicians *heapere* (harper), *bymere* (trumpeter), *pipere* (piper), *fithelere* (fiddler), and *horn-blawere* (horn blower) are all recorded.[46] The feminine forms *fidelestere, hleapestre* and *sangstere* (fiddler, dancer and singer) all appear in the glosses, and as we find a manuscript illustration of a *hleapestre*, there may have also been female musicians and singers.[47]

Dancing, Juggling & Jesting

Cot. Cleo. C. 8 shows two men in martial gear with a horn player and a female dancer.[48] *Tumbian* is the word used for dancing - Herodias' daughter *tumbude* before Herod, hence the term 'tumbler'.[49] Harl. MS 603 also shows dancing.[50] The cup-bearer is serving out wine, a man and a woman seem to be dancing together, another on her own, to the accompaniment of two horns, one larger than the other, a harp, either played by two men, or played by one and supported by a second, and a violin. The step-mother of the young King Edward had in her service a dwarf, a minstrel skilled in various modes of dancing who was sent to entice the young king to her home.[51] Juggling may have been performed to a musical accompaniment, since an illustration in Cot. Tib. C. vi shows a juggler with three balls and three knives, and a musician playing a fiddle with a bow.[52] The same illustration shows King David playing one of the larger eleven-stringed harps, a musician with a curved horn, and another with a straight pipe resting on some sort of support.[53] There are also illustrations of dancing animals and what may be *buffones* (clowns).[54]

Dancing was not just the province of professional entertainers any more than harping or singing was. In the account of the murder of King Ethelbert in 792 we are told that the royal party after dinner spent the whole day with music and dancing in great glee.[55]

At the time of the Winton Domesday John *ioculator* (the jester) paid the king fourpence.[56] A riddle describing a jay or jackdaw has the lines 'who, like an actress, loudly mimic the ways of a clown' (*þe swa scirenige sceawendisan hlude onhyrge*), so there may also have been actresses.[57] Adelina *joculatrix* held lands in Hampshire at the time of Domesday.[58] These two late references would be out of place in the man's world of heroic feasting where the woman's function was virtually that of barmaid.

Riddles

The asking of riddles seems to have been part of the entertainment at a feast since Riddle 42 of the Exeter Book ends:

> ....*nu is undyrne*
> *werum æt wine hu þa wihte mid us*
> *heanmode two hatne sindon*

(now it is revealed to men at their wine how those two mean-spirited creatures are named among us). Riddles are easy to devise, but the skill lies in providing more and more clues without making the answer easier, and also in ambiguity. A number of Anglo-Saxon riddles have an obvious ribald answer, a less obvious polite one. Feasts were also occasions for storytelling.[59]

---

[1] Gollancz/Mackie 1973, *Widsith* l.103 ff.
[2] Zupita 1959, l. 88ff.
[3] Whitelock 1955, 766.
[4] Bruce-Mitford 1983, 724-5.
[5] Owen 1841, 948.
[6] op. cit., 679, 77, 723.
[7] op. cit., 341.
[8] op. cit., 13.
[9] op. cit., 33, 35.
[10] Holmes 1952, 235.
[11] Camb. Univ. Lib. MS Ff. I.23 f.4 v. illustrated in Temple 1976, fig. 249.
[12] Durham Cathedral Lib. B11.30 fol. 81 v.
[13] Bruce-Mitford 1983, 687-8; Temple 1976, No. 249.
[14] Bruce-Mitford 1983, 683, 701.
[15] Whitelock 1955, 234.
[16] Bruce-Mitford 1983, 718.
[17] Evison 1987, 121.
[18] Owen 1841, 475, 477.
[19] op. cit., II 19.
[20] Gollancz/Mackie 1973, *The Fates of Men* l.80 ff.
[21] op. cit., *Deor* l.36 ff.
[22] op. cit., *Widsith* l.53 ff.
[23] op. cit., l. 99.
[24] op. cit., l. 135 ff.
[25] Turner 1828, III 62; Wright 1871, 47; Whitelock 1955, 278.

[26] op. cit., 279.
[27] op. cit., 278.
[28] op. cit.
[29] Gollancz/Mackie 1973, *Widsith* l.65 ff.
[30] Jackson 1971, 132.
[31] Jackson 1969, 100.
[32] Turner 1828, III 567.
[33] Waddell 1932, 210.
[34] Gordon 1954, 307.
[35] Poole 1958, 605; Colgrave 1940, 246-7, 352.
[36] Fowler 1972, 14-5.
[37] Wright 1871, 47.
[38] Whitelock 1955, 437.
[39] Owen 1841, II 19.
[40] Gollancz/Mackie 1973, Riddle 31 l.12.
[41] Turner 1828, III 59.
[42] op. cit., 455 ff.
[43] op. cit., 59.
[44] Temple 1976, fig.305-6.
[45] Holmes 1952, 235.
[46] Turner 1828, III 61.
[47] Fell 1984, 54.
[48] Turner 1828, III 59.
[49] op. cit., 61.
[50] op. cit.
[51] Wright 1871, 47.
[52] Turner 1828, III 59.
[53] illustrated in Wright 1871, 48.
[54] Turner 1828, III 59.
[55] op. cit., 61.
[56] Barlow et al. 1976, 96.
[57] Fell 1984, 54.
[58] op. cit.
[59] Colgrave 1940, 246-7.

Appendix D

Famine Years

439   after a comet

466   caused by 'bad fatal air'

515   'most afflictive'

590   caused by a tempest which raised a great flood

592   caused by a drought from the 10 January to September, and locusts

605   caused by heat and drought

625   'grievous'

680   caused by three years of drought

681   at Selsey, Sussex.[1]

688   Bede says that Cædwalla abdicated and went on a pilgrimage for the good of his soul, but Matthew Paris gives another reason in a marginal gloss. He says it was on account of a widespread famine in England that he fled from the country.[2]

695   famine and pestilence 'so that men ate each other'.[3]
-700

     In the second half of the seventh century the Yellow Plague was raging, and according to Adamnan's *Life of Columba*, about 684 there was 'a mortality upon all animals...for the space of three years so that there escaped not one out of the thousand of any kind of animal'.[4] While there is no record of famine in the chronicles for this year, supplies of animal food must have been scarce, even allowing for sensationalising on the part of the writer. Perhaps this confirms that cereal crops were the principal food resource.

730   great famine.[5]

737   a great drought made the land unfruitful.[6]

793   after many meteors, immense whirlwinds and flashes of lightning.[7] The fact that the pagan invaders slaughtered sheep and oxen no doubt contributed to the natural effects.[8]

800   Contemporary evidence no longer exists for an extensive murrain of cattle in 800, but such is recorded by Roger of Hovenden, who was perhaps using a local copy of the chronicle no longer extant.[9] *Brut y Twysogion* recorded a great mortality of the cattle of the island of Britain for 810.[10]

820   The harvest was spoilt by continuous heavy rains and many men and cattle died. Floods prevented the autumn sowing.[11]

821   harvest devastated by hail, pestilence among men and cattle. The story was told of a town that was afflicted 'each year very frequently by hail so that their crops were destroyed before any reaper could gather the harvest' (*ælce geare oftost þurh hagol swa heora æceras ær wæron aþroxene ær ænig ryftere þæt gerip gaderode*).[12] While this presumably happened in France since St Martin prayed for the afflicted and there was no more hail there during his lifetime, it indicates how devastating hailstorms were for the harvest.

867   a great dearth.[13]

868   a great famine with mortality of men and cattle.[14] There were almost certainly local shortages that went unrecorded, but the great plunder of cattle the invading Danes made in 870 on their way to Peterborough would have taken some seasons to replace, to take only one example.[15] Danish campaigns would certainly have disrupted supply in the areas they were conducted, even if famine is not necessarily recorded as a result.

872   'from ugly locusts'.[16]

879   universal famine.[17]

887   grievous two years.[18]

893   The invading Danes were surrounded at Buttington on the Severn and were reduced to eating their horses, but even so a number died of starvation.[19] (Many Danes also died of hunger in 914, when similar tactics were employed)[20].

896   The English people were much more seriously afflicted by the mortality of cattle and men than by the Danes in these three years.[21] In 894 they had been 'oppressed with lack of food' (*mid metelieste gewægde*).[22]

900   famine.[23]

        In the reign of Athelstan Olaf and his Northmen set fire to crops, 'the green crops withered in the fields, the blighted cornfield mocked the husbandman's prayers'.[24]

954   great famine which lasts four years.[25]

962   famine caused by frost.[26]

969   all grain burnt by the winds.[27]

975   a very great famine recorded in the major versions of the chronicle, interpreted as the vengeance of God.[28]

976   great famine in England, the *micla hungor*.[29] This followed a period of frost, from the 1st November to the end of March.[30]

986   great mortality of cattle (*yrfcwealm*) in England.[31]

988   famine from rain and barren land.[32]

989   great drought and famine followed a period of much snow and rain when there could be no sowing.[33]

1004   such a famine as no man could remember.[34] (This is presumably the famine referred to for 1005).

1005   great famine throughout England - such that no man ever remembered one so cruel.[35] Perhaps this is what motivated the departure of the Danish fleet.

1012   endless multitudes died of famine in England and on the continent.[36]

1016   famine throughout Europe because of hail, thunder and lightning.[37]

1025   famine because of rains.[38]

1031   famine because of great rains and locusts.[39]

1041   weather inclement all the year, great mortality among cattle.[40]

1044   a dreadful famine in England and on the continent so that a sester of wheat cost above 60 pence.[41] Henry of Huntingdon says that a sester of wheat was the burthen of one horse. The famine lasted seven years.[42]

1047   great famine from snow and frost.[43]

1051   an extreme dearth in which many thousands perished.[44]

1054   terrible famine after a comet, wheat at fifteen shillings a quarter.[45] This compared with an average price for the previous fifty or so years of three shillings and sixpence.[46]

1065   'Morkere and his horde from the north harried Northamptonshire, burnt corn, took all the cattle so that the shire and other shires near were for many winters the worse'.[47]
In the south-east counties which suffered most from the campaigns which followed Hastings there is frequent reference to the reduction in hideage on account of the waste and devastation.[48] This was the background to the famines recorded after the Conquest, and presumably led to local shortages.

1068   famine (and plague) after a severe winter.[49]

1069   after harrying by William I the northern countries and other parts of the realm suffered a great dearth.[50]

1073   famine followed by mortality so fierce the living could neither take care of the sick nor bury the dead.[51]

1086   murrain of animals and intemperate weather.[52]

1087   pestilence followed by famine.[53]

1093   great famine and mortality.[54]

1096　famine from summer rain, tempests and bad air.[55]

1099　famine from rains and floods.[56]

[1] Walford 1879, 5.
[2] Bonser 1963, 87.
[3] Walford 1979,5.
[4] Whitelock 1955, 690.
[5] Walford 1879, 5.
[6] Whitelock 1955, 259.
[7] Walford 1879, 5; Whitelock 1955, 167, 247.
[8] op. cit., 242.
[9] Bonser 1963, 87.
[10] op. cit.
[11] Turner 1828, II 55.
[12] Skeat 1881, *St Martin* l.1215.
[13] Walford 1879, 6.
[14] Turner 1828, II 550.
[15] op. cit., I 524.
[16] Walford 1879, 6.
[17] op. cit.
[18] op. cit.
[19] Whitelock 1955, 187.
[20] op. cit., 195.
[21] op. cit., 188.
[22] Bosworth & Toller 1898, I 463.
[23] Walford 1879, 6.
[24] Whitelock 1955, 209.
[25] Walford 1879, 6.
[26] op. cit.
[27] op. cit.
[28] Whitelock 1955, 209.
[29] op. cit., 210; Walford 1879, 6.
[30] Turner 1828, II 551.
[31] op. cit.
[32] Walford 1879, 6.
[33] Turner 1828, II 551.
[34] Walford 1879, 6.
[35] Whitelock 1955, 218.
[36] Walford 1879, 6.
[37] op. cit.
[38] op. cit.
[39] op. cit.
[40] Turner 1828, II 551.
[41] op. cit.
[42] Walford 1879, 6.
[43] op. cit.
[44] Turner 1828, II 325.
[45] Walford 1879, 6, 257.
[46] op. cit.
[47] Douglas and Greenaway 1953, 140.
[48] Loyn 1970, 312.
[49] Walford 1879, 7.
[50] op. cit.
[51] op. cit.
[52] op. cit.
[53] op. cit.
[54] op. cit.
[55] op. cit.
[56] op. cit.

Bibliography

Addyman, P. 1973 Late Saxon Settlements in the St Neots Area *Proc. Camb. Antiquarian Soc.* LXIV 45-99.

Agricultural Research Council: *Institutes and Units of the Agricultural Research Service* n.d.

Alcock, L. 1987 *Economy, Society & Warfare among the Britons & Saxons* Cardiff.

Allen Brown, R. 1985 ed. *Anglo-Norman Studies VIII: Proceedings of the Battle Conference* The Boydell Press.

Arnold, C. J. 1984 *Roman Britain to Saxon England* Croom Helm.

Arrhenius, B. 1985 Chemical analyses of Organic Remains in Archaeological Contexts *ISKOS* 5 339-343.

Ascardi, G. & Nemeskeri, J. 1970 *History of Human Lifespan & Mortality* Budapest.

Ashley, Sir W. 1928 *The Bread of our Forefathers* Oxford.

Aston, M. 1988 *Medieval Fish, Fisheries & Fishponds in England Part ii* BAR British Series 182 (ii).

Attenborough, F. L. 1922 *Laws of the Earliest English Kings* Cambridge.

Austin, Thomas 1888 *Two Fifteenth-Century Cookery Books* EETS reprinted 1964.

Ayrton, E. 1975 *The Cookery of England* Book Club Associates/Andre Deutsch.

Bachrach, B. S. in Allen Brown 1985 Some observations on the military administration of the Norman Conquest 1-25.

Bailey, R. N. 1980 *Viking Age Sculpture in England* Collins 1980.

Baillie, M. 1981 *Current Archaeology* Vol. 7 No. 2 August 1980, Mag. No. 73 Dendro-chronology: the Irish view & Horizontal Mills 61-3.

Bammesberger, A. 1985 ed. *Problems of OE Lexicography: Studies in Memory of Angus Cameron* Regensburg.

Banham, D. 1990 *Anglo-Saxon Food Plants* University of Cambridge Ph.D. thesis.

Banham, D. 1991 *Monasteriales Indicia* Anglo-Saxon Books.

Barlow, F., Bidden, M., von Feilitzen, O., Keen, D. J. 1976 *Winchester in the Early Middle Ages: an edition & discussion of the Winton Domesday* Winchester Studies 1 ed. M. Biddle Oxford.

Barton, F. T. 1912 *Cattle, Sheep and Pigs: their practical breeding and keeping* London.

Barton Lodge, Rev. 1872, 1879 *Palladius, On Husbondrie* EETS

Battiscombe G 1949 *English Picnics* Harvill Press London.

Beasley, Brown & Legge 1987 *Ark* January Ageing cattle by their teeth 22-25.

Bell, M. 1977 Excavations at Bishopstone, Sussex. *Sussex Archaeol. Collections* Vol. 115.

Bencard, M. 1984 ed. *Ribe Excavations 1970-6* Vol. 2 Esbjerg.

Bennett, R. & Elton, J. 1899 *History of Corn Milling* Vol II London.

Biddick, K. 1984 ed. *Archaeological Approaches to Medieval Europe* Kalamazoo.

Bingham, S. 1977 *Dictionary of Nutrition* Barrie & Jenkins.

Bishop, S. n.d. *Interim* Vol. 2 No. 2 Bishophill 14-16.

Blackburn, M. A. S. 1986 ed. *Anglo-Saxon Monetary History: Essays in memory of Michael Dolley* Leicester Univ. Press.

Bland, A. E., Brown, P. A., Tawney, R. H. 1914 *English Economic History - Select Documents* G. Bell & Sons London.

Bloch, M. 1961 *Feudal Society* Routledge & Kegan Paul.

Bonser, W. 1963 *The Medical Background of Anglo-Saxon England* Wellcome Historical Medical Library.

Boorde, A. 1542 *A Compendyous Regyment or a Dyetary of Helth* R. Wyre for John Goughe London.

Bosworth, J. and Toller, T. Northcote 1898 An *Anglo-Saxon Dictionary* (I) and *Supplements* (II) OUP.

Bourdillon, J. Town Life & Animal Husbandry in the Southampton Area *Proc. Hants. Field Club & Archaeol. Soc.* 36 181-191.

Bourdillon, J. & Coy, J. 1980 (in Holdsworth 1980) *Statistical Appendix to Accompany the Animal Bone Report on Material from Melbourne Street*

Bowie, S. H. U. 1988 *Ark* December Cattle for Calf raising 442.

Brett, G. 1968 *Dinner is Served* Rupert Hart-Davis.

Brillat-Savarin, J.-A. 1970 *The Philosopher in the Kitchen* Penguin.

Brinklow, D. 1979 Sites Review: Walmgate 27-32 *Interim* Vol. 6 No. 2 YAT.

British Ornithologists' Union 1971 *The Status of Birds in Britain & Ireland* Blackwell Scientific Pubs.

Brondsted, J. 1940 *Danmarks Oldtid* Copenhagen.

Brooks, C. 1980 Pot Spot: Torksey Ware 39-42 *Interim* Vol. 6 No. 4 YAT.

Brothwell, D. & P. 1969 *Food in Antiquity* Thames & Hudson.

Brothwell, D. & Higgs, E. eds. 1963 *Science in Archaeology* Thames & Hudson.

Brown, L. 1987 *Three Course Newsletter* No. 4 March 1987.

Bruce-Mitford, R. 1975 ed. *Recent Archaeological Excavations in Europe* Routledge & Kegan Paul.

Bruce-Mitford, R. 1983 *The Sutton Hoo Ship Burial* British Museum Publications Vol. 3 i & ii ed. A. Care Evans.

Buckland, P. C., Holdsworth, P. and Monk, M. 1976 The Interpretation of a Group of Saxon Pits in Southampton *Jour. Archaeol. Science* 3 61-9.

Bullough, D. 1984 in L. Fenske et al. *Institutionem, Kultur & Gesellshaft in Mittelalter* Sigmaringen Albuinus deliciosus Karoli regis 73-92.

Burnet, Sir Macfarlane & White, D. O. 1972 *Natural History of Infectious Disease* CUP.

Bynum, C. W. 1987 *Holy Feast & Holy Fast: the religious significance of food to medieval women* Univ. California.

Cameron, K. ed. 1975 *Place-name evidence for the Anglo-Saxon Invasions & Scandinavian Settlements* English Place Name Soc.

Cameron, K. 1985 *Place-Names of Lincolnshire* Part 1 English Place-Name Soc.

Campbell, J. 1962 ed. *Chronicle of Æthelweard* Nelson.

Carter & West see East Anglian Archaeology Report 1980.

Cassidy, P. 1989 *Ark* April Food for thought 115; June What, How Many, Where & Why 195.

Casteel, R. W. *Estimation of size . . . by means of fish scales* in Clason, A. T. 70-86.

Chaplin, R. E. 1971 *The Study of Animal Bones from Archaeological Sites* Seminar Press London & New York

Chapman, N. & D. 1970 *Fallow Deer* British Deer Soc.

Clair, C. 1964 *Kitchen and Table* Abelard-Schuman.

Clarke, H. & Carter, A. 1977 *Excavations in Kings Lynn 1963-1970* Society for Medieval Archaeology Series Monograph 7.

Clarke, H. forthcoming Allecto ed. D/day.

Clarke Hall, J. R. 1950 *Beowulf & the Finnsburgh Fragment* 3rd ed. Allen & Unwin.

Clason, A. T. 1975 ed. *Archaeozoological Studies* North Holland Publishing Co. Amsterdam.

Clemoes, P. & Hughes, K. 1971 *England before the Conquest* CUP.

Clemoes, P. 1972 *Anglo-Saxon England* I CUP.

Clifton, C. 1983 *Edible Flowers* Bodley Head London.

Cockayne, O. 1851 *Leechdoms, Starcraft & Wortcunning* I-III Rolls Series reprint 1961 Holland Press.

Re: *Lacnunga.* Roman numerals refer to Bonser's numbering.

Cole-Hamilton, I. & Lang, T. 1986 *Tightening Belts: A Report on the Impact of Poverty on Food* London Food Commission.

Coles, J. M. & Simpson, D. *Life of St Cuthbert, Anon. Life of St Cuthbert* CUP.

Commissioners 1819 *Reports from the Commissioners...respecting the Public Records of the Kingdom 1800-19.*

Connor, R. D. 1987 *The Weights & Measures of England* HMSO.

Constable, G. 1964 *Monastic Tithes from their Origins to the Twelfth Century* CUP.

Copley, G. J. 1958 *An Archaeology of SE England* Phoenix House London.

Corran, H. S. 1975 *A History of Brewing* David & Charles.

Cox, Charles J. 1905 *The Royal Forests of England* Methuen & Co.

Crane, Eva 1983 *The Archaeology of Bee-Keeping* Duckworth.

Crabtree, P. 1984 *Studies in Medieval Culture* XIII The Archaeozoology of the Anglo-Saxon Site at West Stow, Suffolk 223-235.

Cramp, R. 1984 *Corpus of Anglo-Saxon Stone Sculpture* Vol.1 OUP.

Creighton, C. A. 1891 *History of Epidemics in England* Two vols. CUP reprinted 1965.

Crossley, D. W. 1981 *Medieval Industry* CBA Report No. 40.

Cunliffe 1964 *Winchester Excavations* 1949-60 Vol. 1 City of Winchester Museums & Libraries Committee.

Cunliffe, B. 1976 *Excavations at Porchester Castle* Vol. II Saxon Soc. of Antiquaries of London Reports of Research Committee 33.

Darby, H. C. 1940 *The Medieval Fenland* David & Charles.

Darby, H. C. & Terrett, I. B. 1954 *The Domesday Geography of Midland England* CUP.

David, E. 1960 *French Provincial Cooking* Penguin.

David, E. 1977 *English Bread & Yeast Cookery* Penguin.

Davies, S. M. 1980 Old Down Farm, Andover Part I *Proceedings of the Hants. Field Club and Archaeol. Soc.* 36 161-180.

Davies, W. 1982 *Wales in the Early Middle Ages* Leicester Univ. Press.

Davison, B. K. 1977 Excavations at Sulgrave, Northants. 1960-76 *Archaeol. Journal* CXXXIV 105-114.

Deegan, Marilyn 1986 '...sing a chant against a curly worm' *Popular Archaeology* Feb. 1986 16-21.

De Vriend, H. J. 1984 The *OE Herbarium & Medicina de Quadrupedibus* EETS.

Dickens, J. S. W. & Mantle, P. G. 1974 *Ergot of Cereals & Grasses* MAFF Advisory Leaflet.

Dimbleby, G. W. 1967 *Plants & Archaeology* John Baker.

Dix, J. draft (in Bedford Museum) *Wells at Harrold and Odell, Beds.*

Dix, J. 1981 *Saxon wells near Harrold Beds. Mag* Vol. 18 No. 138 69-71.

Dodwell, C. R. 1982 *Anglo-Saxon Art: a new perspective* Manchester Univ. Press.

Dony, J. G. 1974 *English Names of Wild Flowers* Butterworth.

Douglas, D. C. & Greenaway, G. W. 1953 *English Historical Documents 1042-1189* Eyre & Spottiswoode.

Drummond, J. & Wilbraham, A. 1958 rev. edn. of:

Drummond, Sir J. & Wilbraham, A. 1939 *The Englishman's Food* Jonathan Cape.

Duncan, P. & Acton, B. 1967 *Progressive Winemaking* The Amateur Winemaker.

Dunning, G. C., Hurst, J. G., Myres, J. N. L. & Tischler, F. 1959 *Anglo-Saxon Pottery: A Symposium* CBA Research Report 4 (reprinted from *Med. Archaeol.* III).

Dyer, A. 1984 What to Read on Medical History *The Local Historian* Vol. 16 No. 1 Feb. 1984.

Earle, J. 1884 *Anglo-Saxon Literature* Soc. for Promoting Christian Knowledge.

East Anglian Archaeology Report 1980 No. 9. ed. Carter & West Norfolk Museums Service, Gressenhall.

Eckwall, E. 1960 *The Concise Oxford Dictionary of English Place-Names* Oxford.

Edlin, H. L. 1949 *Woodland Crafts in Britain* Batsford.

Elliott, R. M. W. 1963 rep. *Runes* Manchester Univ. Press.

Ellis Davidson, H. R. 1964 *Gods & Myths of Northern Europe* Penguin.

Ellis Davidson, H. R. & Webster, L. 1967 *The Anglo-Saxon Burial at Coombe (Woodnesborough) Kent* Med. Archaeol. 1967 II 1-41.

Erlichman, J. 1986 *Gluttons for Punishment* Penguin.

Evans, G. Ewart 1960 *The Horse in the Furrow* Faber.

Evans, G. Ewart 1969 *The Farm & the Village* Faber.

Evison, V. I. 1981 *Angles, Saxons & Jutes* Oxford.

Evison, V. 1987 *Dover: the Buckland Anglo-Saxon Cemetery* Hist. Buildings & Monuments Comm. for England Archaeol. Report No. 3.

Eydoux, H.-P. 1966 *The Buried Past* Weidenfeld & Nicolson.

Fell, Christine 1974 OE *Beor Leeds Studies in English* New Series Vol. VIII 76-95.

Fell, Christine 1981 *A note on OE Wine Terminology: the Problem of* Caeren Nottingham Medieval Studies 1-12.

Fell et al. 1983 (C. Fell, P. Foote, J. Graham-Campbell, R. Thomson, eds.) *The Viking Age in the Isle of Man* UCL London.

Fell, Christine 1984 *Women in Anglo-Saxon England and the impact of 1066* with contributions by Cecily Clark & Elizabeth Williams Colonnade Books.

Fenton, A. & Kisban 1986 *Food in Change: Eating Habits from the Middle Ages to the Present Day* John Donald with National Museums of Scotland.

Fenton, A. & Owen, T. M. 1981 eds. *Food in Perspective* Edinburgh.

Fenwick, V. 1978 *The Graveney Boat: a tenth-century find from Kent* BAR British Series 53.

Field, J. 1972 *English Field Names: A Dictionary* David & Charles.

Finberg, H. P. R. 1972 *The Early Charters of the West Midlands* Leicester Univ. Press.

Flower, B. & Rosenbaum, E. 1958 *Apicius, A Roman Cookery Book* Harrap.

Foote, P. G. & Wilson, D. M. 1970 *The Viking Achievement* Sidgwick & Jackson.

Fowler, P. J. 1981 *Farming in the Anglo-Saxon landscape: an archaeologist's review* Anglo-Saxon England No. 9 263-80 CUP.

Fowler, R. W. 1972 *Wulfstan's Canons of Edgar* EETS.

Fox, C. 1948 *The Archaeology of the Cambridge Region* (with supplement) Cambridge.

Fraser, H. M. 1931 *Bee-Keeping in Antiquity* London.

Fraser 1955 rev. edn of above.

Fream, W. 1932 *Elements of Agriculture* John Murray.

Freeman, S. T. 1970 *Neighbors: The Social Contract in a Castilian Hamlet* Univ. Chicago Press.

Furnivall, F. J. *Early English Meals & Manners* 1868 London.

Gair, R. & Lee, J. E. 1978 *Cereal Pests & Diseases* Farming Press Ltd.

Garmonsway, G. N. 1978 *Aelfric's Colloquy* Univ. of Exeter.

Garmonsway, G. N. 1953 *Anglo-Saxon Chronicle* J. M. Dent & Sons.

Gelling, M. 1979 *The Early Charters of the Thames Valley* Leicester Univ. Press.

Gerard, J. 1597 *The Herball or Generall Historie of Plants* London.

Godwin, H. The Ancient Cultivation of Hemp *Antiquity* XLI Part 161 42-49.

Gollancz, I. see Mackie.

Goodwin, C. W. 1848 *The Anglo-Saxon Version of the Life of St Guthlac, Hermit of Crowland* John Russell Smith.

Gordon, I. L. 1960 ed. *The Seafarer* Methuen OE Texts.

Graham-Campbell, J. & Kidd, D. 1980 *The Vikings* BM Publications.

Graham-Campbell, J. 1980 *Viking Artefacts: a select catalogue* BM Publications.

Grant, Annie 1974 (unpub.) *Excavations at St John's, Bedford* (Bedford Museum).

Grattan, J. H. G. & Singer, C. 1952 *Anglo-Saxon Magic & Medicine* London.

Green, F. J. 1975 Plant Remains in Excavations at Westgate St., Gloucester *Medieval Archaeol.* Vol. 23 186-90.

Green, F. J. 1979 Ed. Collection & Interpretation of Botanical Information from medieval urban excavations in Southern England in *Festschrift Maria Hopf Archaeophysika* Vol. 8 35-55.

Gregory, V. L. 1974 Excavations at Becket's Barn, Pagham, W. Sussex *Sussex Archaeological Collection* 114 207-17.

Grigson 1984 ed. *Five Hundred Points of Good Husbandry: Thomas Tusser* OUP.

Groundes-Peace, Z. 1971 *Mrs Groundes-Peace's Old Cookery Notebook* David & Charles.

Grube, F. W. 1934 Cereal Foods of the Anglo-Saxons *Philological Quarterly* XIII 1934 140-158.

Hall, A. 1981, The cockle of rebellion... *Interim* Vol. 8 No. 1 5-8 YAT.

Hall, A. R. & Kenward, H. K. 1982 *Environmental Archaeology in the Urban Context* CBA Research Report 43.

Hall, A. R., Kenward, H. K., Williams, D., Greig 1983 JAR *The Archaeol. of York Vol. 14* Fasc. 4 *The Past Environment of York* CBA for YAT.

Hall, R. 1979, Sites Review: Coppergate *Interim* Vol. 6 No. 2 9-17 YAT.

Hall, R. 1982, Sites Review: Coppergate *Interim* Vol. 8 No. 2 16-24 YAT.

Hall, S. 1989 Running Wild *Ark* January 12-15.

Hamilton, N. E. S. A. 1870 ed. William of Malmesbury *De Gestis Pontificum Anglorum* iv Rolls Series.

Harcourt, R. A. 1974 The Dog in Prehistoric & Early Historic Britain *Journal of Archaeol. Science* Vol.1. Part 1 151-175 .

Harmer, F. E. 1952 *Anglo-Saxon Writs* Manchester Univ. Press.

Harris, B. 1961, *Eat the Weeds* Keats Publishing Corp. New Caanan Conn.

Harris, B. E. 1987 *The Great Roll of the Pipe for the fourth year of the reign of Henry III* Pipe Roll Soc.

Harris, M. 1986 *Good to eat: riddles of food and culture* Allen & Unwin.

Hart, C. R. 1975 *The Early Charters of Northern England and the N. Midlands* Leicester Univ. Press.

Hartley, Dorothy 1954, *Food in England* Macdonald.

Hartley, Dorothy 1978 *Water in England* Macdonald & Jane's.

Harvey, J. 1981 *Medieval Gardens* Batsford.

Haslam, J. 1980 with L. Biek & R. F. Tylecote et al. A Middle Saxon Iron Smelting site at Ramsbury, Wilts . *Med. Archaeol.* XXIV 1-68.

Haslam, J. 1984 ed. *Anglo-Saxon Towns in Southern England* Phillimore.

Hawkes, S. C., Campbell, J., Brown, D. eds. 1985 *Anglo-Saxon Studies in Archaeology & History* No. 4 Oxford see Matthews & Hawkes.

Heighway, C. M., Garrod, A. P., & Vince, A. G. 1975 The Plant Remains in Excavations at Westgate, Gloucester *Med. Archaeol.* XXIII 186-90.

Helbaek, H. 1959 Comment on *Chenopodium Album* as a Food Plant in Prehistory *Berichte Geobotanischen Institues Der Eidgenossischen Technischen Hochschule Stiftung Rubel* Vol. 31 16-19.

Henderson, P. 1959 ed. *The Poems of John Skelton* Dent London.

Henel, H. ed. 1970 reprint Aelfric's *De Temporibus Anni* EETS.

Henson, Elizabeth 1982 *Rare Breeds in History* RBST.

Herzfeld, G. 1900 *An Old English Martyrology* EETS.

Hickin, N. E. 1964 *Household Pests* Hutchinson.

Hieatt, C. B. 1980 The Roast, or Boiled, Beef of Old England *Book Forum* 5 294-99

Hieatt, C. B. & Butler, S. 1985 *Curye on Inglisch* EETS.

Hieatt, C. B. & Jones R. F. 1986 Two Anglo-Norman Culinary Collections ed. from BL MSS Addit. 32085 & Royal 12.C.xii *Speculum* 61/4 859-882.

Higgs, E. S. & White, Peter J. 1963 Autumn Killing *Antiquity* Vol. 37 282-9.

Hill, David 1981 *An Atlas of Anglo-Saxon England* Blackwell.

Hill, J. 1939 *Wild Foods of Britain* Adam & Charles Black London.

Hills, M. 1988 *Curing Illness the Drug-Free Way* Sheldon Press.

Hinde, T. 1985 *The Domesday Book, England's Heritage Then & Now* Hutchinson.

Hindle, B. P. 1982 *Medieval Roads* Shire Archaeol.

Hobhouse, H. 1985 *Seeds of Change* Sidgwick & Jackson.

Hodges, R. 1982 *Dark Age Economics: the Origins of Towns & Trade* Duckworth.

Hodgson 1960 *The Franklin's Tale* CUP.

Holdsworth, Jane n.d. Pot Spot: Tating Ware *Interim* Vol. 2 No. 3 36-7.

Holdsworth, P. 1980 *Excavations at Melbourne St., Southampton 1971-76* Published for Southampton Archaeol. Research Comm. by the Council for British Archaeol.

Holdsworth, P. 1981 Hamwih *Current Archaeology* No. 79 Vol.7 No. 8 October 243-249.

Holmes, U. T. Jr. 1952 *Daily Living in the Twelfth Century* Univ. Wisconsin Press.

Hope-Taylor, B. 1950 Excavations on Farthing Down, Coulsdon, Surry *Archaeological Newsletter* Vol. 2 Part 10 170.

Hope-Taylor, B. 1977 *Yeavering: An Anglo-British centre of early Northumbria* Dept. of the Environment Archaeol. Reports No. 7 HMSO.

Howes, F. N. 1948 *Nuts* Faber & Faber.

Huizinga, J. 1970 *Homo Ludens: A Study of the Play Element in Culture* Temple Smith London.

Jackson, K. H. 1969 *The Gododdin* Edinburgh Univ. Press.

Jackson, K. H. 1971 *A Celtic Miscellany* Penguin.

Jaine, T. 1987 ed. *The Barefoot Baker* T. Jaine, Blackawton, Devon.

Jember, G. K. et al. 1975 *English-Old English, Old English-English Dictionary* Boulder, Colorado.

Jessen, K. & Helbaek, K. 1944 *Cereals in Great Britain & Ireland in Prehistoric & Early Historic Times* Copenhagen.

Jones, A. 1980 in *East Anglian Archaeol. Report No. 9* (North Elmham) ed. Carter & West Norfolk Museums Service, Gressenhall.

Jones, Andrew K. G. undated paper ?1985 *The End Product* York Environmental Archaeology Unit.

Jones, G. 1980 *Eirik the Red and other Icelandic Sagas* OUP.

Jones, G. & Jones, T. 1949 *The Mabinogion* Dent.

Jones, J. 1988 Pridings Farm *Ark* December 430-432.

Jones, M. & Dimbleby, G. W. eds.1981 *The Environment of Man: the Iron Age to the Anglo-Saxon period* Brit. Arch. Reports British series 87.

Jones, P. E. 1976 *The Butchers of London* Secker & Warburg.

Kemble, J. M. 1843/1848 *Dialogue of Salomon & Saturnus Poetry of the Codex Vercellensis* Aelfric Soc.

Kemble, J. M. 1879 *The Saxons in England* London.

Kemp, R. 1986 Pit your 'wics' *Interim* Vol. 11 No. 3 8-16 YAT.

Kenward, H. K. & Hall, A. R. (& Williams, D.) 1982 *The Archaeol. of York* Environmental Evidence from Roman deposits at Skeldergate Vol. 14 Fasc. 3 CBA for YAT.

Kenward, H. K. 1990 A skeptical view of the Coppergate 'beehive' *Interim* Vol. 14 No 4 20-24 YAT.

Ker, N. R. 1957 *A Catalogue of Manuscripts containing Anglo-Saxon* OUP.

Knowles, Dom. David 1940 *The Monastic Order in England* 943-1216 OUP.

Kuper, J. 1977 ed. *The Anthropologist's Cookbook* Routledge & Kegan Paul.

Kylie, E. 1911 *The English Correspondence of St Boniface* Chatto & Windus.

Lamb 1981 Climate from 1000BC to AD1000 in Jones & Dimbleby 1981 53-66.

Lamond, E. 1890 *Walter of Henley's Husbandry together with an Anonymous Husbandry, Seneschaucie & Robert Grosseteste's Rules* Longmans, Green & Co.

Langdon, J. 1986 *Horses, Oxen & Technological Innovation* CUP.

Lappe, F. Moore 1971 *Diet for a Small Planet* Ballantine Books.

Lauwerier, R. C. G. M. 1986 The Role of meat in the Roman diet *Endeavour* New Series Vol. 10 No.1 208-212.

Laver, H. 1916 *The Colchester Oyster Fishery* Colne Fishery Board.

Le Roy Ladurie, E. 1978 *Montaillou* Penguin.

Leslie, R. F. 1966 *The Wanderer* Manchester Univ. Press.

Lester, R. *The Fruitful Interaction: the Food Producer & the Engineer* 62nd Thomas Hawksley Lecture for the Institution of Mech. Engineers.

Lethbridge, T. C. 1936 A Cemetery at Shudy Camps, Cambs. *Proc. Camb. Antiquarian Soc. xxxvi.*

Lethbridge, T. C. & Tebbutt, C. F. 1933 Huts of the Anglo-Saxon period *Proc. Camb. Antiquarian Soc. xxxiii* 133-51.

Lever, C. 1977 *The Naturalised Animals of the British Isles* Hutchinson.

Levison, W. 1946 *England and the Continent in the Eighth Century* Oxford.

Levi-Strauss, C. 1972 *From Honey to Ashes* Jonathan Cape.

Levi-Strauss, C. 1973 *Introduction to a Science of Mythology* Vol.3 Jonathan Cape.

Liebermann, F. 1898 *Die Gesetze der Angelsachsen* Vol. 1 Halle.

Lodge, B. & Herrtage, S. J. 1872, 1879, reprint.1973 *Palladius on Husbandrie* EETS.

Logeman, H. 1888 *The Rule of S. Benet* EETS.

Lovell 1988 Barefoot Baker 1 T Jaine Blackawton, Devon.

Lowe, P. R. 1933 The Differential Characters...of *Gallus & Phasianus*...Ibis 332-43.

Loyn, H. R. 1970 *Anglo-Saxon England & the Norman Conquest* Longman.

Mabey, R. 1972 *Food for Free* Collins.

Mackie, W. S. 1934 *The Exeter Book* EETS.

Mackie, W. S./Gollancz I. 1972-3 reprint *The Exeter Book* EETS.

Mackreth, D. F. n.d. *Saxons in the Nene Valley* Nene Valley Research Committee.

MacNeill, J. T. & Gamer, H. M. 1938 *Medieval Handbooks of Penance* Columbia Univ. Press.

MAFF 1972 rev. *Brucellosis* Advisory Leaflet No. 93.

Magnusson, M. & Palsson, H. 1960 *Njal's Saga* Penguin.

Magnusson, M. & Palsson, H. 1965 *The Vinland Sagas:Graenlendinga Saga and Eirik's Saga* Penguin.

Maltby, J. M. 1979 *Faunal Studies on Urban Sites: The Animal Bones from Exeter 1972-5* Exeter Archaeology Reports No. 2 Univ. of Sheffield.

Marchenay, P. 1979 *L'homme et L'abeille* Berger Levrault Paris.

Margeson, S. 1983 (in Fell et al.) On the iconography of the Manx crosses 95-106.

Marshall, L. 1961 Sharing, Taking and Giving: relief of social tensions among Kung Bushmen *Africa* 31 231-49.

Masefield, G. B., Wallis, M., Harrison, S. G., Nicholson, B. E. 1986 *The Oxford Book of Food Plants* OUP.

Mason, E. 1980 *The Beauchamp Cartulary Charters 1100-1268* Pipe Roll Soc.

Matthews, C. L. R. & Hawkes, S. C. 1985 Early Saxon Settlements & Burials on Puddlehill, Nr. Dunstable, Beds. *Anglo-Saxon Studies in Archaeol. & Hist.* No. 4 59-115.

Mawer, A. and Stenton, F. M. 1969 in collaboration with F. T. S. Houghton *The Place-Names of Worcestershire* CUP.

McArthur, W. P. 1949 The Identification of some pestilences recorded in the Irish Annals *Irish Historical Studies* 6 169-188.

McGee, H. 1986 *On Food and Cooking: The Science and Lore of the Kitchen* Allen & Unwin.

McGraill, S. & Switsur, R. 1979 Log Boats *Med. Archaeol.* XXIII 229-31.

McGregor, A. 1982 Anglo-Scandinavian Finds from Lloyds Bank, Pavement & other sites *The Archaeol. of York* Vol. 17 Fasc. 3 CBA for YAT.

McKendry, M. 1973 *Seven Centuries of English Cooking* Weidenfeld & Nicolson.

McNeill, F. Marion 1963 *The Scots Kitchen: its lore and recipes* Blackie.

McNeill, W. H. 1977 *Plagues and Peoples* Basil Blackwell.

Mead, W. 1931 *The English Medieval Feast* Allen & Unwin.

Meaney, A. L. & Chadwick Hawkes, S. 1970 *Two Anglo-Saxon Cemeteries at Winnall, Winchester* Soc. Med. Archaeol. Monograph series No.4.

Meaney, A. L. 1981 *Anglo-Saxon Amulets and Curing Stones* BAR 96.

Mellows, W. T. 1980 *The Peterborough Chronicle of Hugh Candidus* Peterborough Museum Soc.

Miles, A. E. N. 1969 The Dentition of the Anglo-Saxons *Proc. Royal Soc. of Medicine* 62 1311-1315.

Miles, A. E. N. 1972 Some morbid skeletal changes in the Anglo-Saxons *British Dental Assoc. J.* 133 309-311.

Miller, T. 1890-1 *OE version Bede's Ecclesiastical History* Vols. I & II EETS.

Miller, W. 1965 *Russia* Newnes.

Min. of Ag. see MAFF.

Mintz, S. 1985 *Sweetness and Power* Elisabeth Sefton Books/Viking.

Mitford, M. 1986 *Our Village* Sidgwick & Jackson London.

Moberg, V. 1973 *A History of the Swedish People* Vol. II Heinemann.

Monk, M. 1977 *The Plant Economy & Agriculture of The Anglo-Saxons in southern Britain with particular reference to the 'mart' settlements of Southampton & Winchester* Univ. of Southampton thesis.

Monson-Fitzjohn, G. 1927 *Drinking Vessels of Bygone Days* Herbert Jenkins.

Morgan, J. 1975 *Nutrition: trace element deficiencies* Medical News June 26 4.

Morris, C. 1983 A late-Anglo-Saxon hoard of iron & copper artefacts from Nazeing, Essex. *Med. Archael.* XXVII 27-39.

Morris, C. 1985 Pole-lathe Turning *Woodworking Crafts Magazine* Issue 16 Aug/Sept/Oct 1985 20-4.

Morris, I. 1990 Surviving with Soays *Ark* XVII, No. 11 Nov. 401-3.

Moryson, F. 1617 *An Intinerary* Vols. I-IV Glasgow 1907.

Moss, P. 1958 *Meals through the Ages* Harrap.

Moulden, J. & Tweddle, D. 1986 Catalogue of the Anglo-Scandinavian sites s.w. of the Ouse *The Archaeol. of York* Vol. 8 Fasc. 1 CBA for YAT.

Munby, J. ed.1982 *Domesday Book Vol. 4: Hampshire* Phillimore.

Musty, J. 1969 The Excavation of two barrows, one of Saxon date, at Ford...Wilts. *Antiquaries J.* 49 98-117.

Napier, A. 1916 *The OE Version of the Rule of Chrodegang* EETS.

Nix, J. 1985 *Farm Management Pocket Book* Wye College, Kent.

Noddle, B. A. 1975 *A Comparison of the Animal Bones from Eight Medieval sites in Southern Britain* in Clason AT 248-260.

Noddle, B A 1977 Animal Bone in *Excavations in Kings Lynn 1963-1970* Clarke, H. and Carter, A. eds. 378-403.

O'Connor, T. with Wilkinson, M. 1982 *The Animal Bones from Flaxengate, Lincoln c.870-1500* The Archaeology of Lincoln CBA Vol. XVIII-1.

O'Connor, T. P. 1984 *Selected Groups of Bones from Skeldergate & Walmgate* The Archaeology of York Vol. 15 Fasc. 1 CBA for YAT.

O'Connor, T. P. 1984 Archaeogastronomy *Interim* Vol. 10 No.1 26-7.

O'Connor, T. P. 1985 Shellshock *Interim* Vol. 10 No. 2 29-32.

O'Connor, T. P. 1988 The Case of the Absent Rat *Interim* Vol. 13 No. 4 39-41.

Olsen, O. & Schmidt, H. 1977 *Fyrkat: en jysk vikingeborg* Vol.1 Copenhagen.

Ordish, G. 1953 *Wine Growing in England* Rupert Hart-Davis.

Ordish, G. 1977 *Vineyards in England and Wales* Faber.

Oschinsky, D. 1971 *Walter of Henley and other treatises on estate management & accounting* Oxford.

Ottaway, P. 1983 Any old iron *Interim* Vol. 9 No. 1 20-4 YAT.

Ottaway, P. 1985 We're getting it off our chests *Interim* Vol. 10 No. 4 7-12 YAT.

Owen 1841 A *The Ancient Laws & Institutes of Wales* Record Commission.

Page, R. I. 1985 *Anglo-Saxon Aptitudes* Cambridge.

Page, R. I. 1985 Some Problems of Meaning in Bammesberger, A, 221-7.

Palliser, D. M. 1978 The Medieval Street Names of York *York Historian* No.2 2-16.

Palsson, H. 1971 *Hrafnel's Saga & other stories* Penguin.

Pennant, W. 1772 *Tours in Wales.*

Petch, A. 1987 *Newsletter* p.1 Kings Nympton, Devon.

Pheifer, J. D. 1974 *Old English Glosses in the Epinal-Erfurt Glossary* Clarendon Press Oxford.

Platt, B. S. 1968 *Tables of representative values of foods commonly used in tropical countries* HMSO.

Platt, C. 1969 *Medieval Archaeology in England: A Guide to the Historical Sources* Pinhorns.

Platt, C., Coleman-Smith, R. et al. 1975 *Excavations in Medieval Southampton 1953-1969* Leicester Univ. Press.

Poole, A. L. 1958 *Medieval England* Oxford.

Poole, R. L. 1912 *The Exchequer in the Twelfth Century* Frank Cass (Blackwell, Oxford).

Pope, J. C. 1967 *Homilies of Aelfric* EETS.

Prummel, W. 1983 *Excavations at Dorestad* 2 Amersfoort.

Pullar, Philippa 1970 *Consuming Passions* Hamish Hamilton.

Rackham, O. 1984 in Biddick 1984 The Forest: Woodland and Wood Pasture in Medieval England 70-101.

Radley, J. 1971 Economic Aspects of Anglo-Danish York *Med. Archael.* XV 37-57.

Raffald, E. 1784 *The Experienced English Housekeeper* printed for R. Baldwin London.

Rahtz, P. & Hirst, S. 1974 *Beckery Chapel, Glastonbury 1967-8* Glastonbury Antiquarian Soc.

Rahtz, P. 1979 *The Saxon & Medieval Palaces at Cheddar Excavation* 1960-2 BAR Series 65.

Rare Breeds Survival Trust *Soay Sheep* undated.

Redfern, M. 1987 Killer of Kings & Emperors *The Listener* 5 March 16.

Renfrew, Jane 1985 *Food and Cooking in Prehistoric Britain* English Heritage.

Riche, P. 1978 *Daily Life in the World of Charlemagne* Univ. of Pennsylvania.

Richards, A. 1932 *Hunger and Work in a Savage Tribe* Routledge.

Roach, F. A. 1985 *Cultivated Fruits of Britain: their origin & history* Blackwell.

Robertson, A. J. 1925 *The Laws of the Kings of England from Edmund to Henry I* CUP.

Robertson, A. J. 1939 *Anglo-Saxon Charters* CUP.

Robertson-Smith 1889 *Lectures on the Religion of the Semites* D. Appleton New York.

Robins, D. 1988 A spin through the past *New Scientist* 25 Feb. 1988 49-52 London.

Robinson, F. N. 1957 *The works of Geoffrey Chaucer* Cambridge.

Roesdahl, E. 1977 *Fyrkat: en jysk vikingeborg Vol. II* Copenhagen.

Roesdahl, E. 1982 *Viking Age Denmark* B.M. Publications.

Roesdahl, E. et al. 1987 *The Vikings in England.*

Rogerson, A. ed. 1976 *East Anglian Archaeol. 2* Norfolk Museums Service.

Rothamsted Experimental Station Library Catalogue of Printed Books & Pamphlets on Agriculture 1471-1840.

Rowley, T. 1981 *The Origins of Open Field Agriculture* Croom Helm.

Rumble, A. 1983 *Essex Domesday* Phillimore.

Ryder, M. L. 1961 Livestock Remains from Four Medieval Sites in Yorkshire *Agric. Hist. Review* 9 105-110.

Ryder 1987 Feral Goats - their origin & uses *Ark* September 305-11.

Sabine, E. L. 1933 Butchering in Medieval London *Speculum* 8 335-353.

Salisbury, C. 1980 The Trent, the story of a river *Current Archaeol.* No. 74 Vol. VII Pt. 3 88-91.

Sass, Lorna 1975 *To the King's Taste* John Murray.

Sayce, R. U. 1946 Food through the Ages *Montgomeryshire Collections* XLIX Part II.

Schaumann, B. & Cameron, A. 1977 A Newly found leaf of Old English from Louvain *Anglia* XCV 289-312.

Seebohm, F. 1883 *The English Village Community* Longmans, Green & Co.

Seebohm, M. 1952 rev. ed. *The Evolution of the British Farm* Allen & Unwin.

Severin, T. 1978 *The Brendan Voyage* Book Club Associates.

Simpson, A. W. B. 1984 *Cannibalism and the Common Law* Univ. Chicago Press.

Skeat, W. W. 1869 *Piers the Plowman* OUP.

Skeat, W. W. 1881 *Aelfric's Lives of the Saints* EETS.

Small, A., Thomas, C., Wilson, D. M. 1973 *St Ninian's Isle & its Treasures* OUP.

Schmidt, M. 1980 *Eleven British Poets* Methuen London.

Smith, A. H. 1964 *The Place-Names of Goucestershire* Parts 1-3 CUP.

Smith, A. H. 1970 *The Place-Name Elements 1 & 2* CUP.

Southampton Archaeol. Research Committee 1980 *Saxon Southampton: the Archaeology & History of the port called Hamwih* Southampton Archaeol. Research Committee.

Spencer, P. J. 1979 Fish that men gnawed upon *Interim* Vol. 6 No. 1 9-11.

Spriggs, J. 1977 Roll out the barrel *Interim* Vol. 4 No. 4 11-15.

St Clare Bryne, M. 1925 *Elizabethan Life in Town & Country* Methuen.

Steane, J. M. & Bryant, G. F. 1975 Excavations at the DMS at Lyvenden, Northants. *Northants. Museum Journal* 12 3-160.

Stenton, F. M. 1936 The Road System of Medieval England *Econ. Hist. Review* Nov. 1936 1-21.

Stenton, D. M. 1965 *English Society in the Early Middle Ages* 4th ed. Penguin.

Stevenson, W. H. 1929 *Early Scholastic Colloquies* Oxford.

Stewart, K. 1975 *Cooking and Eating* Hart-Davis Macgibbon.

Stone, L. 1977 *The Family, Sex and Marriage in England 1500-1800* Weidenfeld & Nicolson.

Storms, G. 1948 *Anglo-Saxon Magic* Martinus Nijhoff The Hague.

Stratton, J. M. 1969 *Agricultural Records AD 220-1968* John Baker.

Svensson, O. 1987 *Saxon Place-Names in East Cornwall* Lund.

Swanton, M. 1975 ed. *Anglo-Saxon Prose* Dent.

Symons, T. 1953 *The Monastic Agreement of the Monks and Nuns of the English Nation* Nelson.

Talbot-Rice, D. 1965 ed. *The Dark Ages* Thames & Hudson.

Tannahill, Reay 1973 *Food in History* Methuen.

Tannahill, Reay 1975 *Flesh and Blood: A History of the Cannibal Complex* Hamish Hamilton.

Taylor, T. 1925 *The Life of St Sampson of Dol* London.

TeBrake, W. H. 1984 Early Medieval Agriculture in Coastal Holland: The Evidence from Archaeology & Ecology In Biddick 171-189.

Temple, E. 1976 *A Survey of Manuscripts illuminated in the British Isles 900-1066* Harvey Miller.

Thomas, C. 1971 *Britain & Ireland in Early Christian Times AD 400-800* Thames & Hudson.

Thompson, M. 1989, Poultry Evolution & Development *Ark* Jan. 25 24-5.

Thorn, C. & F. 1980 *Somerset Doomsday* Phillimore.

Thorpe, B. 1843 ed. *The Homilies of Aelfric* Aelfric Soc.

Thorpe, L. 1978 *Gerald of Wales* Penguin.

Ticehurst, N. F. 1923 Some birds of the fourteenth century *British Birds* 17 29-35.

Tickner, Edwards 1917 *The Lore of the Honey Bee* 8th edn.

Todd, M. 1975 *The Northern Barbarians 100BC-AD300* Hutchinson Educational.

Todd, M. 1987 *The South-West to AD 1000* Longmans.

Tooke, J. Horne 1805 *The Diversions of Purley* London.

Trow-Smith, R. 1951 *English Husbandry from the Earliest Times to the Present Day* Faber & Faber.

Trow-Smith, R. 1957 *British Livestock Husbandry to 1700* London.

Turner, Sharon 1828 *The Anglo-Saxons* London.

Tusser, Thomas 1984 reprint *Five Hundred Points of Good Husbandry* OUP.

Tylecote, R. F. 1962 *Metallurgy in Archaeology* Edward Arnold.

Tylecote, R. F. 1967 The Bloomery Site at W. Runton *Norfolk Archaeol.* 34 187-214.

Ucko & Dimbleby 1971 *Domestication and Exploitation of Plants & Animals* Duckworth.

van Es, W. A. with Verwers, W. J. H. 1980 *Excavations at Dorestad Vol. 1. The Harbour: Hoogstraat 1* Nederlandse Oudheden 9 R.O.B. Amersfoort.

Victor, Paul-Emile 1955 *The Great Hunger* Hutchinson.

von Matt, L. & Hilpisch, S. 1961 *St Benedict* Burns & Oates London.

Waddell, Helen 1932 *The Wandering Scholars* Penguin.

Wade-Martins, P. 1984 Excavations in Thetford 1948-59 & 1973-80 *East Anglian Archaeology 22* Norfolk Museums Service.

Wade-Martins, P. 1986 Breeding Manx Loghtans: is it worth it? *Ark* May 168-171.

Walford, C. 1879 *The Famines of the World Past & Present* Statistical Soc of London.

Walker, C. & Cannon, G. 1986 *The Food Scandal* Century Arrow.

Walker, M. & Bennett, H. 1980 *Somerset Folklore* Somerset Rural Life Museum.

Wartburg, W. von 1928 reprint 1948 + suppl. 1969 *Franzosisches Etymologisches Worterbuch* Bonn & Leipzig.

Waterman, D. M. 1954 Excavations at Clough Castle, Co. Down *Ulster J. of Archaeol.* XVIII Third Series 103-168.

Webster, L. 1975 Medieval Britain *Med. Archaeol.* XIV 220-60.

Weicholt, R. P. 1987 Barefoot in the Netherlands *Three Course Newsletter* No. 4 March 1987 52-47.

Welch, M. G. 1983 *Early Anglo-Saxon Sussex* BAR 112 (i).

Wells, Calvin 1960 Animals bones assoc. with cremations at Illingworth, Norfolk *Antiquity* XXXIV No. 133 March 1960

Wells, Calvin 1964 *Bones, Bodies & Disease* Thames & Hudson

Wells, Calvin 1975 Prehistoric & historical changes in nutritional diseases and associated conditions *Progress in Food and Nutrition Science* No. 1 756.

Wells, Calvin 1977 Disease of the Maxillary Sinus in Antiquity *Medical Biology Illustrated* Vol. 27 173-8.

West, S. E. 1963 Excavations at Cox Lane (1958) and at the Town Defences, Shire Hall Yard, Ipswich (1959) *Proc. Suffolk Inst. Archaeol.* 29 233-303.

West, Stanley 1982 *The Early Saxon Site at West Stow (5th-7th centuries)* Doctoral Thesis Birkbeck Coll. London.

Wheeler, Alwyn 1969 *The Fishes of the British Isles and N.W. Europe* Macmillan.

Wheeler, Alwyn 1979 *The Tidal Thames: the History of a River and its Fishes* Routledge & Kegan Paul.

Wheeler, A. & Jones, A. K. G. 1976 Fish remains Excavations on Fuller's Hill, Great Yarmouth, *East Anglian Archaeol.* 2 131-245.

Whitelock, D. 1952 *The Beginnings of English Society* Penguin.

Whitelock, D. 1955 *English Historical Documents Vol. 1* c.500-1042 Eyre & Spottiswoode.

Whitelock, D. 1968 *The Will of Aethelgyfu* New Collection Roxburghe Club.

Whittock, M. J. 1986 *The Origins of England* Croom Helm.

Wikander, Orjan 1986 *Archaeol. Evidence for Early Water Mills - an Interim Report* History of Technology Lund.

Wilkins 1982 *Butter-making* Acton Scott Farm Museum

Wilkinson, M 1979 *The Fish Remains* in Maltby 1979

Wilkinson, M 1986 *Withowinde* LXXVII 16.

Williams, J. 1984 From Palace to Town: Northampton & Urban Origins *Anglo-Saxon England* XIII 113-136.

Wilson, C. Anne 1973 *Food & Drink in Britain* Constable.

Wilson, D. G. 1975 Plant Remains from the Graveney Boat & the Early History of *Humulus Lupulus L.* in W. Europe *New Phytologist* LXXV 627-648.

Wilson, D. G. 1977 *The Making of the Middle Thames* Spur Books.

Wilson, D. M. 1960 *The Anglo-Saxons* Thames & Hudson.

Wilson, D. M. 1964 *Anglo-Saxon Ornamental Metalwork, 700-1100, in the British Museum* BM Publications.

Wilson, D. G. 1975 Plant Remains from the Graveney Boat & the Early History of *Humulus Lupulus L.* in W. Europe *New Phytologist* LXXV 627-648.

Wilson, D. G. 1977 *The Making of the Middle Thames* Spur Books.

Wilson, D. M. 1960 *The Anglo-Saxons* Thames & Hudson.

Wilson, D. M. 1964 *Anglo-Saxon Ornamental Metalwork, 700-1100, in the British Museum* BM Publications.

Wilson, D. M. ed. 1976 *The Archaeology of Anglo-Saxon England* CUP.

Wilson, D. M. 1984 *Anglo-Saxon Art: from the Seventh Century to the Norman Conquest* Thames & Hudson.

Wilson, D. M. 1985 *The Bayeux Tapestry* Thames & Hudson.

Wilson, D. M. 1986 Trade *Proceedings of Spoleto Conference.*

Wilson, J. 1909 *The Evolution of British Cattle* Vinton & Co.

Wiseman, J. 1986 *A History of the British Pig* Duckworth.

Wiseman, J. 1988 Comments on Corsican Pigs *Ark* May 176-9.

Wolters, J. B. 1967 *Wijster* Palaeohistoria XI Groningen.

Wright & Wulcker 1884 see

Wright, T. & Wulcker, R. P. 1968 reprint *Anglo-Saxon & OE Vocabularies* Vols. I & II Second Edition Darmstadt.

Wycliffe-Goodwin, Charles 1851 *Saxon Legends of St Andrew & St Veronica* Camb. Antiquarian Soc. Series 1.

Yonge, C, M. 1966 *Oysters* New Naturalist Series Collins.

Zeuner, F. E. 1963 *A History of Domesticated Animals* Hutchinson.

Zinsser, Hans 1934 *Rats, Lice and History* Little, Brown & Co. Boston Mass.

Zupita, J. 1959 *Beowulf: facsimile and notes...*EETS.

Personal Communications

B. Adams, Verulam Museum
A. Cook, A. Cook & Son, Heddon, Filleigh, Devon
Dr. D. J. Drewry, Scott Polar Research Institute, Cambridge
The late Professor J. McN. Dodgson, UCL
J. Fensom, Northend Farm, Stagsden, Beds.
Dr. J. Graham, Shuttleworth Agricultural Institute, Old Warden, Beds.
R. K. Hagen, Manshead Archaeol. Soc., Dunstable, Beds.
P. Holdsworth, Formerly Director, Southampton Excavats.
D. Maule, R & D, Whitbreads Brewery, Luton, Beds.
A. Milton, Chapelton Barton, Umberleigh, Devon.
I. Newman, Village Farm, Stagsden, Beds.
D. Smallridge, Chasestead Engineering, Letchworth, Herts.
W. Smallridge, Instow, Devon.
P. Walsh, Guinness Museum, Dublin.

The Author

Ann Smallridge Hagen was born at Kempston, Bedford. After leaving Bedford High School, she had a number of jobs, from toffee apple wrapping to metallurgical analysis. She read English with Honours at University College London, 1965–8, taking Anglo-Saxon Archaeology as a special paper. On leaving university she worked as a Museum Educational Officer, before becoming an English teacher. She was also a partner in a firm of antique restorers for ten years, additionally bringing up a family during this time. She enrolled as a postgraduate student at University College London, and was awarded her M.Phil. in 1992. She lives in Haynes, Bedfordshire, with her three children, and is a freelance lecturer and writer.

The Service of Prime
from the Old English Benedictine Office:
Text and Translation

Prepared by Bill Griffiths

UK £2·50 net   ISBN 0–9516209–3–2   40pp

Alfred's Metres of Boethius

Edited by Bill Griffiths

In this new edition of the Old English *Metres of Boethius*, clarity of text, informative notes and a helpful glossary have been a priority, for this is one of the most approachable of Old English verse texts, lucid and delightful; its relative neglect by specialists will mean this text will come as a new experience to many practised students of the language; while its clear, expositional verse style makes it an ideal starting point for all amateurs of the period.

In these poems, King Alfred re-built the Latin verses from Boethius' *De Consolatione Philosophiae* ("On the Consolation of Philosophy") into new alliterative poems, via an Old English prose intermediary. The stirring images and stories of Boethius' original are retained - streams, legends, animals, volcanoes - and developed for an Anglo-Saxon audience to include the Gothic invasion of Italy (Metre 1), the figure of Welland the Smith (Metre 10), and the hugely disconcerting image of Death's hunt for mankind (Metre 27). The text is in effect a compendium of late classical science and philosophy, tackling serious issues like the working of the universe, the nature of the soul, the morality of power - but presented in so clear and lively a manner as to make it as challenging today as it was in those surprisingly Un-Dark Ages.

UK £12·95 net   ISBN 0–9516209–5–9   212pp

Beowulf: Text and Translation

Translated by John Porter

The verse in which the story unfolds is, by common consent, the finest writing surviving in Old English, a text that all students of the language and many general readers will want to tackle in the original form. To aid understanding of the Old English, a **literal word-by-word translation** by John Porter is printed opposite an edited text and provides a practical key to this Anglo-Saxon masterpiece.

UK £7·95 net   ISBN 0–9516209–2–4   192pp

Monasteriales Indicia
The Anglo-Saxon Monastic Sign Language

Edited with notes and translation by
Debby Banham

The *Monasteriales Indicia* is one of very few texts which let us see how life was really lived in monasteries in the early Middle Ages. Written in Old English and preserved in a manuscript of the mid-eleventh century, it consists of 127 signs used by Anglo-Saxon monks during the times when the Benedictine Rule forbade them to speak. These indicate the foods the monks ate, the clothes they wore, and the books they used in church and chapter, as well as the tools they used in their daily life, and persons they might meet both in the monastery and outside. The text is printed here with a parallel translation. The introduction gives a summary of the background, both historical and textual, as well as a brief look at the later evidence for monastic sign language in England. Extensive notes provide the reader with details of textual relationships, explore problems of interpretation, and set out the historical implications of the text.

UK £6·95 net   ISBN 0–9516209–4–0   96pp

The Battle of Maldon:
Text and Translation

Translated and edited by Bill Griffiths

The Battle of Maldon was fought between the men of Essex and the Vikings in AD 991. The action was captured in an Anglo-Saxon poem whose vividness and heroic spirit has fascinated readers and scholars for generations. *The Battle of Maldon* includes the source text; edited text; parallel literal translation; verse translation; review of 86 books and articles.

UK £6·95 net   ISBN 0–9516209–0–8   96pp

Wordcraft
Concise English/Old English Dictionary and Thesaurus

Stephen Pollington

This book provides Old English equivalents to the commoner modern words in both dictionary and thesaurus formats.

Previously the lack of an accessible guide to vocabulary deterred many would-be students of Old English. Now this book combines the core of indispensable words relating to everyday life with a selection of terms connected with society, culture, technology, religion, perception, emotion and expression to encompass all aspects of Anglo-Saxon experience.

The Thesaurus presents vocabulary relevant to a wide range of individual topics in alphabetical lists, thus making it easily accessible to those with specific areas of interest. Each thematic listing is encoded for cross-reference from the Dictionary. The two sections will be of invaluable assistance to students of the language, as well as to those with either a general or a specific interest in the Anglo-Saxon period.

UK £9·95 net   ISBN 1–898281–02–5   224pp

Anglo-Saxon Verse Charms, Maxims and Heroic Legends

Louis J Rodrigues

The Germanic tribes who settled in Britain during the fifth and early sixth centuries brought with them a store of heroic and folk traditions: folk-tales, legends, rune-lore, magic charms, herbal cures, and the homely wisdom of experience enshrined in maxims and gnomic verse. In the lays composed and sung by their minstrels at banquets, they recalled the glories of long-dead heroes belonging to their Continental past. They carved crude runic inscriptions on a variety of objects including memorial stones, utensils, and weapons. In rude, non-aristocratic, verse, they chanted their pagan charms to protect their fields against infertility, and their bodies against the rigours of rheumatic winters. And, in times of danger, they relied on the gnomic wisdom of their ancestors for help and guidance.

Louis Rodrigues looks at those heroic and folk traditions that were recorded in verse, and which have managed to survive the depredations of time.

UK £7·95 net   ISBN 1–898281–01–7   176pp

Anglo-Saxon Runes

John. M. Kemble

Kemble's essay *On Anglo-Saxon Runes* first appeared in the journal *Archaeologia* for 1840; it draws on the work of Wilhelm Grimm, but breaks new ground for Anglo-Saxon studies in his survey of the Ruthwell Cross and the Cynewulf poems. It is an expression both of his own indomitable spirit and of the fascination and mystery of the Runes themselves, making one of the most attractive introductions to the topic.

For this edition, new notes have been supplied, which include translations of Latin and Old English material quoted in the text, to make this key work in the study of runes more accessible to the general reader.

UK £6·95 net   ISBN 0–9516209–1–6   80pp

Spellcraft

Old English Heroic Legends

Kathleen Herbert

The author has taken the skeletons of ancient Germanic legends about great kings, queens and heroes, and put flesh on them. Kathleen Herbert's extensive knowledge of the period is reflected in the wealth of detail she brings to these tales of adventure, passion, bloodshed and magic.

The book is in two parts. First are the stories that originate deep in the past, yet because they have not been hackneyed, they are still strange and enchanting. After that there is a selection of the source material, with information about where it can be found and some discussion about how it can be used. The purpose of the work is to bring pleasure to those studying Old English literature and, more importantly, to bring to the attention of a wider public the wealth of material that has yet to be tapped by modern writers, composers and artists.

Kathleen Herbert is the author of a trilogy, set in sixth century Britain, that includes a winner of the Georgette Heyer prize for an outstanding historical novel.

UK £6·95 net   ISBN 0–9516209–9–1   288pp

For a full list of publications send a s.a.e. to:

Anglo-Saxon Books

25 Malpas Drive, Pinner, Middlesex. HA5 1DQ

Tel: 081-868 1564

Available in North America from:
Paul & Company
Publishers Consortium Inc.
c/o PCS Data Processing Inc., 360 West 31 St., New York, NY 1001

Þa Engliscan Gesiðas

Þa Engliscan Gesiðas (The English Companions) is a historical and cultural society exclusively devoted to Anglo-Saxon history. Its aims are to bridge the gap between scholars and non-experts, and to bring together all those with an interest in the Anglo-Saxon period, its language, culture and traditions, so as to promote a wider interest in, and knowledge of all things Anglo-Saxon. The Fellowship publishes a journal, *Wiðowinde,* which helps members to keep in touch with current thinking on topics from art and archaeology to heathenism and Early English Christianity. The Fellowship enables like-minded people to keep in contact by publicising conferences, courses and meetings that might be of interest to its members. A correspondence course in Old English is also available.

For further details write to:

Janet Goldsbrough-Jones, 38 Cranworth Road,
Worthing, West Sussex, BN11 2JF, England.

Regia Anglorum

Regia Anglorum is a society that was founded to accurately re-create the life of the British people as it was around the time of the Norman Conquest. Our work has a strong educational slant and we consider authenticity to be of prime importance. We prefer, where possible, to work from archaeological materials and are extremely cautious regarding such things as the interpretation of styles depicted in manuscripts. Approximately twenty-five per cent of our membership, of over 500 people, are archaeologists or historians.

The Society has a large working Living History Exhibit, teaching and exhibiting more than twenty crafts in an authentic environment. We own a forty foot wooden ship replica of a type that would have been a common sight in Northern European waters around the turn of the first millennium AD. Battle re-enactment is another aspect of our activities, often involving 200 or more warriors.

For further information contact:

K. J. Siddorn, 9 Durleigh Close, Headley Park,
Bristol BS13 7NQ, England.

The International Society of Anglo-Saxonists

The International Society of Anglo-Saxonists (ISAS) is an organization open to all persons interested in any aspect of the culture of Anglo-Saxon England. ISAS intends to provide scholars interested in the languages, literatures, arts, history, and material culture of *Anglo-Saxon England* with support in their research and to encourage exchanges of ideas and materials within and between disciplines. All of this is accomplished primarily through biennial meetings of the Society during which members present papers and discuss topics of mutual interest. Many of the papers appear in a revised form in *Anglo-Saxon England*.

Benefits of membership include discount subscriptions to *Anglo-Saxon England* and other publications. Only members of the Society can attend and present papers at its meetings.

To join ISAS contact:

Patrick W. Conner, ISAS, Dept. of English, 231 Stansbury Hall, West Virginia University, Morgantown, WV26506, USA.

Old English Newsletter

The *OEN* is a journal produced by, and for, scholars of Old English. It is a refereed periodical. Solicited and unsolicited manuscripts (except for independent reports and news items) are reviewed by specialists in anonymous reports. Four issues are published each (American) academic year for the Old English Division of the Modern Language Association by the Centre for Medieval and Early Renaissance Studies at the State University of New York at Binghamton.

General correspondence should be addressed to the Editor:

Paul E. Szarmach, CEMERS; SUNY-Binghamton, PO Box 6000, Binghamton, New York 13902-6000, USA.